Aviation Elite Units

4th Fighter Group 'Debden Eagles'

Aviation Elite Units • 30

4th Fighter Group 'Debden Eagles'

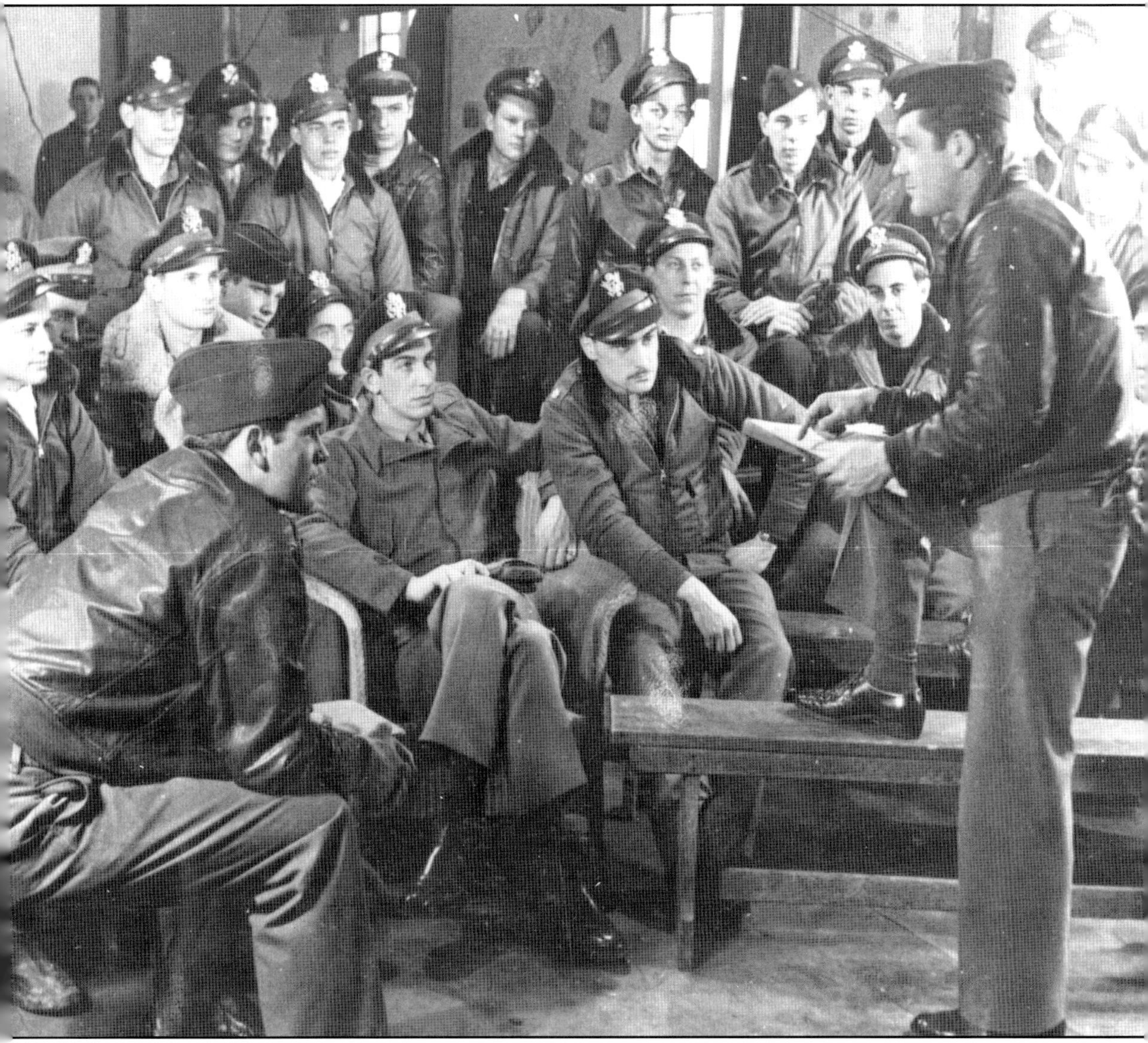

Chris Bucholtz

Series editor Tony Holmes

Front Cover
On 2 July 1944, after the second leg of the *Frantic I* shuttle mission to the USSR, the 4th FG was assigned to fly a sweep ahead of a Fifteenth Air Force mission to Budapest, which saw 700 bombers attack oil targets in the Hungarian capital. The 4th (and one squadron from the 352nd FG) ran into I./JG 302 and the Hungarian 101st Fighter Group, both equipped with Bf 109s. Nine Axis fighters were duly shot down in a swirling dogfight, with three falling to ace Capt Howard Hively of the 4th FG's 334th FS.

One section of Bf 109s became intertwined with Hively's section so that an eight-aeroplane train of alternating Mustangs and Bf 109s found themselves in a turning fight. Hively destroyed his first victim, but then a 20 mm cannon shell exploded against his canopy, wounding him in the face and injuring one of his eyes. Squadronmate 1Lt Grover Siems in his P-51D-5 Mustang 44-13322 *Gloria III* then drew a bead on Hively's attacker and sent him spiralling down in flames. He was then attacked himself.

As Hively shot down two more Bf 109s, Siems' Mustang was hit by cannon fire, wounding him in the shoulder, neck and chin. Siems extricated himself from the fight, and when he landed at Foggia, in Italy, he was too weak to open his canopy and was ignored by airfield personnel until he fired his guns. When Siems was removed from his Mustang, he was so weak from blood loss that he could not move, and was therefore assumed to be dead. After being covered with a sheet and taken to the morgue, Siems was finally able to wiggle a finger to capture the attention of an orderly, who quickly gave him a blood transfusion and saved his life (*Cover artwork by Mark Postlethwaite*)

First published in Great Britain in 2008 by Osprey Publishing
Midland House, West Way, Botley, Oxford, OX2 0PH
443 Park Avenue South, New York, NY, 10016, USA
E-mail; info@ospreypublishing.com

ISBN 13: 978 1 84603 321 6

Edited by Tony Holmes
Page design by Mark Holt
Cover Artwork by Mark Postlethwaite
Aircraft Profiles by Chris Davey
Index by Alison Worthington
Originated by PDQ Digital Media Solutions,
Printed and bound in China through Boolbuilders

08 09 10 11 12 10 9 8 7 6 5 4 3 2 1

ACKNOWLEDGEMENTS
First and foremost, I must thank Wade Meyers, whose research on the 4th FG, as well as his vast archive of photographs, was put at my disposal, which made writing this book a considerably easier effort. Also, Brett Stolle at the National Museum of the Air Force Museum was a tremendous help. Thanks also go to Robert Burman, Tom Cleaver, Roy Sutherland, Steve Eisenman, Mike Meek, Bob Fisher and the readers of *Hyperscale*, who helped narrow down the profile choices from a vast field. And, most important of all, to my wife Elizabeth, who indulges my love of aviation and who supports my efforts to preserve history.

EDITOR'S NOTE
To make this best-selling series as authoritative as possible, the Editor would be interested in hearing from any individual who may have relevant photographs, documentation or first-hand experiences relating to the world's elite pilots, and their aircraft, of the various theatres of war. Any material used will be credited to its original source. Please write to Tony Holmes via e-mail at: tony.holmes@zen.co.uk

CONTENTS

'EAGLES' TO THE ARMY AIR FORCE

When the United States entered World War II in December 1941, its as-yet untapped capacity to manufacture weapons was unmatched anywhere in the world. What it did lack was military experience, and especially experienced fighter pilots. Europe had been at war for two years, and Asia for longer than that. This meant that the air arms of Great Britain, Germany, Japan and Italy had a tremendous head start when it came to developing combat-seasoned flyers.

While the US Army Air Corps prepared to carry out its doctrine of strategic daylight bombing, the fighter took a back seat. But observers to the first two years of war in Europe saw how badly unescorted bombers, first British, then German, fared by daylight when opposed by fighters. If the American philosophy of daylight bombing was to succeed, a substantial effort needed to be made to build a formidable force of both fighter aeroplanes and pilots to accompany the bombers.

In England, at least, the core of this group of pilots was already in place. The 4th Fighter Group (FG) was born on order of VIII Fighter Command on 12 September 1942 at Bushey Hall, in Hertfordshire. The group's real purpose was to absorb the men of the RAF's 'Eagle' Squadrons (Nos 71, 121 and 133 Sqns), which would become the 334th, 335th and 336th Fighter Squadrons of the USAAF.

These American volunteers had been flying combat missions since long before the US entry into the war, and as such they were accorded status in the press in both the UK and back at home that was in excess of their accomplishments. In fact, at one point, Air Marshal Sir Sholto Douglas, head of RAF Fighter Command, accused the 'Eagles' of being prima donnas, and during a fact-finding mission Commander-in-Chief of the USAAF, Gen Henry 'Hap' Arnold said that if they did not show

Plt Off Don Gentile claimed a Ju 88 and an Fw 190 destroyed whilst supporting the disastrous Dieppe landings on 19 August 1942. Flying with No 133 Sqn at the time, he became a founder member of the 4th FG's 336th FS when the 'Eagle' Squadrons switched from RAF to USAAF control the following month. Gentile is seen here posing with his Spitfire VB BL255, which bore the nickname *"BUCKEYE-DON"* and two victory symbols on its port side. The fighter's name referred to its pilot's Piqua, Ohio, origins (*via Wade Meyers*)

Three pilots pose with a 336th FS Spitfire VB freshly painted in US markings. The new insignia did not come with USAAF codes, 4th FG Spitfires instead retaining their RAF codes – in this case, 'MD' for the 336th FS. The group flew its final Spitfire mission on 8 April 1943 (*Jack Raphael via Wade Meyers*)

improvement soon the RAF should consider disbanding the squadrons and sending the pilots home!

In any event, the 'Eagles' were credited with 73.5 aerial victories, and in exchange 82 pilots gave their lives in combat and in accidents from September 1940 through to September 1942. The pilots also gained something other US aviators were sorely lacking – combat experience.

As this administrative shift was taking place, the squadrons continued to fly missions in their Spitfires. On 21 September, 2Lts William Kelly and John Slater of the 335th FS flew a shipping reconnaissance mission and spotted a German convoy escorted by a number of flak ships off the Dutch coast. Former bus driver 'Wild Bill' Kelly decided to make a strafing pass, during which flak hit Slater's Spitfire. He radioed that he was baling out, but before he could jump his aeroplane suddenly dove into the English Channel. Slater became the 4th FG's first combat fatality.

Three days later the 335th FS received a contingent of pilots from the RAF, including Maj William Daley, who assumed command of the squadron. On the 26th, in a mission supporting B-17s, 11 of 12 Spitfire IXs from the 336th FS were lost to a combination of German fighters, fuel starvation, bad weather and poor navigation. Four pilots were killed – 1Lt William Baker and 2Lts Gene Neville, Leonard Ryerson and Dennis Smith – six were taken prisoner and one, 2Lt Robert Smith, evaded back to England. One of the PoWs, Flt Lt Edward Brettell, was later executed by the Germans for his role as the mapmaker in the 'Great Escape' of 76 PoWs from *Stalag Luft III*. One Fw 190 fell to Capt Marion Jackson.

Only 2Lt Richard Beaty made it back to England, and he was badly injured when he crash-landed his Spitfire on the Cornish coast. There was also one abort that day – 2Lt Don Gentile had engine trouble and returned to base.

On 29 September, the men of the former 'Eagle' Squadrons assembled at RAF Debden, in Essex, as their command was officially handed over to

'Eagle' Squadron personnel stand at attention on 29 September 1942 as control of RAF Debden is turned over to the USAAF (*National Museum of the USAF*)

the newly formed US Eighth Air Force. The ranks stood in a driving rainstorm as Air Marshal Sholto Douglas handed over the units, officially consolidated as an American fighter group, to Maj Gen Frank Hunter, commander of VIII Fighter Command, and Maj Gen Carl Spaatz, head of the Eighth Air Force. Col Edward Anderson was named the group's first commanding officer, while Wg Cdr Raymond Duke-Wooley was assigned as operational air commander.

The group's heritage was reflected in the way its pilots spoke. Instead of 'the 335th Fighter Squadron', they referred it to as '335 Squadron', in typically clipped RAF fashion. Aeroplanes were 'kites', missions were 'shows'. Indeed, the use of RAF jargon was another aspect that would set the 4th FG apart from other VIII Fighter Command groups.

The group flew its first major mission – escorting bombers to the Calais/Dunkirk area – on 2 October. The 334th and 335th FSs engaged enemy fighters at 24,000 ft, and Fw 190s fell to Capt Oscar Coen and Lts Gene Fetrow and Stanley Anderson. Wg Cdr Duke-Woolley and Lt Jim Clark shared in the destruction of another Fw 190.

On 20 October, two Spitfires from the 334th FS were on convoy patrol (a duty left over from the unit's RAF days) when 2Lt Anthony Seaman's Spitfire VB suffered an engine problem and crashed into the channel ten miles east of Harwich. The pilot's body was never found.

Following a month of fruitless sweeps over France, the group finally stirred up some action on 16 November when 2Lts Jim Clark and Robert Boock led an attack on Saint-Valery-en-Caux, in Normandy. For Clark, the trip was made more exciting when he hit a tree while ducking flak at low-level. Another 'Rhubarb' (offensive patrol) three days later concluded with Lt Frank Smolinsky of the 335th FS shooting down an Fw 190 over the English Channel.

Future six-kill ace 2Lt Roy Evans bagged a rare Fieseler Fi 156 army communications aircraft on 20 November near Furnes, but he was soon hit by flak. His damaged Spitfire carried him to within a few miles of the English coast before he had to bale out. Smolinsky circled overhead the downed pilot until Evans was recovered safely by an RAF rescue launch.

Two 4th FG Spitfire VBs beat up Debden before departing on one of a seemingly endless series of convoy patrols in the late autumn of 1942 (*National Museum of the USAF*)

On 22 November, Maj Daley's tour of duty was complete and command of the 335th FS passed to the vastly experienced Capt Don Blakeslee. The hard-charging Blakeslee was already something of a legend, having seen combat with the RCAF since mid-1941. He initially resisted a transfer to the 'Eagle' Squadrons due to the units' reputation for overclaiming. Fellow 4th FG ace James 'Goody' Goodson also recalled that Blakeslee was not fond of authority, recalling in his autobiography *Tumult in the Clouds*, 'While no one questioned his talent in the air, many in the top command had less confidence in his behavior on the ground'.

According to Goodson, Blakeslee firmly established his already colourful reputation at the time of his transfer to the 4th by choosing the night before Gen Hunter's visit to Debden to entertain two female WAAF officers in his barracks room. Hunter started his tour early the next morning. 'Warned of the approaching danger, the two WAAFs just had time to cover some of their embarrassment and scramble out the barracks window, right into the path of the general and his staff', wrote Goodson. 'Told that Blakeslee would be demoted and transferred, Gen Hunter remarked, "For one, maybe. But for two, he should be promoted!"' Blakeslee's personality would duly leave an indelible mark on the group.

Sneaking in missions between bouts of bad weather, the 4th FG flew a 'Rodeo' along the French coast on 4 December, and two days later escorted B-17s to the Lille/Fives locomotive works. On the way home Lt Gene Fetrow tangled with an Fw 190 and was credited with a probable.

Small-scale 'Rhubarbs' and convoy patrols occupied the 4th FG for the rest of December. Two group missions escorting bombers were launched on 13 January, marking its first major missions of 1943. The next day, Anderson and Boock were concluding yet another 'Rhubarb' near Ostend when they were bounced by a pair of Fw 190s. Anderson chopped his throttle and skidded violently, causing the German fighters to overshoot, then straightened out his Spitfire and

Lt Col 'Pete' Peterson, Maj Oscar Coen, Capt Don Blakeslee and 2Lt Evans talk with Lt Gen Ira Eaker, commander of the Eighth Air Force, at Debden in late 1942 (*National Museum of the USAF*)

2Lt Steve Pisanos and Capts Don Blakeslee and Vernon Boehle pose in front of a Spitfire VB in late 1942. Boehle was the only one of the three to start as an 'Eagle', Pisanos having previously flown with other RAF units, as had Blakeslee, who resisted transfer because he thought the 'Eagles' played fast and loose with kill claims. Note the unofficial 336th FS emblem on the aircraft parked behind them (*via Wade Meyers*)

followed the enemy aeroplanes in a right turn, opening fire at 200 yards. One of the Fw 190s skidded and crashed into the ocean.

Meanwhile, Boock had spotted two more Focke-Wulfs closing in on Anderson from astern. Turning his Spitfire VB into them, he fired, and the leading Fw 190 climbed abruptly and then dived into the Channel.

On 20 January the 335th FS set out on another 'Rhubarb' over France, and Boock shot up a locomotive during the unit's brief sweep over enemy territory. That same day, future five-kill ace 2Lt Spiros 'Steve' Pisanos of the 334th FS crashed his Spitfire VB whilst taking off from Debden and suffered minor injuries.

After two uneventful escort missions on 21 January, the 335th FS took the bombers to St Omer the next day. As they flew over the French coast they were bounced by Fw 190s, one of which was shot down by 2Lt Boock northwest of Dunkirk. His fighter was also shot up, however, with German rounds shattering the Spitfire's cockpit and ripping Boock's goggles away. 336th FS CO Maj Coen and Lt Joseph Matthews also claimed kills. Later in the mission, the Spitfire VB of 335th FS pilot Lt Chester Grimm was hit by flak and he baled out. Although the young pilot was seen in his dinghy, he was never recovered.

On 26 January, the 336th FS flew a 'Ramrod' to Bruges, in Belgium, during which Lt Boock was hit by flak. His aircraft quickly caught fire, but Boock stayed with the Spitfire until the flames started to melt his boots and he lost control of the fighter. He baled out six miles off the coast, and Fetrow, Kelly, Frank Fink and Victor France orbited his position for fear that he would be strafed by Fw 190s reported in the area. A merchant ship had to weigh anchor to get underway to rescue Boock, who was having difficulty with his dinghy in the frigid waters. Luckily, he was picked up safely and returned to base.

Sitting in its revetment at Debden in February 1943 is Spitfire VB BM309/AV-V of the 335th FS. On 22 January it had been used by 2Lt Robert A Boock to destroy an Fw 190 northwest of Dunkirk in the 4th FG's last big engagement with the Spitfire (*D Young via R C B Ashworth*)

SPITFIRES TO THUNDERBOLTS

From early January 1943 onwards, the battle-weary Spitfire VBs assigned to the 4th FG would soon be replaced by another aircraft on the Debden flightline – the Republic P-47C Thunderbolt. The largest single-seat, piston-engined American fighter to see combat, the immense P-47 was more than twice the weight of the Spitfire. Pilots, especially the old hands who had flown with the 'Eagle' Squadrons, were dubious about the Thunderbolt. 'Goody' Goodson recalled discussing the machine with a horrified Don Blakeslee. Goodson said that the Thunderbolt would catch anything in a dive, to which Blakeslee shot back, 'It damn well ought to be able to dive – it sure as hell can't climb!'

Full group conversion to the P-47 would not be complete until late March, so in the meantime squadrons continued to fly Spitfire VBs in combat. On 5 February, Capt 'Wild Bill' Kelly spotted a large convoy near Walcheren Island, off Holland, and as he dove in to attack his aircraft suffered a direct hit from a destroyer's guns at 1200 ft. With his fighter on fire, he initially tried to make the Dutch coast, then turned back to ditch near the convoy. As his aircraft was consumed by fire, Kelly tried to roll it onto its back and take to his parachute, but he became stuck halfway out of the cockpit. The aeroplane nosed into the water and sank immediately.

The Channel claimed another victim eight days later when the Spitfire VB of 2Lt Jap Powell suffered engine failure during a convoy patrol. The pilot baled out, but by the time rescuers reached him Powell had drowned.

After now-Maj Blakeslee led a 'Ramrod' to St Omer on 19 February, orders were received at Debden to apply identification markings to the group's growing ranks of P-47s. These consisted of a white band to the leading edge of the cowling, a star-and-bar insignia below each wing, a 12-inch stripe on the vertical fin and an 18-inch stripe on the horizontal stabilizers. The still-unfamiliar fighter was being misidentified as an Fw 190, and these touches, it was hoped, would avoid mistakes.

On 26 February, the group flew three missions escorting bombers sent to strike an armed raider docked at Dunkirk. The next day, another mission to Dunkirk found the raider had departed, so the group shot up and bombed the docks instead.

By 8 March, the group had gone 17 days without seeing an enemy aircraft, and although the 335th and 336th FSs spotted seven Fw 190s menacing RAF bombers during a 'Ramrod' to Rouen that day, the Germans fled the moment the Spitfires turned to engage them.

Forty-eight hours later, the 334th FS gave the P-47 its operation debut in the ETO when 14 aircraft, led by 4th FG Executive Officer Lt Col Chesley Peterson, were sent on a sweep of Ostend. All the fighters returned safely to Debden. The 335th and 336th FSs took their Spitfires to France on 12 March, where they were bounced by two Fw 190s. One

Lt Col Chesley Peterson (leaning over the chart table) briefs two sections from the 4th FG prior to the group flying a 'Rhubarb' over France in the spring of 1943. Peterson survived a close call when flying 1Lt Victor France's P-47C *Miss Dallas* on 13 April 1943, as the fighter's engine failed over the Channel and he was forced to take to his parachute (*National Museum of the USAF*)

German fighter was damaged, but at a cost of a 336th FS Spitfire VB shot down and its pilot, 1Lt Hazen S Anderson, captured.

On 16 March, the 335th FS officially spent its final day flying Spitfires. Men from the unit who had been temporarily assigned to the 336th FS to learn how to fly the Thunderbolt returned to the 335th to teach their fellow pilots about the idiosyncrasies of the P-47. A week later the first Republic fighters were issued to the 335th. A dozen more Thunderbolts arrived on 27 March. After several days of bad weather, 334th FS CO Maj Coen went up on 3 April for a recognition flight with B-17 crews and, at 25,000 ft, his supercharger caught fire. When he baled out, the shroud caught on his arm and he broke his shoulder. That same day, 2Lt Frank Smolinsky of the 335th FS was killed when he too suffered engine failure in a P-47C and stalled in from 150 ft while attempting a forced landing at Sawbridgeworth airfield, in Hertfordshire.

10 April saw two pilots from the 335th FS fly the group's last mission with the Spitfire. The following day, Maj Blakeslee led six P-47s on a

Groundcrew survey the landing gear of P-47C *WELA KEHAO*. Assigned to 1Lts Stanley Anderson and Walter 'Lulu' Hollander of the 334th FS, the Thunderbolt's art was created by prolific 4th FG groundcrewman Sgt Don Allen to honor Hollander's Honolulu, Hawaii, home, but the pilot was transferred to the 6th Fighter Wing before he could fly any missions in this particular aircraft. *WELA KEHAO* was eventually passed on to the 495th Fighter Training Group (FTG) (*via Wade Meyers*)

Above left
This P-47 remains something of a mystery machine, but it is clearly another example of Sgt Don Allen's nose art (*via Wade Meyers*)

Above centre
Capt Ervin 'Dusty' Miller's P-47C 41-6529 *Hi! R.P.M.* commemorated the birth of his son, Robert Paul Miller. A native of Oakland, California, Miller had previously been a member of No 133 'Eagle' Sqn prior to the unit becoming the 336th FS (*via Wade Meyers*)

Above right
336th FS P-47C 41-6573 wore this artwork while assigned to 1Lt Andrew Stephenson. The machine was later passed on to 1Lt Peter Lehman, who was the son of the governor of New York at the time. Lehman added the acronym *B.E.V.O.A.P.A.B.M*, which he said stood for 'Bird's Eye View of a Pig's Arse by Moonlight'! Note the white star on the fighter's wheel cover – a frequently seen marking on Eighth Air Force P-47s in 1943 (*via Wade Meyers*)

sweep over France that was intended to draw enemy fighters up before Allied bombers launched their mission. No German aircraft were sighted, however. On 13 April, a 'Ramrod' to Bruges and a 'Rodeo' to Berck were again uneventful, but one P-47 was shot down by British anti-aircraft after flying over Dover at low altitude. The pilot was able to walk away from his destroyed P-47.

Two days later, Lt Col Peterson led a 'Rodeo' to Cassel. As the 335th FS headed for the Continent at 27,000 ft, it spotted five Fw 190s and peeled off to attack. Peterson shot down one Focke-Wulf (for his seventh, and last, kill), but as he turned to re-enter the fray, a cylinder blew out in the engine of his P-47C. Peterson nursed the aircraft back across the Channel, only for it to catch fire 30 miles from the coast. Jumping from his blazing fighter, his bulky parachute opened only seconds before he hit the water. An RAF Walrus quickly scooped Peterson up, shaken, but sporting only a cut lip and two black eyes as souvenirs of his escape.

Meanwhile, Maj Blakeslee had spotted three Fw 190s ahead of him, and they made the mistake of trying to dive away from him. He closed in and sent two bursts into one fighter, which caught fire and crashed – the first kill for the 4th's P-47, and Blakeslee's fourth overall.

Lt Boock saw a P-47 under attack and latched onto the attacker's tail. The Fw 190 hit its quarry, then split-S'ed away. Boock stayed on the German fighter and fired, the Fw 190 bursting into flames and crashing into the sea. Lt Gover also bagged an Fw 190, and Capt Richard McMinn also reportedly destroyed one, but he and Capt Stanley Anderson (both from the 334th FS) were in turn shot down and killed.

A lone Fw 190 flew through the 335th FS during a 'Ramrod' to Antwerp on 4 May, and Lt George Carpenter managed to damage the fighter and send it spiralling earthwards. On the way back, 334th FS pilot Lt John Lutz suffered an engine problem, and at 2500 ft his P-47C rolled over and dove into the Channel two miles south of Flushing. Lutz baled out and was seen floating unconscious in the water, but rescue aeroplanes could subsequently find no trace of him.

A 'Ramrod' to Antwerp on 14 May saw the 335th FS bounce some Fw 190s, with Blakeslee claiming one destroyed for his all important fifth victory. Lt Col Peterson and Lt Gover were credited with probables.

1Lt Duane Beeson, Maj Jim Clark, and Lt Col Don Blakeslee are seen at the door of the Red Cross's alcohol-free Eagle Club in London in the autumn of 1943. More often, the pilots could be found at the nearby Crackers Club, where no such prohibition on beverage choice existed (*National Museum of the USAF*)

1Lt James Goodson's P-47D 42-7959 bore the diving eagle emblem he would later have applied to his P-51B Mustang. Goodson was flying this aeroplane when he shot down an Fw 190 near Hulst on 22 July 1943 for his first of 14 kills. The fighter was subsequently lost in October 1944 while flying with the 404th FG in Belgium (*via Wade Meyers*)

On the 18 May 'Rodeo' to Bruges, Bf 109s jumped and shot down 2Lt Robert Boock, who was killed when his P-47 crashed into the Channel. Squadronmates Capt T J Andrews and 2Lt Duane Beeson set off in pursuit of the Messerschmitts, using the P-47's unmatched speed in a dive to close on them. Despite being pursued by two more Bf 109s, both 334th FS pilots turned into their pursuers and shot them down. These were the first Bf 109 kills credited to the Thunderbolt.

With 200 sorties under his belt, Lt Col Chesley Peterson was relieved of flying duties on 19 May and succeeded as 4th FG Executive Officer by Maj Blakeslee. Two days later, a 'Rodeo' to Ostend by the 334th FS encountered a pair of Fw 190s, one of which was reportedly engaged by 1Lt Brewster Morgan. His P-47C was, however, hit by the German fighter, forcing him to ditch off Ostend – Morgan spent the rest of the war as a PoW. Squadronmates Lts Pisanos, Gordon Whitlow and Leland MacFarlane went after the second Fw 190, with Pisanos firing a short burst that drew white smoke from the fighter. Whitlow and MacFarlane attempted to follow it inland, but were killed when their Thunderbolts collided northwest of Bruges.

Fw 190s were next encountered during a sweep of the coast near Brest on 29 May, when one got on Lt Earle Carlow's tail and hit his fighter with several 20 mm shells. He made it home thanks to the cockpit armour.

During a 12 June 'Rodeo' to Roulers and Ypres, 1Lt Ernest Beatie of the 335th FS developed engine trouble in his P-47C and baled out over the Channel. Luckily, an RAF Walrus plucked him from the water and returned him safely to England. Three days later, during a weather-cancelled 'Ramrod', the engine in 1Lt Howard Hively's P-47C also let go mid-Channel, forcing him to bale out over the water. The future ace was circled by 335th FS pilot 1Lt Cadman Padgett, who guided a launch to rescue him.

On 22 June, Maj Blakeslee led a 'Ramrod' to Antwerp, and the rendezvous with the bombers was missed. By the time the group picked up the bombers on their way out, the B-17s were under attack from 20 German fighters. The 335th and 336th FSs engaged the fighters while the 334th FS flew top cover. In the melee which ensued, the 4th FG claimed three Fw 190s and a Bf 109 shot down. Two victories were credited to 1Lt Beatie, thus proving that he was fully recovered from his dunking in the Channel ten days earlier.

He and his section saw four straggling B-17s under attack from a quartet of Fw 190s. 'I overshot the last '190 and attacked the one in front of him', Beatie reported. 'I saw strikes and a big ball of black smoke as he snapped over and went straight down.' Although Beatie blacked out and turned sharply away from the Fw 190, squadronmate 1Lt Paul Ellington saw the fighter dive into the ground near the Dutch islands of Beveland-Walcheren.

When Beatie came to, he found himself surrounded by ten Bf 109s. 'Three went directly in front of me as I pulled over in a tight chandelle', he said. 'I dove on the last in a line and got in strikes on his cockpit and he started over in a roll and went down. I followed him until he started pulling up. I was very close to him, and was just pushing the firing button when he baled out.' 1Lt Fonzo 'Snuffy' Smith knocked down another Fw 190, then outran two more enemy fighters, and 1Lt 'Goody' Goodson of the 336th downed the third Fw 190 near Hulst for his first kill.

Four days later, the group provided withdrawal support for B-17s, which they picked up around Dieppe – along with the now mandatory swarm of enemy aircraft. In the resulting scrap, 334th FS pilots Lts Raymond Care and Duane Beeson (both flying P-47D-1s) each downed a Bf 109, with Lt Dale Leaf damaging a third. 'Six Bf 109s came in under us head-on about a mile east of me', said Care. 'I turned and followed them inland. Two of them broke away and turned out to sea. I picked the leading aircraft and fired four or five bursts. I closed to 250 yards and gave two more bursts, which hit the enemy aircraft in the cowling and cockpit. Fire burst out of his engine and the enemy aircraft slid down into the sea.'

The 4th suffered its next combat loss on 14 July when 2Lt Ward Wortman of the 335th FS set off after an Fw 190 northeast of Amiens and failed to return to Debden. He was later confirmed as having been killed in action.

1Lt 'Mike' Sobanski's P-47D 42-7924 and another 334th FS aircraft – both equipped with 200-gallon external tanks – prepare for take-off at Debden. The ungainly external tank was referred to as a 'baby' by the crews, and when first employed, the store could not be jettisoned in flight. This was quickly rectified by groundcrews, who modified the tank mounts, but the drag-inducing 200-gallon store was soon replaced by streamlined, pylon-mounted, 75- and 108-gallon tanks (*National Museum of the USAF*)

Streaming glycol from its engine, a Bf 109G takes hits on the wings in this gun camera film still taken from 1Lt Beeson's P-47 on 28 July 1943 during the group's first mission to Germany. This fighter went down (*National Museum of the USAF*)

On 19 July, the 4th FG received orders stating that the star-and-disc national insignia on its P-47s was to be complemented by two white bars on either side. The new marking was to be outline in red.

The group was also issued with 200-gallon belly tanks for its fighters at this time, and these were first used on the 25 July 'Rodeo' to Ghent.

Two days later, the group was forced to abandon an escort for B-26s when its 'tankerless' P-47s ran low on fuel. After this mission, the 200-gallon external tanks were installed on all serviceable aircraft. The big tanks made possible the next day's 'Ramrod' to Westhoof-Emmerich – the group's first foray into Germany airspace. On the way to the rendezvous, the group found a bomb wing of B-17s under attack by more than 30 Bf 109s and Fw 190s. Diving headlong into the enemy fighters, the 4th fought a large-scale dogfight over the Dutch city of Utrecht. The group was subsequently credited with the destruction of five Bf 109s and four Fw 190s, although 2Lt Henry Ayres of the 336th FS was forced to bale out over Holland when his fighter was shot up by Luftwaffe ace Major Rolf-Günther Hermichen, adjutant of III./JG 26.

1Lt Beeson jumped on a single Bf 109 and fired. 'I saw many strikes, his left wingtip blew off and then there was an explosion just in front of his cockpit, when he lurched violently and went down smoking. While climbing back to rejoin [my section], an Fw 190 got on my tail and Lt Care closed up behind me and opened fire. There were many strikes and the pilot baled out.'

Maj Carl Miley's P-47C 41-6579 wears the early US star-and-disc on the wings and fuselage and Sgt Don Allen's rendition of 'Donald Duck' on its nose. Miley downed a Bf 109 in this machine on 27 July. The fighter was later turned over to 2Lt Conrad 'Connie' Ingold, who demolished it in a landing accident on 16 September 1943 (*Keith Hoey via Wade Meyers*)

Some 22 P-47Cs from the 335th (closest to the camera) and 336th FSs assemble for take-off around Debden's west runway prior to heading on yet another sweep into France in May 1943. Note how well the fighters' white ETO bands stand out (*via Wade Meyers*)

Capt Carl Miley and Capt Gover each scored single kills, while 4th FG CO Col Edward Anderson downed two Bf 109s for his only aerial victories of the war. Other fighters fell to Capt Roy Evans, Lt Frank Boyles and Lt Leon Blanding.

After two uneventful missions on 29 July, the following day the 335th FS, led by unit CO Maj Gilbert Halsey, conducted a 'Circus' to Westhoof-Emmerich that ran into more than 50 enemy aircraft. 1Lt Frederick Merritt was killed when he was shot down by Major Rolf-Günther Hermichen of III./JG 26, who claimed his second victory over a 4th FG P-47 in just three days. The outnumbered Thunderbolts downed five Fw 190s in return, however.

Lt Aubrey Stanhope saw three Fw 190s in vic formation and attacked the one on the right, 'getting hits on his tail and left wing. He side-slipped and went down. I then turned to the one on the left, firing a long burst from 15 degrees deflection to dead astern. I saw strikes on his tail and left wing. Then there was a violent explosion in his left wing where his gun was. There was a huge flash, pieces flew off, and all his wing outboard of his gun came off clean. The plane then tumbled tail over nose and spun down smoking badly.'

2Lt Pierce McKennon's P-47C 41-6621 displays a single kill marking, denoting his victory over an Fw 190 on 30 July 1943 – the first of his 11 aerial successes (*National Museum of the USAF*)

2Lt Pierce McKennon saw a 'bomber being clobbered by two Fw 190s. I cut my throttle and dove on one as he broke away and went into a diving turn.' The Fw 190 went into a sharp climbing turn to port. McKennon 'firewalled everything and closed to within about 150 ft and got in a three- or four-second burst. Something flew off his port side and large quantities of white smoke came pouring out. He flicked violently to starboard, and I almost hit him. Passing within just a few feet of him, I saw his engine on fire with long streamers of flame and smoke.' McKennon had just claimed the first of his 11 kills.

Former No 71 'Eagle' Sqn pilot 1Lt Steve Pisanos claimed three kills with the P-47 in 1943–44, before 'making ace' in the P-51B. Unlike most other members of the 4th FG, he had flown an Allison-engined Mustang I during his brief spell with the RAF (*National Museum of the USAF*)

Lt Ken Smith saw a fighter below him, and as he throttled back and manoeuvred to stay with it, he suddenly realized it was an Fw 190 – it was, in fact, the aircraft flown by Feldwebel Ernst Christoff of I./JG 26, who had just shot down B-17F 42-30290 *Lucky Lady II* of the 388th BS/96th BG. 'I opened fire at about 75 yards', he said. 'I immediately saw flashes at the wing root and cockpit area. I broke off as he rolled and went into a spin.' Christoff got out of the aeroplane, but his 'chute snagged on the fighter's tail and the nine-kill ace was dragged to his death. The 4th FG's final tally for this mission was five kills for the loss of 1Lt Merritt.

The group saw no further aerial opposition until a 12 August escort to Sittard, in northern Holland. Near the back of the formation, 1Lt Cadman Padgett's section saw a group of enemy fighters shy away at the sight of the escort. 'One of them, who must have taken us for friendly aircraft, started to formate on us at our exact altitude on our starboard side', he recalled. 'I did a slow turn to starboard, a slow turn to port and then closed in behind him. I sat there for a few seconds lining up my sights. When I had closed to within 150 yards I fired a two-second burst and he lit up like a Christmas tree.' Padgett fired a second burst, and 'immediately something exploded so violently that he was completely obscured from my vision. I broke away sharply as I was afraid of ramming him.' 334th FS pilots 1Lt William O'Regan, 1Lt Pisanos and future 10.5-kill ace Capt James Clark also claimed Fw 190s destroyed.

Four days later, Maj Blakeslee led a 'Ramrod' to Paris. The P-47s were attacked by small groups of six to eight fighters, and almost all of the Thunderbolts were forced to land at advance bases in southern England on their return as a result of damage and a lack of fuel.

'I was 2000 ft above and slightly northeast of the first box of B-17s', reported Maj John DuFour, CO of the 336th FS. 'I noticed that enemy fighters were making head-on attacks on this box of bombers, so I dove down to a position directly in front of the B-17s and attacked two Me 109s who were just turning to make their attack.' DuFour damaged one fighter and sent it diving away, then saw two more Bf 109s preparing an identical attack. In a turn, he fired and saw no hits. 'I took one last look at the '109 and saw his left wing suddenly peel back and fly off. The '109 immediately flicked into a peculiar, uneven type of spin, and when last seen was headed straight down completely out of control.'

336th FS pilot 1Lt Goodson had his section above and to the left of the B-17 formation when he saw several German fighters angling for head-on attacks. Goodson and 2Lt Kendall 'Swede' Carlson overshot a yellow-nosed Fw 190, and seconds later another German fighter crossed in front of Goodson, intent on attacking the bombers from behind. 'I closed to

Newly delivered attrition replacement P-47Cs are given the once-over in the summer sunshine at Debden in late August 1943. Note the embellishment already added to the wheel cover of the Thunderbolt in the foreground (*National Museum of the USAF*)

dead astern and about 75 yards or less. I observed many strikes, saw the enemy aircraft roll on its back and I followed until I saw him crash straight into a woods north of Paris', Goodson reported. He and Carlson then climbed back up to the bombers, only to find another Fw 190 lining up for an identical shot at them. 'I fired from 250 yards and closed, observing many strikes, including a violent flash in the cockpit', said Goodson. The Focke-Wulf fell to earth in a spin.

Capt Roy Evans' section from the 335th FS was covering the front box of bombers when he bagged his Bf 109. 'I saw three Me 109s start to attack a straggling "Fort" out of the sun. I was 3000 ft above the enemy aircraft

Also a former member of No 71 'Eagle' Sqn, future six-kill ace 1Lt Henry Mills scored his first two victories (both Fw 190s) on 16 August 1943 – a day when the 4th FG was credited with downing 18 German aeroplanes. Promoted to major, and made operations officer for the 334th FS, Mills failed to return from an escort mission to Berlin on 6 March 1944. He spent the rest of the war as a PoW (*National Museum of the USAF*)

Included in the first batch of Thunderbolts delivered to the 4th FG (on 16 January 1943), P-47C 41-6197 *Sand Man* belonged to 336th FS pilot 1Lt Donald Nee. It was labelled *Cisco* on the opposite side of the cowling. This, like much of the 4th FG's nose art, was the handiwork of Sgt Don Allen. Nee, who was a former No 133 'Eagle' Sqn pilot, transferred to the 354th FG in November 1943 (*via Wade Meyers*)

334th FS pilot 1Lt Dale Leaf, seen here with Steve Pisanos' P-47D 42-7945 *Miss Plainfield*, was ambushed by four Fw 190s and killed near Formerie on 1 September 1943 (*National Museum of the USAF*)

with my section. I went down to attack these Me 109s. I took one enemy aircraft and my No 2 man, Lt Stanhope, took another. The first burst of about one second hit him in the tail or slightly behind. I moved my bead up and saw strikes around the cockpit, on the engine and at the wing root on the left side. I was closing so fast that I flew past very close to the aircraft – less than 20 yards away. I saw the pilot slumped over in the cockpit and smoke and flame coming from the left side of the engine cowling.'

Future six-kill ace Lt Raymond Care wingman spotted two Fw 190s flying line abreast, parallel to the bombers. 'I attacked from line astern', he recalled, seeing the flash of strikes. The stricken machine's undercarriage dropped down. 'I then skidded over to the second enemy aircraft and gave him a burst from about 150 yards.' Care climbed and turned, watching the enemy aircraft go down. 'I saw one of them hit and explode in a small field on the outskirts of Paris. The other I lost sight of going down and smoking, out of control.' He was credited with a probable for this claim.

In addition, Capt Clark of the 334th FS shot down two Fw 190s before his P-47 was hit by a 20 mm cannon shell that tore a three-foot hole in its port wing. Squadronmate, and future six-kill ace, 1Lt Henry Mills also knocked down two Fw 190s, whilst Lts Hively, Happel, Fink, Stanhope, Young and Fonzo Smith, and Flt Off Clyde Smith claimed single victories. 1Lt Joseph Matthews of the 336th FS also destroyed an Fw 190, but was in turn shot down, probably by Leutnant Friedrich Mayer of

10./JG.2. He successfully evaded and returned to Britain in late 1943.

On 17 August it was announced that Col Edward Anderson was being promoted to brigadier general and taking command of the 65th Fighter Wing, while Col Chesley Peterson was being made 4th FG CO.

Peterson, the youngest 'full-bird' colonel in the Army at just 23 years of age, led the group on a sweep near Formerie on 1 September. Almost a dozen enemy fighters bounced the 334th FS, and 1Lt Dale B Leaf was shot down. His P-47D was last seen diving with four Fw 190s on its tail. Leaf was killed in action.

1Lt Paul Ellington's P-47C 41-6217, equipped with a 108-gallon belly tank, sits ready before a mission at Debden. Ellington rose to the rank of captain during his 17 months with the group before being forced to bale out of his P-51B after it suffered engine trouble over the Dutch coast on 4 March 1944. He spent the rest of the war as a PoW (*National Museum of the USAF*)

Two days later, the group escorted bombers of the 1st Air Task Force, and as the formation neared Abbeville, enemy aircraft made a try for the 'heavies'. The 336th FS Squadron broke up the attack. A short while later, while providing withdrawal escort for the same B-17s, the 335th FS arrived at the rendezvous point to find the bombers under attack from 15 yellow-nosed Fw 190s. The latter dove away at the sight of American fighters. A few minutes later, a lone Focke-Wulf tried to press home an attack and was shot down by newly promoted Maj Roy Evans.

Although no kills were recorded on 7 September, the 335th FS broke up an enemy attack on bombers near Daynze before it could get started. As the bombers approached Hulst, the 334th FS accomplished the same feat, but in the process, 1Lt Aubrey Stanhope's P-47 was hit by flak while chasing an Fw 190 at low altitude and he baled out. He was soon captured.

On the 9th, more than 30 enemy fighters went after B-17s near Elbeu. The 334th and 336th FSs broke up their attack, reformed and then

Mission time. Groundcrew prepare to plug the auxiliary power unit (near the starboard undercarriage leg) of this replacement P-47D into its receptacle to start the fighter's engine. Note that the pilot is receiving last-minute instructions from the operations officer of the 336th FS (*National Museum of the USAF*)

1Lt Willard Millikan of the 336th FS prepares to take off in 1Lt Jack Raphael's assigned P-47C 41-6529 *Eager Beaver*/*MISS BETH*. Millikan scored a kill over an Fw 190 in his own Thunderbolt (P-47C 41-6180) on 27 September (*Jack Raphael via Wade Meyers*)

scattered another group of 16 German fighters. Despite the group's best efforts, at least three B-17s went down, as did two P-47s from the 4th. 1Lt Frank Fink of the 335th suffered an engine failure in his P-47C and he baled out over Paris, where he became a PoW.

Capt Vernon Boehle of the 334th FS was the other pilot lost. 'I dove after an Fw 190 that was attacking a "Fort"', he said. 'I followed, but pulled up unable to get into firing range. Climbing back up, another Fw 190 dove to attack me.' This was the aircraft flown by Oberleutnant Artur Beese of I./JG 26, who would ultimately score 22 kills prior to his death. 'I took evasive action, ending up in a spin and dive and eventually coming out at 10,000 ft. The Fw 190 followed, firing at every opportunity as I manoeuvred. I was able to get in a short burst at him, but saw no strikes. I then dove for the deck. He followed, still firing, until, apparently out of ammo, he broke off and climbed.'

Boehle duly headed for home, nursing the P-47 until, suddenly, there was a terrific vibration and the engine broke loose and fell away! 'With some difficulty, I baled out at about 15,000 ft', said Boehle. 'I landed in

1Lt 'Mike' Sobanski climbs into his P-47C 41-4924 prior to flying his next mission in the autumn of 1943. Like many of the group's pilots at this time, Sobanski has opted for RAF flying gear. British flying helmets and 'Mae Wests' were hangovers from the days when these men had flown Spitfires (*National Museum of the USAF*)

Capt Jim Clark prepares to taxi our in P-47C 41-6413 in the early autumn of 1943. At various times, this 334th FS aircraft was assigned to Maj Oscar Coen, Lt Col Chesley Peterson and 1Lt Thomas Andrews. Clark, who scored 10.5 kills, downed four German fighters flying Thunderbolts in 1943 (*via Wade Meyers*)

the water about 30 miles off Dieppe.' He released his dinghy, inflated it and climbed in, getting 'as comfortable as possible'. After midnight on his second night adrift, Boehle heard British motor torpedo boats and flashed the torch on his 'Mae West'. 'They finally saw me and picked me up after 43 hours in the water'.

On a 15 September 'Ramrod' to Paris, 1Lt Winslow 'Mike' Sobanski led his section in to break up several Fw 190s attacking the bombers. No victory claims were made, but the P-47s drove off the attackers.

The group did not score again until 27 September, when an escort to Rottermeroog Island was attacked by a pair of Fw 190s. They were in turn set upon by the 336th FS, and 1Lt Willard Millikan shot down one of the German fighters to register his first of 13 kills.

Two days prior to this mission being flown, P-51B Mustang 43-6388 had been assigned to the 334th FS for evaluation purposes. Maj Coen and Capt Clark immediately made experimental hops in it, followed by Capt Fonzo Smith of the 335th.

On 2 October, the group watched over B-17s striking Emden, and deflected several waves of enemy fighters. Six Bf 109s attempted to attack the bombers near the target area, but they were engaged by the 335th and 336th FSs. One of the Messerschmitts became the first victory for future 8.5-kill ace Flt Off Albert Schlegel, who was also credited with damaging a second Bf 109.

Later, near Aurich, ten Fw 190s were chased off by the 334th FS. 'These appeared to be positioning themselves for a head-on attack on the bombers', said 1Lt Duane Beeson. 'They were flying in very tight formation, and as I closed up on their rear, they broke in several directions. I watched them to see that none came around on me, then as they split up and headed down, I picked the tail-end Charlie and opened fire at about 250 yards. I saw strikes around his cockpit and engine, then large pieces started coming off and he jettisoned his hood.'

The Jagdwaffe opposed a 'Ramrod' to Bremen on 8 October, the 334th FS spotting 30 enemy fighters up-sun of the rear box of bombers. As they climbed to attack them, the P-47 pilots were bounced repeatedly by groups

On 2 October 1943, the 4th FG downed two German fighters, one of which fell to the guns of 1Lt Duane Beeson (left). He is seen here chatting with 336th FS pilot 1Lt Kenneth Peterson, who, like Beeson, was a former 'Eagle' Squadron pilot. Both men would become PoWs within a week of each other in March–April 1944. Standing between them is group mascot 'Duke' (*National Museum of the USAF*)

A close-up of the nose art that adorned 1Lt Jack Raphael's P-47. This fighter had been previously been Capt Ervin Miller's *Hi! R.P.M.*, seen on page 13, but its name was changed to reflect its new pilot's Pacific Northwest heritage (*Jack Raphael via Wade Meyers*)

After being told by old hands that he would have to wait and gain experience before he would be ready to claim his first kill, Flt Off Ralph Hofer bagged a Bf 109 over the Zuider Zee on 8 October 1943 – his very first mission over enemy territory! He would have to wait until 6 February 1944 to down his second victory, however (*Bruce Zigler via Wade Meyers*)

of four to eight fighters. Flt Off Clyde Smith was hit by a Bf 109 early on in the engagement, his cockpit erupting in flames and the pilot baling out. As he was floating down to become a PoW, he gained some measure of satisfaction when he saw 1Lt Beeson shoot down the aeroplane that had got him. This victory made Beeson the 4th FG's first ace, and he claimed his sixth kill (another Bf 109) a few minutes later.

1Lt Robert Patterson of the 335th FS was also downed by a Bf 109, and although he evaded for two months, he was eventually taken prisoner and sent to *Stalag Luft III*.

334th FS pilot Flt Off Ralph 'Kidd' Hofer, on his first mission, spotted a Bf 109 shooting up the P-47 of 63rd FS/56th FG pilot 2Lt Dover Fleming near Amsterdam. Without hesitation, he swooped in and shot down Unteroffizier Franz Effenberger of I./JG 3. He could not, however, save Fleming, who crashed to his death in the Zuider Zee. Capt Clark took his overall tally to 4.5 victories when he also claimed a Bf 109 destroyed.

The day's second mission was also a 'Ramrod' to the Bremen area, and again the Germans tried to intercept. For their efforts, they lost two aeroplanes to the 335th FS, namely an 'Me 210' (almost certainly an Me 410) despatched by 1Lt Donald Ross and an Fw 190 downed by Maj Evans. The latter victory saw Evans crowned as the 4th FG's second ace.

On 3 November the group launched an escort to Wilhelmshaven. They encountered German fighters attacking from up-sun, then swooping back to altitude for another pass. The tactic was designed to force the P-47s to drop their external tanks, as the USAAF pilots could not hope to stay with the enemy fighters in a climb when carrying an underbelly store. With the tanks gone, the 4th FG would have to cut short its mission. 334th FS pilots 1Lt Ivan Moon and Flt Off Frank Gallion fell victim to these tactics, both men being killed when their fighters plunged into the Zuider Zee. In return, 1Lt Alexander Rafalovich of the 334th FS claimed a Bf 109 destroyed and 2Lt Robert Frazer got a probable.

2Lt John Godfrey's first *REGGIE'S REPLY* was this P-47D, 42-7884, which he inherited from his future flight leader, 1Lt Don Gentile. Named after Godfrey's brother, who had perished during the Battle of the Atlantic, this aircraft also bore the name *LUCKY* and an artwork of a dog on the port side of its engine cowling. 'Lucky' was the name of Godfrey's dog. The ace would claim 1.5 kills and one probable (all Bf 109s) in this aircraft in late 1943 (*National Museum of the USAF*)

Two days later, Maj Evans led a 'Ramrod' to Dortmund, and as the bombers reached the initial point, 12 Fw 190s attacked head-on in a series of four-abreast formations. Evans led his 335th FS in to break up the attack, his own fire sending one into a spin. As the squadron turned to chase the 11 remaining aeroplanes away, a further eight attacked the group, and a melee ensued. 'Two Fw 190s appeared in front of me at about 400 yards distance', said Capt Fonzo Smith, 'and I closed to approximately 300 yards and started firing.' Smith saw numerous flashes and explosions along the fuselage and wing roots. 'A large section from his empennage broke off and passed under my port wing.' When B-17s started firing at the Fw 190s, Smith broke off. He was credited with an Fw 190 destroyed.

On 26 November, the group escorted B-24s to Bremen. 1Lt Cadman Padgett's section was covering some stragglers when he saw a Bf 109 lining up behind one of the Liberators. He closed to 200 yards astern of the Bf 109 and opened fire, hitting the left side of the fuselage near the cockpit. He reported, 'As I flew into his slipstream, my sights were momentarily thrown off and a large object, possibly his canopy, passed by to my starboard. I lined him up in my sights again and gave him another two-second burst, observing strikes and a large red flash at his port wing root and fuselage. A shower of fragments flew off the enemy aircraft, which immediately started tumbling downward. As I passed him I noticed his right wheel was down.'

Texan Capt Fonzo 'Snuffy' Smith flew this P-47D (42-7936) during the first of his two tours with the 4th FG. He claimed three Fw 190s destroyed and a Bf 109 as a probable between 22 June and 29 November 1943. An ex-No 121 'Eagle' Sqn pilot, Smith was eventually shot down on 3 August 1944, spending the rest of the war as a PoW (*National Museum of the USAF*)

Padgett's section climbed back up to the bombers, and five minutes later he noticed contrails. 'These two Bf 109s flew parallel and to our rear for a short distance, then made a diving turn to starboard as if to attack the bombers.' Padgett took the section in an orbit to the left and came out on the tail of one of the enemy aircraft as it entered a steep climbing turn to port. 'I fired a short burst at 200 yards but observed no hits. The aircraft flipped over and went down in a vertical dive, while the No 2 enemy aircraft made two aileron turns to port and started off to the southwest.'

Two days later, 'Eagle' Squadron ace Maj Selden Edner led a 'Ramrod' to Bremen, fending off a series of hit-and-run attacks during which 1Lt Beeson and Capt Fonzo Smith claimed Bf 109s probably destroyed.

Promoted to CO of the 336th FS on 29 November, Maj Edner led his squadron on a 'Ramrod' to Solingen on 1 December, during which future 16.333-kill ace 2Lt John Godfrey downed a Bf 109 for his first victory. 'Down below me a lone "Fort" was headed for home and a Bf 109 was jockeying for position sun-up to it', he said. 'I dove down on him from up-sun. I closed in on him very fast from astern. I fired at 250 yards. Immediately, red and white sheets of flame enveloped him. I pulled up to watch him go down, but there was nothing left.'

A lull in operations followed, but losses continued. On 2 December, during a test flight, a 334th FS P-47D caught fire and struck the ground at a 40-degree angle near Kenton, killing Flt Off John McNabb and spreading wreckage over a four-acre area.

Many of the Thunderbolts in the group had the outboard gun in each wing removed, saving weight and helping to stretch range. When belly tanks began to arrive, especially the 108-gallon tanks, the guns were re-installed. Here, armourers wrestle belted 0.50-cal ammunition into the left wing bay of a P-47 (*Jack Raphael via Wade Meyers*)

On 11 December, Maj Evans led a 'Rodeo' to Emden. While en route to the rendezvous point, the 335th FS was attacked by four Bf 109s. Eight more Messerschmitts bounced the 334th FS, and during the ensuing battle 1Lt Victor France downed one of the attackers.

An uneventful 'Ramrod' to Bremen two days later was followed by a second 'Ramrod' to the same target on 16 December. New tactics were introduced on the latter mission, with the group spreading its three squadrons over a 30-mile front, with each unit being 2000 ft apart. A fifth section was also added to each squadron to serve as scouts, flying 500 ft above the rest of the unit and tasked with reporting and attacking approaching enemy fighters. It was hoped that the three new sections would prevent the group from being broken up as it approached its rendezvous point with the bombers. The additional flight also meant that each unit would sortie 20 P-47s on a typical bomber escort mission.

During the operation, German heavy fighters attacked the bombers, and the destruction of a single Ju 88 was shared between future 336th FS aces Capt Don Gentile and 1Lts Louis 'Red Dog' Norley and Vermont Garrison.

334th FS pilot Capt Victor France stands before the third incarnation of *Miss DALLAS* (P-47D 42-7876). The first had been No 71 'Eagle' Sqn Spitfire VB AD196, which was called *Miss NORTH DALLAS*. This was succeeded by the P-47C (41-6414) that Lt Col Chesley Peterson was forced to bale out of on 15 April 1943. Having claimed 4.333 aerial and three strafing kills, France perished on 18 April 1944 when his P-51B43-6832 *Miss DALLAS* struck the ground near Stendal whilst he was chasing a Bf 109 at low-level (*National Museum of the USAF*)

Bremen was the target again on 20 December, and during the mission 1Lt Willard Millikan nailed a Bf 109. Flt Off Ralph Hofer turned back because of engine trouble, and while flying home alone he was bounced by three Bf 109s, which chased him mid-way across the Channel until he escaped. After doing six missions in P-51Bs with the 354th FG for experience – and claiming his first Mustang kill during the 20 December mission – Lt Col Don Blakeslee led a 'Ramrod' to Munster on the 22nd. Near Enschede, 1Lts Allen Bunte, Vasseure Wynn and John Godfrey bounced four Bf 109s. The latter split-S'ed and positioned himself behind one enemy aircraft. 'As I was closing in, another P-47 (flown by Wynn) gave a short burst and hit the No 2 enemy aircraft in the wing and fuselage. The P-47 pulled up, leaving me in a position to fire at the enemy aircraft.' Godfrey's rounds hit the Me 109 in the wings, fuselage and cockpit. The enemy aircraft rolled over, burning.

'I then closed in on the No 1 and started to fire. I saw strikes on the wings, fuselage and cockpit. Bits flew off the aircraft and I watched the pilot bale out as the Me 109 went out of control through the clouds. Another Me 109 pulled up behind me, and as he fired, I felt hits on my aircraft and saw tracers go by. I looked back and saw an Me 109 with a yellow nose firing at me. As I was practically in a stall, I yanked back on the stick, applied rudder and my aircraft toppled over and spun out. I managed to straighten it out and pulled out of the cloud. My height at the time I straightened out was about 50 ft.'

Wynn closed on another Bf 109 that was ahead and to his left. 'I gave him a two-second burst and he blew up, his starboard wing coming off', he said. Both Wynn and Godfrey were credited with 1.5 kills apiece.

1Lt Louis 'Red Dog' Norley's P-47C 41-6183 was the first of his fighters to be adorned with his nickname. It was also the only one of his machines to feature Walt Disney's 'Pluto' (who was tinged scarlet to match the name) on its engine cowling. Norley claimed one kill and one damaged in this aircraft in January–February 1944 (*via Wade Meyers*)

One of the first Mustangs assigned to the 335th FS, P-51C 42-103036 was supposed to have been RAF Mustang III FB142, but it was diverted to the USAAF. This aircraft was later transferred to the 496th FTG (*Keith Hoey via Wade Meyers*)

BLAKESLEE TAKES THE REINS

On New Year's Day 1944, Lt Col Don Blakeslee took over as commander of the 4th FG from Col Chesley Peterson. 'The 4th FG is going to be the top fighter group in the Eighth Air Force', Blakeslee announced. 'We are here to fight. To those who don't believe me, I would suggest transferring to another group. I'm going to fly the arse off each one of you. Those who keep up with me, good. Those who don't, I don't want them anyway.'

His first mission as CO came on 4 January, when he led an uneventful 'Ramrod' to Munster. The following day, Blakeslee headed up a Target Support for bombers heading for Tours airfield. As the 4th neared the target, four Fw 190s literally ran into elements of the 336th FS. Capt Gentile and 1Lt Robert Messenger each knocked one down.

On 7 January the group provided Withdrawal Support for bombers returning from Ludwigshafen, and the hard-flying Blakeslee was nearly undone by his aggressiveness. Near Hesdin, about a dozen Fw 190s attacked straggling B-17s from out of the sun. Blakeslee tried to bounce the enemy aeroplanes, but when he was cut off by some RAF Spitfires, he joined Capt Goodson's Red Section. 'I had climbed up 12,000–14,000 ft when I saw more Fw 190s attacking straggling "Forts"', said Blakeslee. 'I dived on these, being covered by Capt Goodson's section, and chased one enemy aircraft down to between 2000–3000 ft.'

Goodson, with wingman 1Lt Robert Wehrman in tow, followed Blakeslee line astern 'to the best of my ability', he said, although he admitted it was 'a rough ride'. 'Other '190s attempted to attack, but usually broke away down through the clouds when I turned into them.'

Suddenly, Blakeslee was jumped by three Fw 190s. One made a 'determined attack, firing at Lt Col Blakeslee even after I started firing at him', recalled Goodson. 'When I started getting strikes on him, he broke hard to port, but even though he pulled streamers from his wingtips, I was able to pull my sights through him. He suddenly did two-and-a-half flick rolls and then split-S'ed vertically through some light scud cloud. I followed in a steep wingover, and had to pull out hard to miss some trees as the cloud was lower than I had realized. As I did so, I caught sight of an explosion. Since the '190 had gone through vertically, I feel sure he could not have pulled out even if he had not been damaged.'

Goodson soon joined up with Blakeslee again. 'Before I could get close enough to prevent it, a '190 came in on Lt Col Blakeslee and commenced firing at short range', said Goodson. The German scored hits – 71 by the count of Blakeslee's groundcrew! Goodson got on his tail and fired, 'and was relieved to see strikes all over him, and see him peel away and crash in flames on the ground, which was quite close'. He had saved his CO, and 'made ace'. 1Lt Vermont Garrison damaged Blakeslee's third pursuer.

Lt Col Don Blakeslee was just 25 when he was given command of the 4th FG. One of his first acts was to begin a behind-the-scenes campaign to get his group equipped with Mustangs. The first P-51B was seen at Debden on 25 September 1943, but it was not until 28 February 1944 that the group flew its first operational mission with the aircraft (*National Museum of the USAF*)

Despite flying a damaged fighter, the CO of the 4th FG latched onto another Fw 190. 'The enemy aircraft I was attacking suddenly broke off its turn, straightened out and went into haze', said Blakeslee. 'I followed, and as he came out I was dead line astern. I fired a three- to four-second burst, observing strikes on the enemy aircraft's tail and starboard wing. Pieces came from the cockpit. It then did a half-flick to the right and went in. My radio had been shot out and my aircraft was spraying oil badly.'

While Blakeslee nursed his damaged Thunderbolt home, he and his escorts were repeatedly bounced by Bf 109s. By now only Wehrman, on his first combat mission, had ammunition left, leaving Goodson and Garrison to make mock attacks to throw off the Germans' aim. Blakeslee landed at Manston, having survived the mission with his seventh kill.

Exactly one week later, during a freelance sweep of northern France, the 336th FS bounced 15 Fw 190s over Compiegne Wood. Two fell to Capt Don Gentile (thus making him an ace) and 1Lt Vermont Garrison, and Flt Off Robert Richards claimed a single kill.

Gentile, who was flying with Richards as his wingman, saw the German formation fan out into two groups. 'I picked two stragglers flying north and attacked at "eight o'clock" to the enemy aircraft, which were in a 50-degree dive', said Gentile. 'I closed in and fired a long burst at the No 2 '190, and observed strikes around the left side of the cockpit, after which I saw smoke coming out.' Gentile's prey went into a spiralling dive and crashed.

He immediately shifted his attention to the lead Fw 190, closing in to about 250 yards and then opening fire. 'As I was trying to follow him down in his slipstream to get another shot, he hit the woods. I pulled out, just missing the woods myself. Just as I pulled up I was jumped by two '190s, and then the fun really started. The No 1 '190 was so close to me that I heard his guns. I broke and the first '190 went over me. I stayed in a port turn because the No 2 was still coming in.

'In the meantime, the No 1 had pulled up sharply to position himself for another attack, but I quickly swung to starboard and fired a short burst at the No 2, whom I never saw again. All this action took place at treetop height. I swung to port to get away from the No 1 man, who was firing, but giving too much deflection. I used the last of my ammo on the burst at the No 2 '190. I tried to outturn him, but he stayed inside me.'

At about this point, Gentile radioed 'Help! Help! I'm being clobbered!' When 1Lt Willard Millikan calmly asked him for his call sign and position, all he could stammer was 'I'm down here! By the railroad tracks with a '190!

'I suddenly flicked and just about wiped myself out on the trees. Recovering, I reversed my turn to starboard, and there he was, still inside me and still shooting like hell. I kept on turning and skidding. He

1Lt 'Steve' Pisanos and Capt Don Gentile were two former 'Eagle' Squadron pilots who helped make the 4th FG a top-scoring unit in 1943–44 (*National Museum of the USAF*)

Although seen here with a P-51B in early March 1944, 1Lt John Godfrey, Capt Don Gentile, 1Lt Peter Lehman, Capt Jim Goodson and 1Lt Willard Millikan were all veteran P-47 pilots. Godfrey, Goodson and Millikan would all end up as PoWs, Lehman was killed while testing a Mustang and Gentile was sent home after pranging his P-51B following his tour's final mission (*National Museum of the USAF*)

slid under and overshot, and I reversed again. We met head on, and he was still firing. For the next ten minutes we kept reversing turns from head-on attacks, trying to get on each other's tails', Gentile recalled. 'The last time he came in he didn't shoot, so he must have been out of ammunition. He then left and I felt like getting out and doing the rumba. I climbed up slowly and came home.'

Later, near Soissons, the group tangled with a dozen more Fw 190s, and this time it was the 334th FS that made all the kill claims – five in total. 1Lt Beeson was one of the first to attack. 'We saw 10–12 Fw 190s about 8000 ft below us diving inland', he said. 'I picked one of the last four and opened fire at about 250 yards. I saw several strikes and large flashes in the wing roots and observed a large hole in his cockpit hood. The aircraft fell off into a dive, turned over and exploded as it hit the ground.'

2Lt Alex Rafalovich was Beeson's wingman during the attack. He fired two bursts at an Fw 190 at the rear of the formation. 'I observed severe strikes on both wings and I saw fire coming from his engine. I pulled away to avoid an explosion. 1Lt (William) Whalen came in from behind, slightly astern.' The two shared credit for the destruction of the Fw 190, with Whalen also claiming a second kill. Two more Fw 190s were destroyed by future aces 1Lts Hippolitus 'Tom' Biel and Gerald Montgomery.

After five days of fog, Blakeslee led a freelance sweep to the Pas de Calais on 21 January. Flt Off Robert Richards recalled;

'We were vectored to Beauvais to intercept some bandits in that area. When we got near there, there was nothing to be seen except a little flak. My No 1 (1Lt Kenneth Peterson) was still very keen on the way out, and I saw him put his aeroplane on its side. I looked down also and saw four bogies flying south in Spitfire formation. My No 1 started to go down. We started diving from about 24,000 ft, and as we got closer I recognized them as Fw 190s.

'They didn't see us until we got right on top of them, and my No 1 started firing. My No 1 overshot, and at that time another '190 came in from 45 or 50 degrees, under-deflecting all the time. I saw one '190 come in head-on at me, firing. I took a short burst at him. He went over the top of me. I started to pull around to get on his tail when I saw another '190 right in front of me. I had plenty of speed, and I closed in from about 100 yards, firing all the time. I saw strikes all over him. He pulled up to the right to try to break into me. As he did that I laid off a little deflection above him and I hit him all over the cockpit. It looked as if the cockpit was all-ablaze from the strikes. I closed in to about 25 yards and pulled off to the side to watch him go down. He peeled off smoking and headed for the deck out of control.'

On 29 January, the 4th FG flew a Penetration Support mission to Frankfurt. Soon after leaving the bombers over Maastricht, in Holland, the 334th FS spotted 16 Bf 109s (probably from JG 300) some 3000 ft below them. 'As our squadron bounced this group of enemy aircraft, I saw six other Me 109s coming in to get on the squadron's tail', reported 1Lt Beeson. '1Lt Archie Chatterly and I turned into these. One of them put a hole in my tailplane before we could turn into them, but when the turn was completed I saw 1Lt Chatterly on the tail of a '109.'

'My first strike was on the left wingtip', said Chatterly. 'He straightened out and dived. Many strikes were then seen around the cockpit and other sections of the fuselage. Pieces flew off and the enemy aircraft went out of control and down slowly on its back, with dark smoke trailing behind. I lost sight of it as the '109 floated into the clouds.'

'Meanwhile', continued 1Lt Beeson, 'the other Me 109s continued to dive. I got on the tail of the nearest one and opened fire. I saw very severe strikes on the fuselage and wing roots, then a large flash somewhere in the cockpit area and the enemy aircraft flicked violently to the right and went down trailing a long stream of grey-black smoke. The last I saw of the '109, he was going straight down through ten-tenths cloud below.'

Beeson looked down and saw a dogfight below him. 'I started down again when I sighted an aircraft off to starboard, also diving. When I went

On this unidentified group P-47, the armourers took special precautions to prevent the boresighting of their guns from being thrown off by thoughtless groundcrew (*Keith Hoey via Wade Meyers*)

over to investigate, he turned out to be a yellow-tailed Fw 190 with a belly tank. I can't think he saw me, as I was approaching him out of the sun. I fired a burst out of range, trying to slow him down. No results were seen so I continued behind him as he went into a cloud at about 3000 ft, and when we came out below I was about 300 yards behind. I opened fire again and saw many incendiary strikes on his fuselage. He dropped his nose at about 200 ft and went into the deck.'

1Lt 'Steve' Pisanos and his section spotted 15 enemy aeroplanes below them and they too dove to attack. 'I lined up at once and began firing', Pisanos said. His quarry 'went into a dive and I followed him down, firing. Just above the cloud base I saw hits behind the cockpit. The enemy aircraft went out of control and dived straight down into the cloud at 3000 ft. I then started to climb to starboard when I saw another Bf 109 below me and to my port, flying straight and level. I went down and closed on him, opening fire. As he dived into the cloud, I saw hits on the cockpit and fuselage, a lot of fire came out and he rolled over to the right and went in.'

Future six-kill ace Capt Henry Mills also claimed two Bf 109s destroyed, 1Lt Archie Chatterly got one and 1Lt Vic France claimed an Fw 190. 335th FS pilot 2Lt Burton Wyman became the 4th FG's first combat fatality of 1944 when he failed to return to Debden. He had last been seen chasing a German aeroplane down through the undercast, with another enemy fighter on his tail.

335th FS pilot 2Lt Charles Anderson of Gary, Indiana, poses next to the nose of his P-47D 42-74726 *Hell's Belle*, in which he claimed a Bf 109 destroyed and a second damaged on 30 January 1944. Anderson would lose his life on 19 April 1944 when his P-51B crashed in Brussels after suffering mechanical failure. His score at the time of his death stood at ten aerial victories and 5.5 strafing kills (*National Museum of the USAF*)

The next day, during a Penetration Support mission to Brunswick, the 335th FS spotted two groups of enemy aircraft, with 12 at 26,000 ft and 15 more at 12,000 ft. The squadron climbed after the upper group, and the German fighters responded. 'When we were almost up to them, two '109s dived down between my No 3 and me', reported future ten-kill ace 2Lt Charles Anderson. 'Upon seeing my aircraft, they started to climb immediately. I followed them up and fired at the one on the left from about 350 yards. He started smoking badly and turned off to the left. As the two were flying line abreast, I could not follow the one I had fired at for fear the other one would get on my tail.' Anderson later saw the Bf 109 spinning and burning as it entered a cloud.

During the fight, 2Lt Edwin Mead was shot down (shortly after he had probably downed a Bf 109) and wound up a PoW.

On 31 January, Capt Raymond Care led the group on its first ever dive-bombing mission when P-47s targeted Gilze-Rijen airfield in Holland. Two four-aircraft sections in each squadron flew Thunderbolts armed with a single 500-lb bomb on the centreline shackles, while the remaining two sections flew as fighter cover. The 4th duly hit a fuel dump and one of the runways.

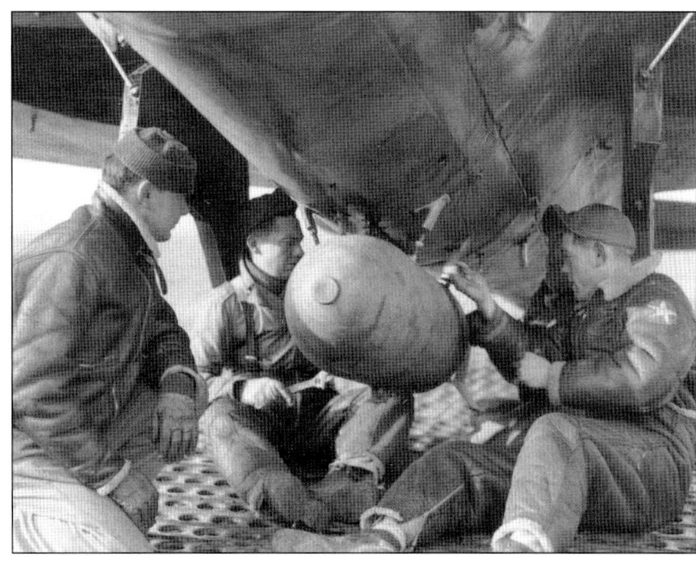

Groundcrew attach a 500-lb bomb to the centreline shackles of a P-47 prior to the 4th FG's historic dive-bombing mission to Gilze-Rijen airfield on 30 January 1944 (*National Museum of the USAF*)

While the bombs were falling, the top cover was attacked by 15–20 Bf 109s. 1Lt Raymond Clotfelter's 335th FS section had dodged four diving enemy fighters when he spotted a Bf 109 'coming in at "nine o'clock", and when he started to pull deflection on me, I called a break and immediately flicked over into an aileron turn. I saw three other enemy aircraft off to my right approximately 1500 yards away. I decided I could catch them, so I pushed everything to the firewall and closed very quickly.' When the Me 109s recovered from their dives, 'I pulled deflection and opened fire', said Clotfelter. 'After a short burst, I pushed my nose through again and fired a longer burst. I closed to 100 yards, seeing strikes all over the cockpit, pieces falling off the tail and a fire. I had to break off to the right, and as I did, I passed within a wing span of the enemy fighter.' The Bf 109 dove to earth and exploded.

Capt 'Mike' Sobanski was leading the top cover, and one Bf 109 made a pass at his section. 'As he broke away, I saw another Me 109 dive head-on past us, and I followed him down', Sobanski reported. 'I gave him a short burst in a 70-degree dive, observing no strikes. He started pulling up, turning left and I fired a 20-degree deflection shot. I observed strikes in the wings and near the cockpit. A large puff of white smoke came out after my last burst, and he flicked left, smoking badly. 1Lt Howard Moulton – my No 2 – saw him go down in flames after he flicked over.'

With the top cover engaged, another group of Bf 109s snuck in behind the aeroplanes that had just bombed. The Thunderbolt pilots thought that they were friendly, and orbited to join up! According to 1Lt Paul Ellington of the 335th FS, 'They turned out all to be Me 109s, about six or eight in number. We engaged them immediately, and three of them dived for the deck.' Future six-kill ace 1Lt Kendall 'Swede' Carlson knocked down a Bf 109 and then saw another P-47 (flown by 335th FS pilot 2Lt William Rowles) with a Messerschmitt behind it. '1Lt Ellington cut inside of me and took him off the '47's tail', said Carlson. The Bf 109 crashed in a pall of smoke and flame on a mud flat. Additional victories fell to 1Lts Garrison and Beeson.

On 3 February, Col Sel Edner led a 'Ramrod' Penetration Support mission to Emden. While no enemy aircraft were encountered, 334th FS pilot Flt Off William Cox became separated from his leader in clouds and icing conditions near the target and was killed when his P-47 crashed.

Three days later, during a Penetration Target Support mission to Romilly, the Luftwaffe was back in force. Some 15 to 20 enemy fighters

During the 30 January 1944 mission to Gilze-Rijen, 2Lt. William Rowles' P-47D was was badly damaged by cannon fire from a Bf 109. Rowles had missed squadronmate 1Lt Kendall Carlson's call to break after the German fighter had been spotted closing on his tail. Fortunately for Rowles, 1Lt Paul Ellington reacted quickly and shot the Messerschmitt off his tail, but not before 42-75112 had been holed in its fuselage, tail, flaps and canopy (*National Museum of the USAF*)

continuously attacked the bombers for 40 minutes. During the fray, Flt Off Ralph Hofer knocked down a Bf 109 and 1Lts Garrison and Robert Hobert from the 336th each destroyed an Fw 190. 1Lt Hubert Ballew of the 335th FS was shot down by an Fw 190, however. Baling out near Paris, he was quickly captured.

Edner was again in command on 10 February when the 4th escorted 'heavies' to Brunswick, and from Lingen to Nienburg the group battled 25 to 30 Fw 190s and Bf 109s. The aggressive German fighters made repeated passes, but they paid for it – an Fw 190 was downed by 1Lt France, and Bf 109s were claimed by 1Lts Montgomery, Biel, Cecil Manning, Millikan, Garrison (giving him ace status) and Norley.

On 14 February the first three P-51Bs issued to the group (one per squadron) arrived at Debden. Blakeslee immediately made it clear that he expected all pilots to check out in the new fighter between flying combat missions. There would be no down time to permit units to transition pilots en masse.

The Thunderbolts were up again on the 20th, performing a Withdrawal Support mission for bombers returning from Leipzig. Minutes after rendezvousing with the combat bomb wings, the group spotted five Bf 109s and Bf 110s attacking with rockets. 'My No 2, 2Lt Bernard McGrattan, and I dived on them', said 1Lt Pierce McKennon, 'and due to so much speed from the dive, I overshot while McGrattan cut in and tried to get him, but couldn't position himself because the '190 broke into a very sharp climbing turn.' McKennon got back on the Fw 190's tail and fired. 'I was going to give him another burst when the '190 half-rolled and the pilot baled out.'

The 335th FS, meanwhile, targeted the Bf 110s, and 1Lts Paul Ellington and Clemens Fiedler downed one apiece, while future 6.5-kill ace 1Lt Paul Riley and his wingman 2Lt Richard Reed shared in the destruction of a *Zerstörer*. The latter pilot was shot down and killed by a pair of Fw 190s near Aachen shortly after destroying the Bf 110.

Five minutes after the Messerschmitts had been engaged, 1Lt Beeson sighted two more Fw 190s beneath the bombers. 'They were about 5000 ft directly below, and as we circled around to come in on their tails, they both began to go around in a circle, and we ended up with Green Section coming at them straight down from above.'

Beeson tried to manoeuvre for an attack, and finally managed to get around behind them just as another Thunderbolt came in, causing them to dive away. 'The other P-47 was nearer than me, and closing fast, so I waited for him to get the last one so I might take the leader. He overshot and they whipped around in a starboard turn, so I closed in on the No 2, who began to climb just as his leader dived for the cloud. I opened fire and got good strikes around his fuselage and on his wings. As I overshot him, he pulled straight up and jettisoned his cockpit hood, then baled out.'

Capt Henry Mills saw a Thunderbolt chasing an Fw 190 below him and started after them. 'The P-47 started to overshoot and broke to the right. I closed in, firing from astern and above. He pulled up ahead of me and I pulled through deflection so that he was under my nose and opened fire, firing until I was less than 50 yards from him. I broke at the last instant to keep from ramming him. The enemy aircraft pulled off slowly to my left, smoking slightly, and the pilot baled out in front of Capt Care, who was following me.' This was Mills' fifth victory.

The next day, Lt Col Blakeslee led a Penetration Support mission for bombers returning from Schweinfurt. Near Aachen, Fw 190s from 6./JG 26 were seen circling a crippled B-17, and they were duly attacked by the 335th FS. *Staffelkapitän* Hauptmann Horst Sternberg abandoned his *kette* and dove on another damaged straggler that he had spotted nearby. Unit CO Maj George Carpenter spotted him and opened fire, causing Sternberg to break hard away from the bomber. After two turns, Carpenter fired again and scored hits that caused pieces of Sternberg's Fw 190 to fly off. At 500 ft, he pulled up and watched Sternberg's Focke-Wulf hit the ground and explode in a ball of flames.

Another pilot in the *kette*, Unteroffizier Paul Gross, was overshot by one of the P-47s, probably flown by Capt Raymond Care, but the Gertman's evasive manoeuvres were too indecisive and the P-47 ended up on his tail again. 'He did two slow rolls before I closed and fired', Care reported. 'I observed many strikes and saw something come off as I broke to avoid collision. As I climbed back up, a 'chute opened down on top of the clouds as the enemy aircraft slid from view.' His 'chute opened, but Gross had been hit by gunfire and he died before reaching the ground.

As the 334th FS's victory tally neared 50 kills, each of the 30 pilots in the unit contributed £1 each to a pot to be claimed by the man who scored the squadron's 50th victory. On 10 February, 1Lts Tom Biel (left), Gerald Montgomery and Vic France each scored what might have been the milestone kill, so they split the prize three ways (*National Museum of the USAF*)

Future six-kill ace 2Lt David Howe also claimed an Fw 190 destroyed during the course of this mission.

On 22 February, the group flew a Withdrawal Support mission, and upon rendezvousing with 24 B-17s from the 1st Bomb Division over the Rhine between Coblenz and Bonn, Maj Carpenter saw a Flying Fortress in trouble.

Just after the first parachute came out of the damaged B-17, Carpenter's wingman spotted two Fw 190s headed for it. 'I manoeuvred into position and opened fire at about 300 yards', the 335th FS pilot reported. 'As soon as my tracers began passing the enemy aircraft, he broke quite violently, but not sufficiently enough to get away. We did a couple of orbits, and every few seconds I was able to draw deflection and get a few strikes on the wings and in the cockpit area. Finally, the enemy aircraft straightened out and went into a gentle dive. At about 1000 ft, I saw many pieces fly off his fuselage. When he hit there was a gigantic orange flash, then burning pieces could be seen strung out beyond him for several hundred feet.'

Future 8.5-kill ace 1Lt Bernard McGrattan claimed an Fw 190 destroyed during this engagement, while 1Lt Pierce McKennon and Flt Off Joseph Goetz shared in the destruction of a second Focke-Wulf fighter.

Two days later, Col Edner led a similar mission for B-24s returning from Schweinfurt. Four Fw 190s made head-on attacks on the Liberators and were then chased off, but near Coblenz ten more German fighters attacked the bombers. 335th FS pilot 1Lt Albert Schlegel was credited with probably destroying an Fw 190, but squadronmate 2Lt Joseph Sullivan was shot down and killed and 2Lt Leighton Read returned to Debden with shrapnel wounds from a 20 mm shell that had exploded in his cockpit. Three more P-47s were shot up and forced to land at advance bases.

That same day, both the 334th and 336th FSs received ten Mustangs apiece, while eleven were suppled to the 335th. A further 15 arrived the following day.

On 25 February Lt Col Edner led a Penetration Escort for bombers headed for Regensburg, Nurnberg, Stuttgart and Augsburg – this was the last mission mounted by Eighth Air Force 'heavies' during the 'Big Week' offensive. Approaching the target, five Fw 190s made a head-on pass on a B-17 and were immediately set upon by the 336th FS.

'I started firing, and I hit this enemy aircraft, seeing several strikes

336th FS groundcrewmen stand beside 1Lt Glenn Herter's P-47C 41-6354. This aeroplane was struck by 1Lt Jack Raphael's P-47C 41-6529 *EAGER BEAVER/MISS BETH* whilst taxiing at Debden on 5 January 1944 and written off (*via Wade Meyers*)

1Lt John Godfrey tells his dog 'Lucky' to stay as he prepares to climb into his P-51B 43-6765. A portrait of 'Lucky' adorned the nose of Godfrey's P-47D 42-7884 (*National Museum of the USAF*)

and then he turned and I overshot him', stated 1Lt Vermont Garrison. 'I whipped around on his tail again. His engine was smoking badly now. I did not catch him the second time until he was down on the deck at about 100 ft. I closed up and started shooting, getting good strikes, and I set his engine on fire. We were right down just above the ground. I hit him several times at close range. I overshot again as his engine was gone and he was slowing down. I slowed down and got behind him, gave him a few short bursts and he went straight into the ground. A wing came off and the engine stopped about 100 yards from the rest of the aeroplane.'

Meanwhile, 1Lt Glenn Herter and Capt Gentile found their own pair of Fw 190s. Herter saw two aeroplanes about 10,000 ft below them, but they were 'hard to identify because of their camouflage, which blended with the dark background', he reported. 'On getting closer, it was an Fw 190 with black camouflage. He was flying straight and level, and apparently did not see me. I held my fire until I reached approximately 125 yards, then opened fire in one long burst. I immediately observed hits from the port wing root to the cockpit. On being hit, the enemy aircraft did a violent flick and the pilot shot out of the aircraft with his 'chute streaming behind him. The Fw 190 continued straight down into the ground, trailing smoke.'

'I closed to about 400 yards for my first burst', said Gentile. 'I opened fire again at about 300 yards, observing many strikes and large and small pieces coming off the '190. My whole aircraft was covered with oil, and my No 2 man was hit by pieces of the enemy aircraft in the cowling and the prop. When I last saw the '190, he was close to the ground going almost straight down. He had definitely "had it".' Capt Gentile and 1Lt McKennon also tallied Fw 190s.

MUSTANGS OVER BERLIN

As mentioned in the previous chapter, on 25 February 1944, 31 Mustangs flew into Debden for the 4th FG. The following morning, Capt 'Mike' Sobanski of the 334th FS took one of the new P-51s up for a weather reconnaissance flight, then became confused about whether his landing gear was up or down and belly-landed back at base. Lt Col Blakeslee was infuriated. 'Why couldn't it have been one of those seven-ton monsters?' he said, referring to the unloved P-47s.

The Thunderbolt's days with the group were at an end, however. On 28 February, 14 more P-51s were assigned to the 334th FS. That same day, with most pilots having only a few hours of familiarization in the new fighter, 334th FS CO Maj Jim Clark led the group's first Mustang mission, with 35 P-51s being despatched as escorts for bombers sent to attack V1 launch ramps near Boulogne-Compiegne. No German fighters were encountered, although a solitary Ju 88 was destroyed on the ground at Soissons. Back at base, 1Lt Robert Frazer of the 334th FS was coming to the end of a familiarization flight in a P-51B when, turning into the pattern, he stalled the fighter, which flipped over onto its back and dove into the ground, killing him instantly.

Such accidents, often due to mechanical failure, were synonymous with early Mustang operations in the ETO, as the P-51B was initially blighted by teething problems with its engine, propeller, wing tanks, cooling system, guns and radio. Despite these maladies, the aircraft had double the range of the P-47D, and was far more agile in combat. One of its early proponents was ranking 336th FS ace Capt Don Gentile, who stated at the time that the Mustang 'could go in the front door of the enemy's home and blow down the back door and beat up all the furniture in between'.

The 4th FG would claim its first kills with the P-51B on the 2 March show to Frankfurt, when Lt Col Sel Edner led a Target Withdrawal Support mission. Over the Rhine town of St Goar, six Bf 109s made a head-on attack on the formation, followed by ten Fw 190s. Two sections from the 334th FS reacted immediately.

'I saw five Me 109s positioning at "11 o'clock" to the bombers', reported 1Lt 'Georgia' Wynn. 'I positioned myself astern the last enemy aircraft. I started firing and closed to 50 yards. The aircraft took slight evasive action and dived for a

1Lt George Villinger of the 336th FS, seen here in the cockpit of his P-47D *Dull Tool*, was the first 4th FG pilot to be killed in action flying a Mustang. He was shot down by Fw 190s near the German town of Linburg during a Target Withdrawal Support mission to Frankfurt on 2 March 1944. Villinger had joined the 336th FS as a replacement pilot in August 1943 (*Jack Raphael via Wade Meyers*)

cloud as I observed strikes. I fired very long bursts and kicked rudder. Glycol started streaming from the enemy aircraft. I followed him through, and I saw the enemy aircraft pull back up. I gave him another long burst and observed strikes on the fuselage. I circled under the cloud base (9000 ft), and soon the enemy aircraft came down, followed by the pilot and 'chute.'

336th FS pilot 1Lt Glenn Herter managed to latch onto one of the Fw 190s from the second formation and shoot it down. These successes were tempered by the loss of Herter's squadronmate 1Lt George Villinger, who was shot down and killed by enemy fighters.

The following day Lt Col Blakeslee led a Target Support mission to Berlin – the 4th FG's first trip to the German capital. Flights from the 335th and 336th FSs broke off from the main body to fend off enemy fighters, with nine Mustangs from the latter unit engaging no fewer than 60 Fw 190s and Bf 110s near Wittenburg. Pilots claimed five German aircraft destroyed, but in turn lost 1Lts Garrison, Herter and Philip 'Pappy' Dunn.

Herter was lured down by the low element of German fighters and was bounced – he died when his Mustang crashed. Dunn got lost on the way home, and with his radio out (a common problem in early P-51Bs) and no way to get a vector to cross the Channel, he headed for Spain. Dunn had already tangled with an 'Me 210' (almost certainly an Me 410) during the mission, and eight miles from the border, he spotted an He 111. Unable to resist, Dunn shot down the bomber – he was credited with a probable, due to the lack of witnesses – then ran out of gas as he circled to watch it crash, ending up a PoW.

The same fate befell Garrison, who had managed to down an Fw 190 (taking his tally to 7.333 kills) and claim a Bf 110 as a probable, despite having only a single operable 0.50-cal machine gun. His P-51B was hit by flak near Boulogne on the way home and he baled out. Finally, 1Lt George Barnes of the 335th FS was last seen off the Dutch coast on his way home, his engine cutting out badly. No trace of him was ever found.

Capt Don Gentile had what he described as a 'hairy' day on the 3rd. 'I took off with my wingman Johnny Godfrey, and the rest of the flight was to join me, but due to weather we never met', he wrote in an account found on the back of his logbook.

Top
Lt Col Blakeslee flew his assigned P-51B (43-6437) during the 4th FG's first mission to Berlin on 3 March 1944. In this photograph, his wheels have just been chocked following his return from the historic mission (*National Museum of the USAF*)

Above
Blakeslee hands his maps to crew chief SSgt Harry East before climbing out of his P-51B after the first Berlin 'show'. The mission was not a rousing success, for although the 4th FG destroyed eight enemy aeroplanes, four of its Mustangs failed to return to Debden. Although a notoriously unreliable aircraft, Blakeslee kept P-51B 43-6437 because of its rare Malcolm hood (*National Museum of the USAF*)

On 3 March 1944, 1Lt Vermont Garrison, pictured in front of 1Lt Andrew Stephenson's P-47C, became the first 4th FG ace to be shot down and captured. Having destroyed an Fw 190 and probably destroyed a Bf 110, all with just one operable 0.50-cal machine gun, his Mustang was hit by flak as he headed for home over Boulogne. Garrison took to his parachute and was soon captured. He would later claim ten MiG-15s destroyed whilst flying F-86Fs with the 335th Fighter Interceptor Squadron/4th Fighter Interceptor Wing in Korea in 1953 (*National Museum of the USAF*)

They broke overcast at 33,000 ft after flying on instruments for an hour. 'After being on course for a couple of hours, still no one joined us, so we decided to continue on alone. When we were approximately 100 miles from the target, the weather seemed to clear up. In the distance, I spotted approximately 50 Do 217s in formation climbing for altitude, and above them were about 100 Fw 190s. They were getting ready to attack the "Big Boys" head on. I called Johnny and asked him if he wanted to go ahead and attack knowing there were no other friendly fighters in this area. As usual, Johnny said "You're the boss".'

Gentile went for the Do 217s, hoping to disrupt their formation so the USAAF bombers could unload before the German fighters could get reorganized. 'I began firing at tail end "Charlie" and the Dos started diving for the deck. About this time Johnny started screaming that the 100+ Fws were coming down on us. The Dos were cross-firing on us at the same time. I had one Do smoking badly when I had to break away due to the 100+ coming in on us. Johnny and I met them head-on, going through the complete German formation. From then on all hell broke loose', Gentile recalled.

'Aeroplanes were going up and down and every which way. I thought this was it. In the midst of twisting and turning, I managed to get on an Fw, who overshot me, and was lucky enough to get him. Johnny started to scream that 50 more were coming in at "six o'clock", so I started to aileron roll for the deck. I had to pull up in a vertical climb into the Fws. At this time I noticed a brightly painted Fw on my tail, blazing away, and Johnny screaming for me to break. I broke so hard that my aeroplane started doing snap-rolls – when I got it under control the Fw was slightly ahead and above, with me on his tail diving and twisting. This lasted a good ten minutes. I managed to get his aircraft on fire and noticed he had had it, so I broke away.'

With their ammunition gone, the two headed for home. 'We had to dive for the clouds with them on our tail, skidding at the same time. By the grace of God we reached the cloud bank, and after flying on instruments for a while, we let down through the bottom of the cloud deck. During the combat I lost my maps, so I didn't know my position, and Johnny didn't know either, so we took the general direction home.'

Gentile and Godfrey landed at Hurn airfield, in Dorset, all but out of fuel. 'Thank God for a good wingman, or I wouldn't be able to write this today', he concluded.

On 4 March the group returned to Berlin. Just before the bombers reached the initial point, 20 Bf 109s and Fw 190s swarmed in to attack, eight from head-on in two sections, with the others as top cover. After the first eight had flown through the bomber formation, the top cover dove on the 4th. 2Lt Hugh Ward of the 335th FS gave chase to a Bf 109 in a dive;

'I opened fire as he started a slow turn to the left. I observed strikes on his wing root. He realized the situation and flicked over, and he dove straight down with me on his tail. I gave him a three-second burst with good strikes. He continued straight down, heading for heavy clouds as I began to overrun him. I pulled back on the throttle and gave him another blast. I got a heavy concentration of strikes all over his cockpit and engine covering. I kept firing as the Me 109 started to come apart. I attempted to back off but was too late.

'A large section of the enemy aircraft smashed my canopy and windscreen, and it must have sheared off most of my tail section. My aeroplane began to snap viciously, end-over-end, and my right wing snapped off. I was stunned momentarily, but I managed to jettison my canopy. I pulled my harness release, which threw me out of the cockpit. I delayed opening my 'chute because of the speed, and I fell through the cloud layer. I opened my 'chute just in time. I landed in the suburbs of Berlin and I was captured by civilians.'

Future 11.833-kill ace 1Lt Nicholas 'Cowboy' Megura of the 334th FS was behind Ward, chasing after a second Bf 109 that had latched onto the tail of the diving Mustang. 'At 18,000 ft, the P-51's wing came off at the root and disintegrated. The canopy and tail came off as I dodged past. Pieces carried away my antenna and hit my stabilizer.' Megura's controls were frozen by compressability, and he had to use trim to pick up the nose.

'The only evasive action taken by the enemy aircraft immediately in front of me throughout this action was a weave to right or left. I barrel-rolled and positioned myself 1000 ft above and to the side of him. I dropped flaps and dove astern. This engagement brought us down to 2000 ft. Just as I was about to fire, the enemy pilot pulled up sharply to 3000 ft, jettisoned his canopy and pilot baled out. The enemy aircraft crashed and burned.'

Clearing his tail, Megura found that he was over a grass airfield, and he set fire to a Ju 52/3m, then attacked a locomotive pulling a dozen wagons. 'Seeing that it was time to "leave out", I set course for home.'

Aside from Ward, the 335th FS also lost 1Lt Paul Ellington when his Mustang suffered engine failure and he baled out over Holland – he became a POW. The group's only fatality on the 4th came at the very end of the mission when 336th FS pilot 1Lt Robert Richards was killed when he crashed near the advanced base at Framlingham.

Lt Col Blakeslee led 5 March's bomber escort mission to Bordeaux, although he soon had to abort due to a rough-running engine – 24 hours earlier, he had returned to base with all four of his guns inoperable. Capt Beeson assumed the role of mission leader. With the primary target completely socked in, the bombers headed for the secondary target. As they made their turn, six Bf 109s attacked. 'Our section immediately dove toward them', said Duane Beeson. 'They saw us coming and whipped into a tight turn.' Twice the fighters turned into Beeson, and twice he fired head-on shots at them.

'There were now several Mustangs around who were trying to get these

Just 24 hours after 1Lt Garrison was shot down, the 336th FS lost its fifth pilot in 72 hours when 1Lt Robert Richards, who had two victories to his credit, was killed while trying to land at the advanced base at Framlingham in P-51B 43-6786 upon his return from the escort mission to Berlin (*National Museum of the USAF*)

Me 109s. As the enemy aircraft went over into a dive, the Mustangs went after them. I had managed to keep my speed pretty high, and was able to get on the tail of one. 1Lt Pisanos also got on the tail of one. Before I opened fire, I saw 1Lt Pisanos getting very good strikes on his aircraft. After opening fire at about 150 yards, and getting more strikes, he began to smoke badly. As I overshot the enemy aircraft, the pilot baled out.'

Squadronmate, and future 12-kill ace, 1Lt Howard Hively noticed four aircraft approaching the bombers from the south. He turned toward them and identified them as Bf 109s, camouflaged 'a dirty-green colour, with bright orange spinners'. Hively attacked from their 'nine o'clock'. They broke into me and we went around and around in a port climbing orbit', he said. 'Two of the enemy aircraft broke to starboard out of the turn and started for the deck. I picked up my flaps, turned and chased. For a second it looked as if I wasn't closing, so I took two short burst at about 800 yards just for meanness.'

Hively was now closing too fast, so he lowered his flaps and throttled back, eventually winding up 50 yards behind one of the fighters;

Pilots pass the time in the 334th FS dispersal at Debden in March 1944. The board in the centre of the room kept a running tally of the squadron's victories, with each kill being listed by type and date (National Museum of the USAF)

'He turned to starboard as I fired, and I observed many strikes on both the bottom and top of the fuselage, as well as the wing root. As I slid by, I saw his starboard wing crumple about two feet from the wing root. I then slid right into the lead enemy aircraft and fired. I observed five or six good hits on his fuselage, underside and just back of the cockpit. He never pulled out. The enemy aircraft went in with a large column of dust and black smoke. Neither pilot baled out.'

Capt Beeson's section then sighted an airfield about 60 miles north of Bordeaux. 'We dove down to the deck about a mile from the aerodrome', said 2Lt Charles Carr of the 334th FS. 'We approached it at about 400 mph. Capt Beeson and Capt (Kenneth) Peterson of the 336th FS turned to port to attack an Fw 200 on the ground. I was on the inside, and I could not turn with them, so I continued to fly straight. I pulled up over a hill and saw what I thought was a Ju 88 in front of a hangar. I fired and saw strikes in front of the enemy aircraft. I raised the nose and kept on shooting. I pulled up over a hangar and continued on for a few hundred yards before pulling up.'

Suddenly, Beeson 'felt a heavy blow on the aircraft and was thrown over on my side. I had great difficulty regaining control. I checked my engine instruments, which were okay, and I reduced speed for better control. The rudders were very stiff, and I was forced to hold hard left rudder all the way back to base.' Flak had blown a large hole in Beeson's rudder.

'About five minutes after our attack, Capt Peterson shot down an Fw 200', Beeson continued. 'I also confirmed one Me 109 shot down by Lt Pisanos.' The latter, who actually downed two Bf 109s to take his tally to five victories, could not claim his victims in person for he had been forced to crash-land his P-51B ten miles south of Le Havre when it suffered mechanical failure. Pisanos evaded and eventually rejoined the group at Debden in September.

335th FS pilot 1Lt Jim Steele had also experienced engine problems with his fighter, and as he headed for England, he came across eight Fw 200s in the circuit over Bergerac airfield and duly shot one of them down. Two Fw 190s then tried to bounce Steele, but he was already heading for home at full speed – he left them far behind. Capt Fonzo Smith and 1Lt Ed Freeburger bagged another Fw 200 between them, then came around and machine-gunned the crew as they ran from the wreck. The day's final kill (an Fw 190) was credited to 1Lt Jim Dye of the 335th.

Lt Col Blakeslee was in the lead again for the Target Support mission to Berlin on 6 March, when the Luftwaffe was up in force. About 30 enemy aircraft made head-on attacks on the bombers, while 40–50 more approached from astern and abeam. One B-17 was hit by an aircraft-fired rocket and exploded, taking its entire crew with it. Three other Flying Fortresses were seen falling from the formation after being hit by fighters.

Fending off the attacks split the 4th FG into flights and sections. 1Lt Archie Chatterly of the 334th FS was flying No 3 in Maj Mills' flight. 'Our section dropped our tanks. Immediately afterwards, I saw an Me 110 attacking a "Fort" that had pulled out of formation. I attacked, and saw strikes with my deflection shots. When I closed to line astern, I saw many strikes. Pieces flew off and smoke streamed back over my windscreen.'

A Mustang pilot then radioed that a 'Ju 88' was on his tail, and Chatterly climbed to assist him;

335th FS groundcrewmen anxiously 'sweat out' the return of their pilots and aircraft from a mission to Germany in early March 1944. The men who spent so long maintaining the aeroplanes were crushed when one was lost in combat, and doubly so when it fell to a mechanical problem – the latter was, sadly, a regular occurrence with the early-build P-51B/Cs that equipped the 4th FG (*National Museum of the USAF*)

'As I climbed up, I began to pull deflection. The German broke away and began to pull very tight, diving turns. The "Ju 88" turned out to be an Me 210, which dove from 28,000 ft down to 2000 ft in a series of tight turns. He never straightened out of his turn until the very last minute. I was on the red line of my air speed following him when someone said the '210 was shedding pieces. He pulled out, made a zoom, dove and crashed.'

Chatterly then formed up with three other Mustangs, and they intercepted a lone Fw 190 head-on. 'All four of us turned and started wide-open racing for him. The '190 started a shallow climb, and we gained on him quickly. I asked Maj Mills if we were going to queue up. "Hell no – first one there gets him", he answered. Maj Mills edged the rest of us out, and I confirmed his claim after seeing many strikes on the enemy aircraft as it dove straight in.'

After strafing a train and an airfield, Chatterly, who had by then paired up with 1Lt John Godfrey from the 336th FS, set off for Debden. 'About ten minutes out from the target, I had to urinate badly. I was just beginning to relieve myself when tracers passed on each side of me, converging in front', Chatterly recalled. '1Lt Godfrey called to break, which I did without putting any of the relief equipment back in place. Strikes hit me just as I broke. 1Lt Godfrey then shot the Me 109 down'.

1Lt Howard Moulton of the 334th FS was flying on 1Lt Whalen's wing when, southwest of Berlin, they saw Capt David Van Epps losing altitude after his oxygen system had failed. '1Lt Whalen and I went down with him', Moulton reported. 'An Me 110 came diving down at "two o'clock" to us. As we went after him, I followed about 500 yards behind 1Lt Whalen. I saw him get very close, line astern to the enemy aircraft. He gave a short burst that was very accurate. The enemy aircraft blew up and many pieces flew back.' Debris from the Bf 110 struck Whalen's Mustang as the enemy fighter spun into the ground near Nienburg. Whalen's aircraft crashed nearby. 'This was the last time I saw 1Lt Whalen', said Moulton.

'I noticed a pilot swinging violently in a back-type chute at 1000 ft', recalled Capt Van Epps. 'About that time an explosion occurred at "two o'clock" to me as if an aircraft had blown up in the air. I presume that 1Lt Whalen baled out after his encounter with the enemy aircraft. His P-51 exploded.' Whalen did not survive this encounter.

Elsewhere, Capt Cecil Manning and his section of 335th FS Mustangs spotted a section of Do 217s that had been lobbing rockets toward the bombers. As they broke downward, Manning 'opened fire on the starboard enemy aircraft at approximately 300 yards and closed to the point I had to break away to keep from colliding with him.

'I observed lots of strikes on the cockpit and out to the port engine, which immediately burst into flames. It flicked into a spin, and I saw two 'chutes come out. I turned into the other two enemy aircraft and fired at one. The rear gunner had been firing up to the point where I observed strikes, which must have killed him. The pilot must also have been killed because the enemy aircraft mushed and fell into a fast spin. One 'chute came out before the enemy aircraft crashed and burned.'

Manning climbed to attack the remaining Do 217, but he ran out of ammunition. 'On the way home, my oil pressure dropped, the engine overheated and the glycol caught fire. I must have caught a slug from the Do 217 which caused me to lose my oil. I baled out at 3000 ft over Sogel, 16 miles inside Germany.' Manning became a PoW.

In all, the group was credited with the destruction of 15 German aircraft, with Lt Col Blakeslee downing an 'Me 210', 1Lt Megura two Bf 110s, 1Lts McKennon and Alex Rafalovich a Bf 109 each, 1Lt McGrattan a 'Ju 88' (actually a Bf 110), 1Lts Anderson and Dye a Do 217 apiece and Flt Off Lloyd Waterman another Bf 110. Moulton and Van Epps shared a Bf 110. In addition to Manning and Whalen, 1Lt Robert Messenger of the 336th FS was shot down by German fighters during the mission and Maj Henry Mills baled out when he suffered engine trouble west of Brandenburg. Both became PoWs.

On another Target Support mission to Berlin on 8 March, opposition was again intense, and 16 aeroplanes were claimed by 4th FG pilots. The only pilot lost by the group on this mission was Lt Col Edner, who was leading the 4th when he and his wingman were bounced by four Bf 109s near Hegensburg. Edner was quickly shot down and became a PoW.

The 4th FG's legendary nose art artist Sgt Don Allen applies kill markings to Nicholas Megura's P-51B *ILL WIND*? Megura scored 11.833 aerial and 3.75 strafing victories, all of which appear to have been marked with a cross on his Mustang's impressive scoreboard. The Eighth Air Force was unique in the USAAF for giving ground kills the same status as aircraft that were shot down (*via Wade Meyers*)

Southwest of Brandenburg, the lead wing of bombers was attacked by six Bf 109s. In short order a further 60 enemy fighters joined the fray. Eight B-17s were seen to go down after enemy attacks.

Maj Jim Clark followed a Bf 109 down to 8000 ft, 'where I fired three short bursts. I observed a few strikes in the cockpit area. The enemy aircraft flicked over and dove straight into the ground.' This success gave Clark his fifth victory.

In the same section was 'Cowboy' Megura. 'I gave chase to an Me 109. I closed and started to fire. At about 25 yards range, I got strikes on his wing and engine, which exploded. Skidding in a turn, I found another '109 on my tail, but I lost him in a couple of turns. I went to help a "Fort" and closed on an Fw 190. I got strikes on his starboard wings and engine. He baled out and the aircraft crashed in smoke and flame.' Megura, too, had just 'made ace'.

'The Jerries all struck just as we joined the "Big Boys", coming down from 30,000 ft in shallow head-on dives', recalled Capt Gentile. 'Godfrey and I were covering the rear box of 300 "Big Boys". I saw a tiny speck flashing in the sunlight far ahead, then I saw 12 to 15 of our bombers going down in flames and blowing up. Then the Jerries broke off to the left for another pass. I said, "Come on Johnny, let's go up there – they're getting set for another pass." I managed to get in front of the oncoming Jerries to break up a head-on pass, which consisted of about 60 to 80 enemy aircraft. We both fired head-on and latched onto them.'

Gentile quickly got two or three bursts into an Fw 190, which streaked down, burning, from 20,000 ft.

'We climbed, twisting and turning, breaking into them to keep them from getting on our tail. I saw two Mes flying abreast, and told Johnny to take the one on the right and I'll take the left one. As usual, Johnny said "You're the boss – let's go". Johnny's blew up and mine caught fire and disintegrated fast, so the pilot baled out. No sooner had we finished with them when two more Me 109s were below us. Johnny turned and got his killed right away, but I went round and round for five minutes. I kept clobbering him, but I guess it was not enough. Suddenly, he gave up and went into a vertical dive, and that enabled me to blow him apart.

'Then I looked around and saw an Me 109 coming around for Johnny's tail. I yelled "Break into him, Johnny!" He did and the Jerry overshot. Johnny got him smoking, but his ammo was gone, so I climbed aboard

A collection of notable 4th FG pilots relax at Debden after a mission in this labelled photograph, taken in the early spring sunshine in March 1944. Of special note is the inclusion of the Alsatian 'Duke' at the right of the scene (*Jack Raphael via Wade Meyers*)

again, and with a few more bursts he was burning viciously, with flames shooting 15 ft behind him. He must have been tough, for he continued fighting for a couple of minutes with his craft an inferno, but he finally rolled over on his back and baled out.'

Two aircraft that ducked away from Godfrey and Gentile emerged right in front of 1Lt France. He closed rapidly on one and opened fire from 100 yards. 'After many strikes, I hit his belly tank, which exploded in a mass of flames and debris', said France. 'He crashed in a forest as I overshot him.'

Poor weather and ongoing mechanical problems with the Mustangs (which were grounded between 13 and 15 March) precluded any further action again until 16 March, when newly promoted Col Blakeslee led the group to Munich. After rendezvousing with the bombers, the group intercepted seven Bf 110s as they tried to attack the bombers from behind. Flt Off 'Kidd' Hofer was flying on Maj Jim Clark's wing when the latter jumped a *Zerstörer*. 'As Maj Clark closed, he discovered his guns would not fire', Hofer reported, 'and he told me to take over. I attacked two Me 110s that jettisoned their rockets and dove for the clouds. I followed one – the rear gunner of the enemy aircraft was firing all the time, and hit my prop. I fired and saw strikes, followed by explosions as the Me 110 nosed down from 300 ft and crashed.'

A little later, a formation of 20 Bf 110s was engaged, and six more twin-engined Messerschmitts went down. Archie Chatterly was involved in this melee. 'I engaged an Me 110 and saw strikes around the cockpit cover and fuselage. It tumbled straight down as if the pilot had been hit.'

The total score was 13 Bf 110s destroyed, with Goodson, Carpenter, future 10.333-kill ace Fred Glover and 'Swede' Carlson each getting two apiece, and Hofer, Chatterly, Kenneth Smith, Bernard McGrattan and Godfrey claiming one apiece. Carpenter's second victim almost got him, however, as its rear gunner peppered his P-51 with rounds, including one that hit the canopy. 2Lt Ernest Skilton of the 336th FS was not so lucky, being killed when his fighter was hit by flak during the battle.

On 18 March, Col Blakeslee led the group back to Munich on a Target Withdrawal Support mission. Eight Bf 109s were sighted 5000 ft below the group, just above the bombers, and four sections of Mustangs descended on them. 'As we started down on the enemy fighters, they were darting in and out of the clouds', said Capt Beeson. 'I closed on one, and my second burst must have hit his belly tank, because the whole aircraft immediately blew up in my face and I was unable to avoid it. I had to fly through it, and I felt pieces of the Me 109 strike my aircraft before I could break clear. I could feel the heat in my cockpit, and I immediately checked my instruments. I looked down and saw what was left of the '109 going down, covered in flame.'

Blakeslee, with Gentile as his wingman, dove at the same time. 'As we approached, the eight enemy aircraft split, with four diving line abreast, so we followed them to the deck', Blakeslee recalled, 'closing to 50 yards before opening fire. I took the No 3 aircraft and Capt Gentile took the No 4. When I finally closed to within 200 yards of the No 3 aircraft, I saw strikes all along the tail, fuselage, cockpit and engine. The cockpit hood fell off, the engine started to smoke and burn and the left undercarriage fell down. I did not see him go in, but Capt Gentile saw him hit the ground.'

Hofer opened fire on a Bf 109 and 'saw strikes and an explosion as pieces flew off and black smoke poured out of the falling enemy aircraft', he

Capt Kenneth Smith (left) of the 335th FS became a PoW on 21 March 1944 when his Mustang was one of seven downed by German flak in the Bordeaux region of France during a four-hour long strafing mission of enemy airfields in the area. Three days earlier, he had been flying with 1Lt Edward Freeburger (right) as his wingman when the latter was shot down and killed by Fw 190s near Nancy (*National Museum of the USAF*)

The man Col Don Blakeslee credited with being the glue that held the 4th FG together was 10.5-kill ace Lt Col Jim Clark, who began his service with No 71 'Eagle' Sqn in June 1942, and then went on to serve in a variety of leadership positions until he left the 4th FG in mid-September 1944 (*National Museum of the USAF*)

reported. 'I fired on an Me 109, which went into the clouds but popped out again as the canopy came off. The pilot baled out.' Hofer had just become the only ETO pilot to attain ace status whilst still a flight officer. He then prepared to attack two more Bf 109s, but his prop ran away. Hofer set course for Switzerland, and he had started to climb to bale out when his prop came back to normal. 'I decided that with a little luck I could make it back home. I landed at Manston with just six gallons of gas.'

Maj Carpenter and 1Lts Chatterly, Biel and 'Cowboy' Megura also destroyed Bf 109s, but there were losses too. Capt Kenneth Smith and 1Lt Edward Freeburger of the 335th FS had taken up position overhead the lead box of B-17s when a gaggle of 20 Fw 190s wheeled around in front of the formation to make head-on attacks on the B-17s.

'There were so many Huns around that I hardly knew which one to go for', said Smith. 'I called 1Lt Freeburger to take one, while I would take the second of the two fighters just below us. I got on the Fw 190's tail and opened fire. I closed in and gave him a long burst. I finally got strikes along the port wing root. The enemy aircraft went into a spin and white smoke started pouring out. Just then 1Lt Freeburger called and said there were four of them on our tail. I broke and started climbing full bore. The four couldn't climb and turn with me so they gave up and started for the deck. I immediately whipped over and started after them.

'These four Fw 190s were still running ahead of me at about 300 ft, going east, but I was catching them fast. When I cleared my tail before starting to attack, I saw six coming down at me, so I started climbing full bore in a slight turn. Those six behind me did not press their advantage. I was alone then, so I climbed back up to the bomber formation. When I joined again, there were two Me 109s making underneath attacks.' Smith drove them off. 'I stayed with them for another ten minutes and then started for home.' Smith made it back, but Freeburger did not. He was killed when his Mustang was shot down near Nancy. 2Lt Woodrow Sooman of the 336th FS also failed to return, having to bale out when his Mustang lost all its glycol over Frankfurt – he was made a PoW.

There was no bomber mission scheduled for 21 March, so the 4th conducted a fighter sweep of the Bordeaux area. The group was led by Maj Clark, who was now the 4th's operations officer. For four hours all three units attacked airfields in the area, and although eight aircraft were shot down and 12 destroyed on the ground, no fewer than seven P-51s were lost to flak and two pilots killed.

Among those to claim strafing victories was 'Kidd' Hofer. 'I came in very low over an aerodrome near Bordeaux, flying line abreast with 1Lt Wynn. I fired on an enemy aircraft which I believe was an He 177. I saw many strikes as it burst into flames.'

The defences quickly came to life. 1Lt Robert Williams was hit by flak near Angers and baled out. He was knocked cold when he hit the stabilizer and came to in his parachute, floating inside a cloud. He landed in a ploughed field, and when he tried to get up, he found he could not – he was suffering from a bad gash on his leg and bruised ribs. Some French children helped Williams into a nearby peasant's home, where he was quickly arrested by the Gestapo. Following interrogation, he was sent to a French hospital and then to a PoW camp.

Capt Van Epps and 1Lt Rafalovich came across a Do 217 trying to land. 'I observed strikes all over it from both of us', said Van Epps. '1Lt Blanchfield reports that the aircraft was burning badly when he came across the 'drome behind us.'

Several Fw 190s tried to break up the 334th FS's initial attack. 1Lts Chatterly and Megura were strafing some buildings when the bounce came. 'As I was pulling inside of one of them, they all broke off and started to run off on the tree tops', reported Chatterly. 'I was pulling strikes on the No 4 man when 1Lt Megura went past me and also got strikes. The Hun's wheels started to come down, he hit some tree tops and spread the aeroplane over a field, where it burst into flames. Regaining height, we saw five Fw 190s below us. I attacked the last one. I fired short bursts and saw strikes. I was still firing as he pulled up, jettisoned the hood and baled out.' Shortly thereafter, the pair spotted another airfield, where Megura 'fired a long burst into an He 177, which started to burn', he recalled.

A taxiing Ju 88 was despatched by Capt Hively. 'I got strikes and observed a fire start under his starboard engine, which soon engulfed the entire aeroplane', he said. His wingman, 1Lt Leonard Pierce, fired at a second Ju 88 but missed. 'I then attacked an Me 110 near a hangar and observed hits and also saw the hangar catch on fire', Pierce said.

After bouncing four Fw 190s, 1Lt Bill Hawkins and his wingman, 1Lt James Dye, were set upon by four more German fighters. 'I was trying to shake two of the Fw 190s from my tail by tight manoeuvres below the tree tops', Hawkins said. 'When I finally lost them, I ran into an Me 110 taking off from a grass-covered field. This aircraft was flying at about 50 ft. I made one pass and gave him a short burst at 45 degrees deflection. The enemy aircraft crashed and burned at the end of the runway.'

Hawkins ran out of fuel on the way home and crashed north of Bordeaux, but he evaded and made it back to the 4th FG after spending four months with the French underground. Dye managed to remain airborne even though he suffered a wound to his leg that bled profusely, forcing him to improvise a tourniquet with his belt. This saved his life.

Flt Off Joseph Goetz was hit at low altitude while strafing. 1Lt Pierce McKennon saw his P-51B hit the ground, and although there was no fire, the wings and engine broke off and the fuselage was left upside down. The pilot was later confirmed to have been killed in the crash. Capt Earle Carlow's P-51B was also hit while strafing, and he went over the side about 15 minutes after being hit. Carlow was last seen by his squadronmates gathering up his parachute. He too became a PoW.

1Lt James Brandenburg was struck by flak too while strafing, and as fire engulfed his cockpit, his wingman, 2Lt Lloyd Waterman, shouted at him to bale out. His parachute opened at tree top height, but Brandenburg died from his injuries. Capt Kenneth Smith also failed to return, having force-landed near Caen – he also became a PoW, as did 1Lt Rafalovich, who baled out north of Bordeaux.

335th FS pilot 1Lt James Dye had two kills under his belt when, during the 21 March airfield attacks, his aeroplane was raked by an Fw 190 that damaged his fighter and seriously wounded him in the leg. Using his belt, Dye fashioned a tourniquet to staunch the bleeding and made it back to Debden. While in hospital recovering from his wounds, Dye had the misfortune of being wounded again during a German air raid! He never flew with the 4th FG again (*National Museum of the USAF*)

WAR OF ATTRITION

Following the one-off fighter sweep of German airfields in France on 21 March, the 4th FG flew a more familiar, and seemingly safer, bomber escort mission to Berlin on the 22nd. No German fighters were encountered, however, prompting Capt Duane Beeson to note in his log book, 'No Huns up today! What's wrong with them?' Things returned to normal the following day, however, when Col Blakeslee led the group to Brunswick. The Mustang pilots rendezvoused with the bombers near Steinhuder Lake, by which point the 'heavies' were already besieged by 25 German fighters.

'I saw several bombers going down, one of them in flames and another minus a wing', Capt Beeson reported. A Bf 109 made a head-on pass through his squadron, then wheeled around as if to make another pass. Beeson turned and gave chase;

'He dived to about 12,000 ft, and as I started to close on him, he suddenly pulled up into a steep climb, so I opened everything. When I was in range I got good strikes on him. He began to smoke and dived for a cloud at 6000 ft. I got on his tail as he came out of the cloud and clobbered him again, but he stuck to his aeroplane and crash-landed in a field. I strafed the aircraft on the ground, but as I came around again I saw the engine beginning to flame and the pilot getting out of the cockpit. He ran very fast across the field and fell behind a fence post as I came over again.'

After making a pass on a freight train, Beeson climbed to cloud level and spotted a Bf 109 flying with its wheels down. He turned to pursue it, but the enemy fighter ducked into a cloud;

'I saw tracers going past my port wing, so I made a quick break to starboard and saw another '109 behind me. He pulled up into a cloud, and as I came around he dived down, allowing me to get on his tail. I fired short bursts and saw flashes, and he jettisoned his hood, so I fired again, got more strikes and oil from the aircraft covered my windscreen. The pilot baled out at 1000 ft but the 'chute did not open. His aircraft crashed nearby and burst into flames.'

Flt Off Ralph Hofer picked out an enemy fighter attacking the bombers and followed it through the clouds, getting strikes. 'A dogfight followed, and this ended when the Fw 190 flicked into the deck', Hofer later reported.

To complete the day's haul, Maj Clark got a Bf 109 and an Fw 190, Maj Goodson and Capt Gentile bagged two Bf 109s apiece and 1Lts Megura, Godfrey, Allen Bunte and Leonard Price added four more Messerschmitts for a total of 13 kills.

SSgt Harry East awaits word from Col Don Blakeslee on issues with his Mustang following a mission to Munich. East fought a losing battle with the temperamental engine fitted to Blakeslee's first P-51B, struggling to get the right bank of its Merlin engine to stop smoking and missing. The fighter was finally replaced, much to East's relief, when it suffered a perforated hydraulic line (*Mark Copeland via Wade Meyers*)

336th FS pilots 1Lts Reuben Simon, John Godfrey and Robert Nelson (identity of individual standing is unknown) rest between sorties. Nelson became a PoW on 21 April 1944 (*National Museum of the USAF*)

On 24 March, the only enemy aircraft encountered during an escort to Schweinfurt was a lone Ju 52/3m, which scuttled off into cloud cover before it could be intercepted.

Three days later, Maj Clark led the group on an escort of three combat wings of bombers that were targeting Cazaux airfield, in France. After the 'heavies' had dropped their ordnance, the 334th and 336th FS dropped down and systematically strafed the 75 enemy aeroplanes scattered across the airfield – 21 were destroyed. 1Lt Gerald Montgomery headed the list of 14 pilots who were credited with strafing kills, being credited with the destruction of two Ju 88s, a Ju 52/3m and an Fw 190. 'I believe this attack was successful because we hit the enemy aerodrome right after the heavy bombers had left, decreasing the danger from light flak', noted Montgomery's squadron-mate Capt Duane Beeson, who claimed 2.5 victories himself. Despite the reduced flak, 1Lt Archie Chatterly still fell victim to flak, baling out near Tours to become a PoW. Earlier in the mission he had been one of four pilots to claim an aerial victory.

On 28 March, Maj Clark led the group on an escort mission to Chateaudun. The 335th FS dropped down and strafed Dreux/Vernavillet airfield, destroying a single unidentified aircraft. Unfortunately, 1Lt Raymond Clotfelter suffered mechanical failure in his Mustang over the target area and baled out into captivity.

The next day, newly promoted Lt Col Clark took the 4th FG to Brunswick in support of the First Air Task Force. Just after the bombers came off the target, Clark spotted 20–25 Fw 190s climbing from the east on the bombers' tails. 'The enemy aircraft made absolutely no pretence of fighting – they dove for the deck before we were nearly in range', said 335th FS CO Maj Carpenter. 'We followed them through the cloud to the ground where they attempted to out-run us.'

'It was a mad rat race', said 1Lt Pierce McKennon, who, like Carpenter, had 'made ace' during the 21 March strafing sweep. 'I saw two Me 109s flying line astern in a diving port turn. I started after them, but some yellow-nosed Mustangs cut me

1Lt 'Tom' Biel gets the final word on his P-51B from his crew chief before a show in March 1944. Biel destroyed a Ju 88 and an Me 410, and shared in the destruction of a second Ju 88 with Capt Duane Beeson, while strafing Cazaux airfield on 27 March (*National Museum of the USAF*)

A wrung-out 1Lt Pierce McKennon tries to answer questions immediately after returning from one of the frenetic missions of March 1944. He 'made ace' on the 21st of that month (*National Museum of the USAF*)

out on the last one so I went after the first '109. Three of my bursts really tore him up. At 5000 ft he was in a gradual dive, which grew steeper until he hit the deck and blew up.'

Hunting as always as a pair, Gentile and Godfrey were at 27,000 ft when eight Fw 190s passed underneath the bombers, which were in turn some 10,000 ft below the patrolling P-51 pilots. 'I bounced the No 4 Fw 190, fired and saw strikes around the cockpit', Gentile said. 'He slowly rolled over in a port turn and went vertically down. I started to level out below cloud, and 1Lt Godfrey told me to break because there were two behind me.' Godfrey was behind his leader because his engine was cutting in and out. 'I broke and evaded them. I made a port orbit, blacking out. When I recovered, there was an Fw 190 in front of me, so I closed to 300 yards and fired. I saw smoke come out and pieces come off. The pilot baled out at 1000–2000 ft.'

Meanwhile, Godfrey had figured out the problem with his engine – he had forgotten to switch tanks! By then he had lost Gentile. 'Under the clouds five Fw 190s with two Mustangs on their tails tried to fire at me', Godfrey reported. 'I dropped flaps and opened my throttle in an upward spiral turn. I looked behind me and saw one of the Fw 190 pilots bale out.' He was the victim of 1Lt Charles Anderson, who had just 'made ace'.

Anderson had seen seven Fw 190s off to his left, and when his section broke into them, 'they ran into the clouds and started down', he said. The Mustangs pursued them through a valley of clouds. 'I closed to good range and fired at one, and he went into a cloud with me right behind him.

Sporting white theatre bands and a somewhat dented drop tank, a red-nosed Mustang is towed from a blast-proof revetment at Debden. Nocturnal German air raids on Eighth Air Force bases were still a very real threat well into 1944 (*via Wade Meyers*)

When we came out of the cloud a few seconds later, I found myself overshooting badly. I could see that the prop was just windmilling and the cockpit was empty.'

Godfrey and Anderson then gave chase to the four remaining Fw 190s on the deck at full throttle. 'I queued up behind one', said Godfrey. 'Firing short bursts, I noticed strikes most every time. After the fifth or sixth burst, he dropped his wing and went straight in. He blew up right in front of me.'

'I fired at another in quite a tight turn and saw him flick and go into the deck', said Anderson 'I can't say whether this Fw 190 crashed due to my fire or due to the pilot trying to tighten his turn enough to evade me, but instead causing it to flick off out of control. Maj Carpenter and I chased two more Fw 190s on the deck and I fired at one and observed strikes. I ran out of ammunition, and someone came in and finished the aircraft off.'

1Lt Clemens Fiedler 'saw a gaggle of something coming in head-on at the same level', he said. He and his section 'continued climbing, and passed over them at about 1000 ft. I saw that they were 12 Me 109s. I turned in behind and began the attack in an attempt to get the leader. The '109 leader saw me and began turning, thus ruining my deflection. I decided to hell with him and started opening fire on his No 3 man, observing strikes on the engine. Grey smoke began streaming backwards. On a second burst I observed strikes on the cockpit and fuselage. 1Lt Paul Riley, flying on Fiedler's wing, 'saw the aircraft pour black smoke and explode as he went straight into the deck'.

Riley then spotted a Bf 109 split-S'ing away to his left. 'I split S'ed after him, closing so rapidly I had to chop off my throttle', he said. 'With a dead line-astern shot, I shot off his belly tank and observed plenty of strikes. Still closing, he shot huge flames right over my aircraft as I pushed the stick hard forward to clear him.'

At the same time, Gentile was getting back into the fight;

'I told another Mustang to join up and we started toward the bombers again. The Mustang with me was attacked by two Me 109s. I told him to break, but apparently he did not hear me for he continued to fly straight and level. I broke into the '109s, which half-rolled and went into cloud. The Mustang was no longer in sight, but he hadn't been hit, and I found out later that he got home okay. I was bounced by another '109 and broke into him. Just as he started to disappear behind me, I reversed my turn to starboard and fell astern of him. When I opened fire, glycol started streaming out and the pilot baled out.'

Three of the 4th FG's top four aces (according to the contemporary Eight Air Force practice of counting strafing kills – the missing pilot is Ralph Hofer) engage in a staged game of poker for photographers from *Illustrated* magazine. They are, from left to right, Capts Duane Beeson and Don Gentile and Maj James Goodson. These three pilots claimed 20.5 aerial victories between them in March 1944 (*National Museum of the USAF*)

Carpenter saw Godfrey and Flt Off Fred Glover share in the destruction of an He 111 shortly thereafter. Thirty seconds later Carpenter attacked another Bf 109. 'I closed to point-blank range, and he made a circuit and crash-landed in a field', Carpenter recalled. The latter then made an orbit and strafed the downed aeroplane for good measure.

'Due to there being a P-51 on the tail of practically every Hun, I couldn't immediately find a target', related 1Lt Allen Bunte, 'so I dove for the deck, got under the approximate battle area and waited. I noticed a group of aircraft flying due east, and in my direction. Taking what advantage I could of trees, hills and buildings for hiding, I made a large circle and came in behind what I was now certain were Huns. There were 11 of them flying very good formation at about 800 ft.'

After ten minutes, Bunte had closed in on the unsuspecting fighters. 'I picked my Hun and waited until I was directly behind him. I fired about a three-second burst and broke violently for home, full bore. From the time I pushed the button, I saw a profusion of strikes on wing roots and fuselage. As I finished my break, I looked back and saw the enemy aircraft in a glide with flames streaming back from the fuselage. I claim one Fw 190 destroyed, and a hell of a lot of intrepidity!'

In the day's battle, 20.5 German aircraft had been shot down by the 4th FG, for the loss of just three fighters. 1Lt Glen Smart of the 335th FS had suffered mechanical failure in his P-51B over the Channel and baled out. An ASR Walrus and a Spitfire both spotted the Mustang as it broke out of the cloud and splashed into the sea, and they waited for Smart to float into view. Although hauled aboard the Walrus within ten minutes of him entering the water, he was already showing signs of hypothermia. Had it not been nearby, Smart's fate would have been far different.

Near Brunswick, Smart's squadronmate 1Lt William Newell entered into a dogfight with an Fw 190 at 5000 ft. He closed in and fired, and saw strikes on the left side of the fuselage and the left wing root that caused the aeroplane to explode. Just then, a 20 mm shell went off next to his canopy, blasting the Plexiglas out of the left side and causing a coolant leak. After about 15 minutes, the engine seized. Newell baled out northwest of Dummer Lake and was taken prisoner. Finally, former No 133 'Eagle' Sqn pilot Capt Kenneth Peterson of the 336th FS was also shot down and captured. He had single-handedly attacked 12 Fw 190s near Braunschweig in an effort to save the crew of a crippled B-17, and he was awarded the Distinguished Service Cross for his actions.

Capt Ken Peterson and a canine friend pose for the camera at Debden. An ex-No 133 'Eagle' Sqn pilot, Peterson destroyed two Fw 190s on 29 March 1944 prior to being shot down himself defending a crippled B-17. He spent the rest of the war as a PoW (*National Museum of the USAF*)

By the end of March, the 4th FG had been credited with an incredible 156 kills in a single month. The Mustang was clearly proving its worth, even if it was still suffering from myriad technical problems. Col Blakeslee challenged his pilots to score 200 victories in April.

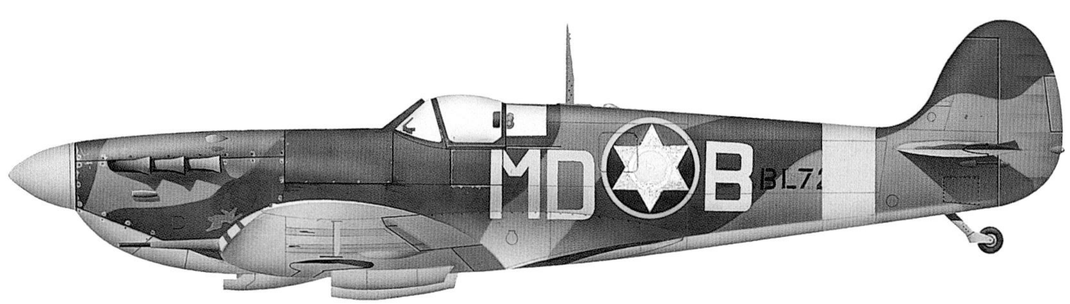

1
Spitfire VB BL722 of 2Lt James Goodson, 336th FS, Debden, October 1942

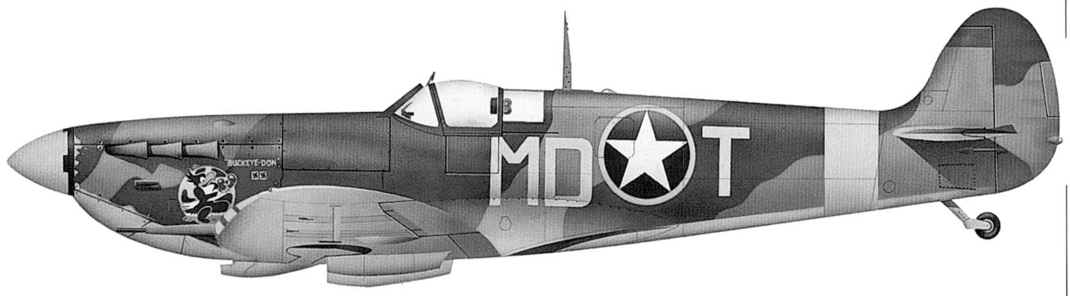

2
Spitfire VB BL255 *BUCKEYE-DON* of 1Lt Don Gentile, 336th FS, Debden, October 1942

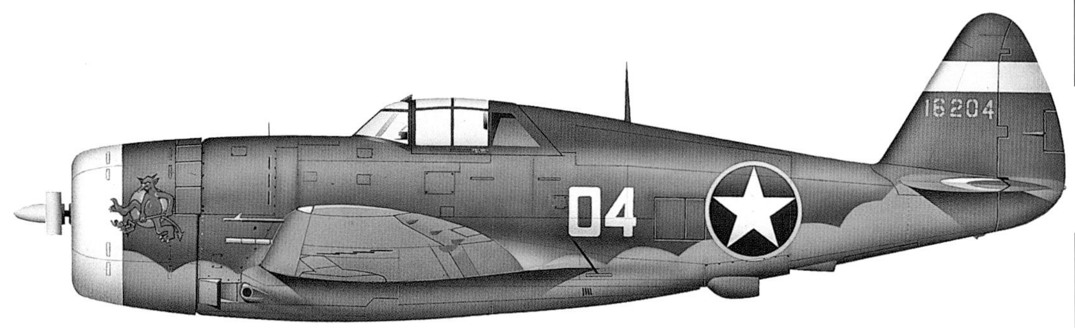

3
P-47C-2 41-6204 of Capt Richard D McMinn, 334th FS, Debden, February 1943

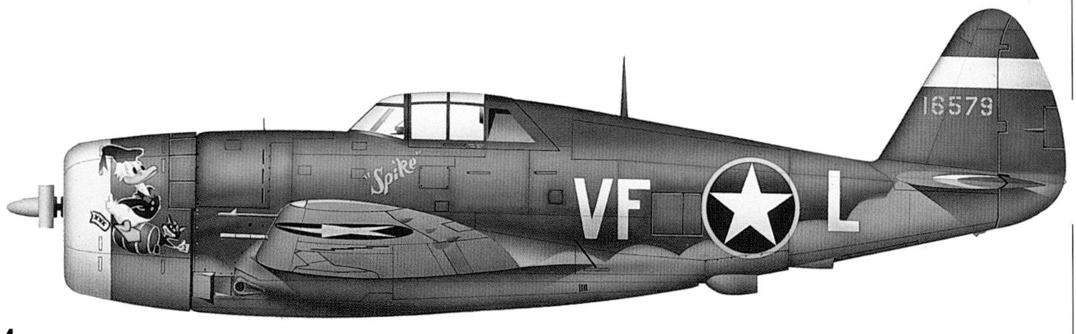

4
P-47C-5 41-6579 of Maj Carl 'Spike' Miley, CO of the 336th FS, Debden, March 1943

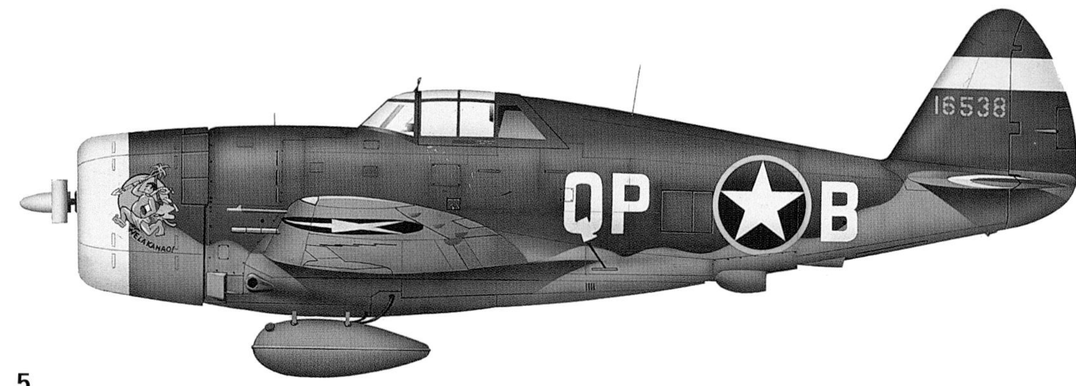

5

P-47C-5 41-6538 *WELA KAHAO!* of Capts Walter Hollander and Stanley Anderson, 334th FS, Debden, April 1943

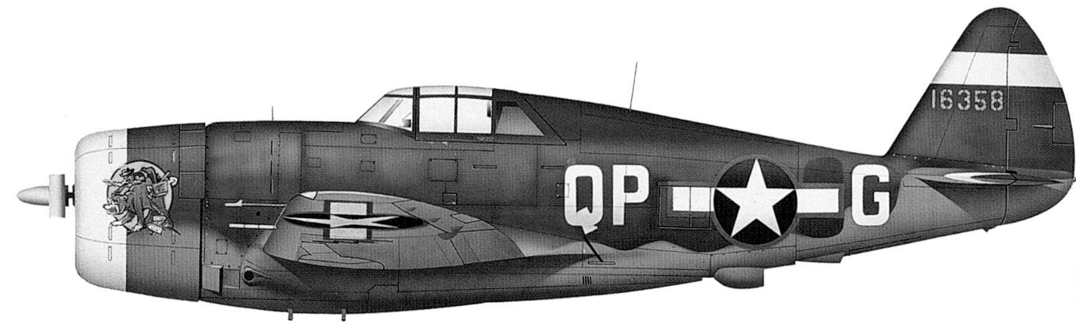

6

P-47C-5 41-6358 *CALIFORNIA OR BUST* of 1Lt Archie Chatterley, 334th FS, Debden, April 1943

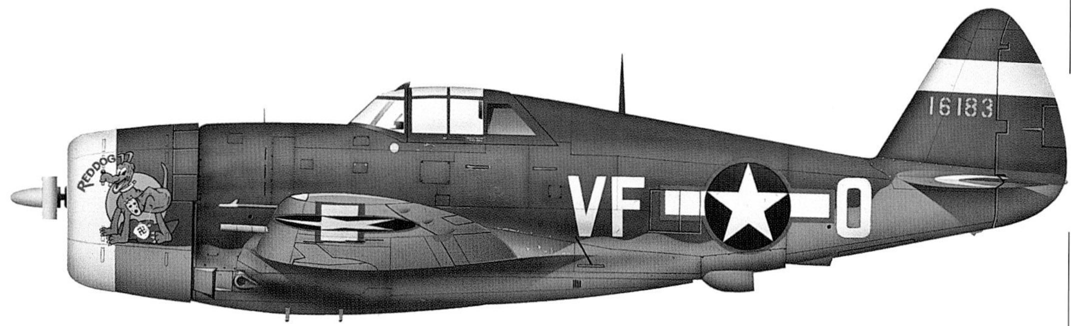

7

P-47C-2 41-6183 *Red Dog* of Capt Louis Norley, 336th FS, Debden, August 1943

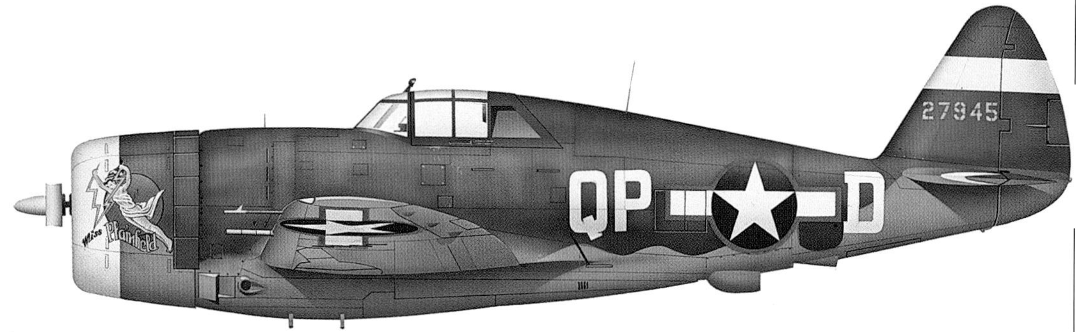

8

P-47D-1 42-7945 *Miss Plainfield* of 2Lt Spiros 'Steve' Pisanos, 334th FS, Debden, May 1943

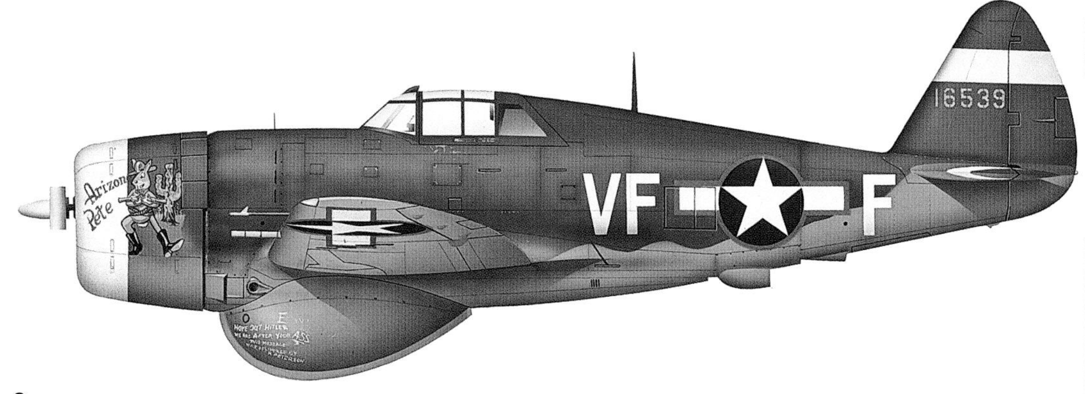

9

P-47C-5 41-6539 *Arizona Pete* of 2Lt Kenneth Peterson, 336th FS, Debden, June 1943

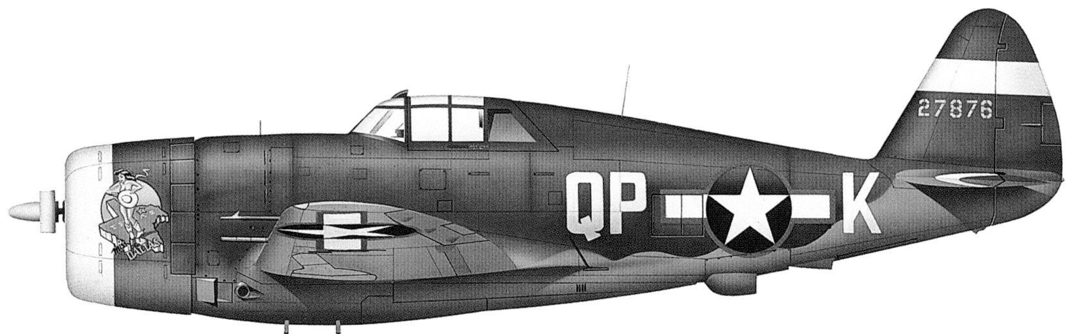

10

P-47D-1 42-7876 *Miss DALLAS* of 1Lt Victor France, 334th FS, Debden, June 1943

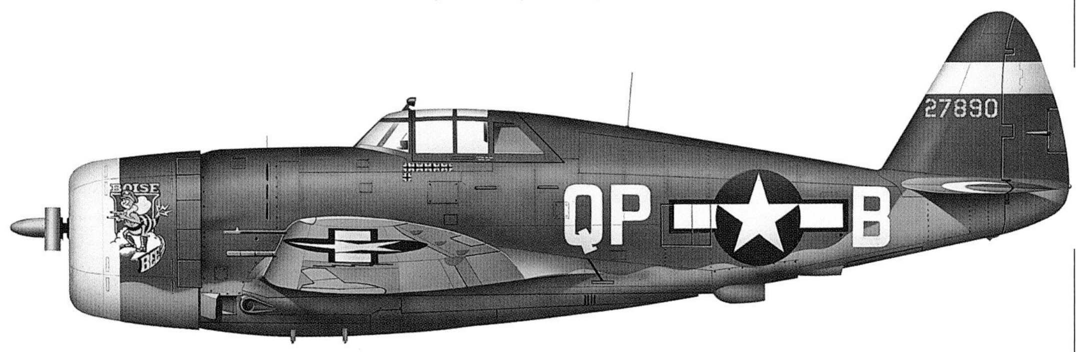

11

P-47D-1 42-7890 *BOISE BEE* of 1Lt Duane Beeson, 334th FS, Debden, September 1943

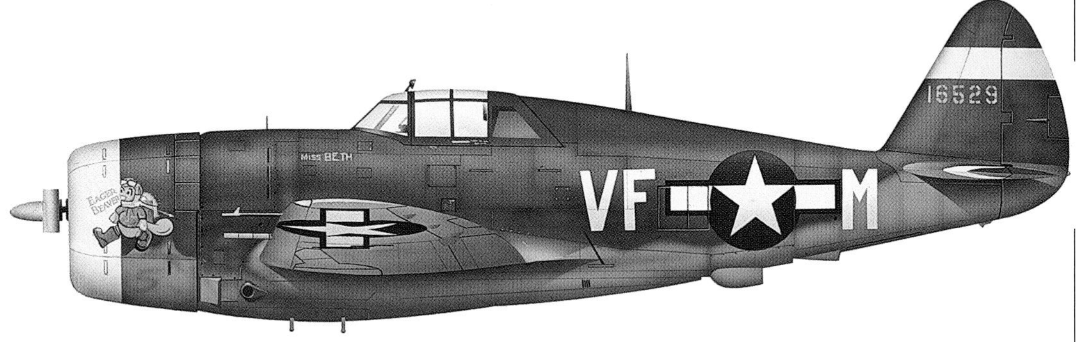

12

P-47C-5 41-6529 *Eager Beaver/MISS BETH* of 1Lt Jack Raphael, 336th FS, Debden, October 1943

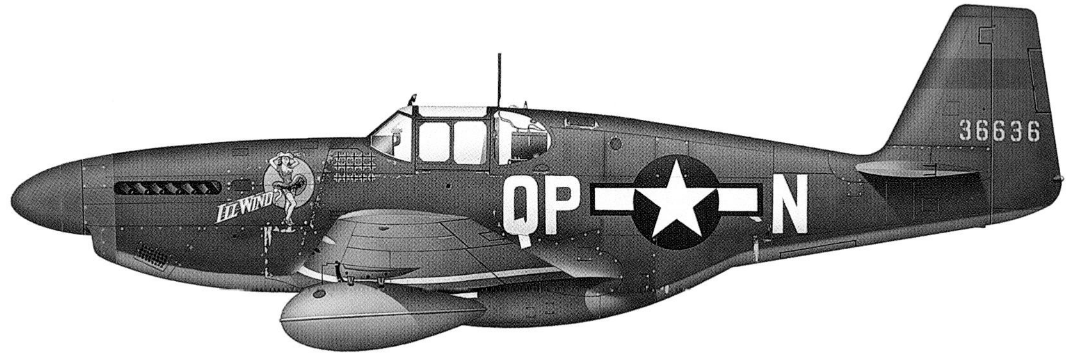

13
P-51B-5 43-6636 *ILL WIND* of 1Lt Nicholas Megura, 334th FS, Debden, March 1944

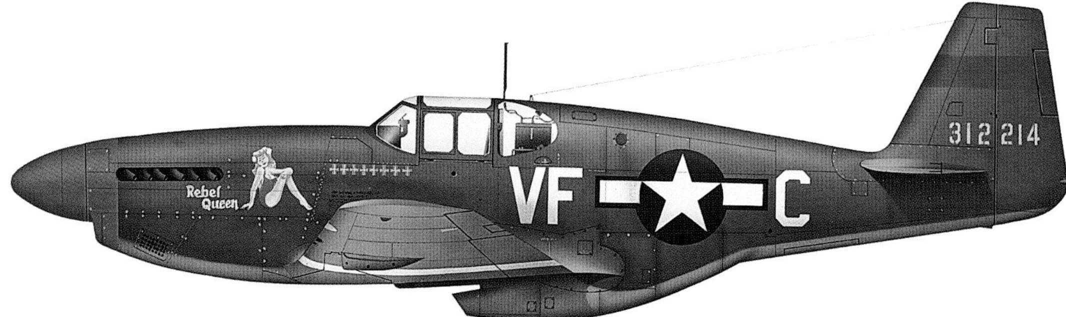

14
P-51B-1 43-12214 *Rebel Queen* of Flt Off Fred Glover, 336th FS, Debden, March 1944

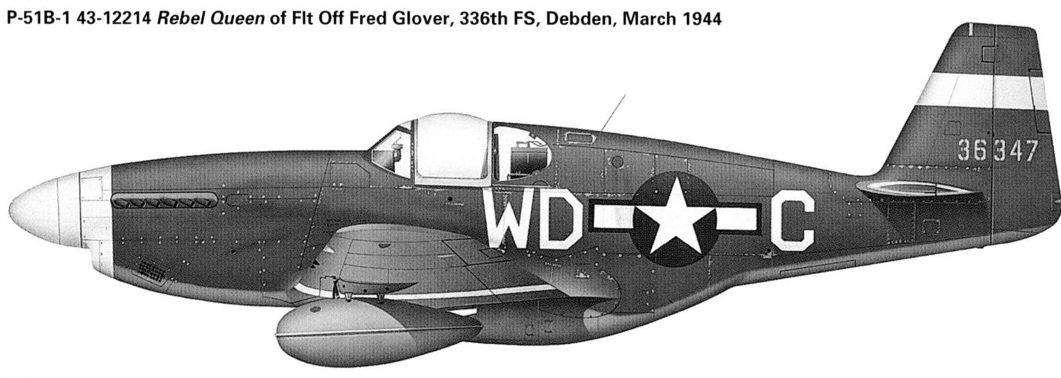

15
P-51B-5 43-6347 of Col Don Blakeslee, CO of the 4th FG, Debden, March 1944

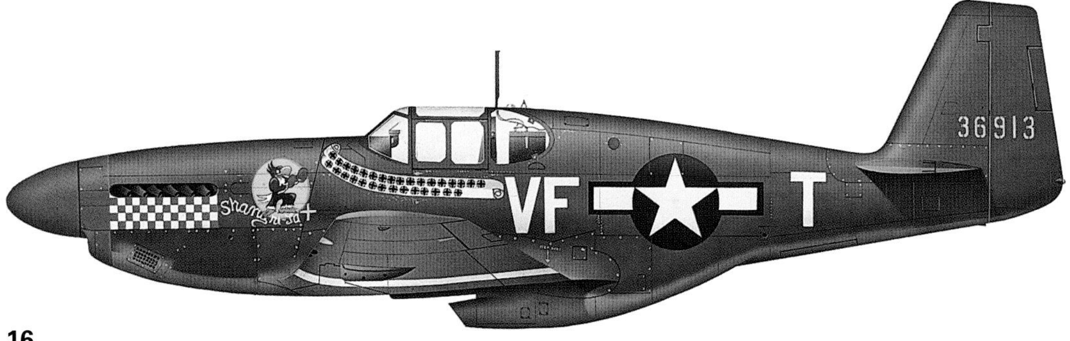

16
P-51B-7 43-6913 *Shangri-La* of Capt Don Gentile, 336th FS, Debden, April 1944

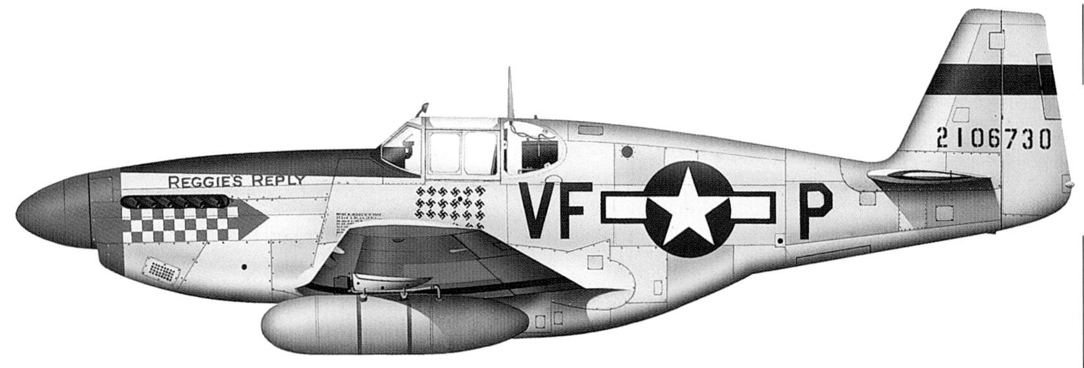

17
P-51B-10 42-106730 *Reggie's Reply* of 1Lt John Godfrey, 336th FS, Debden, April 1944

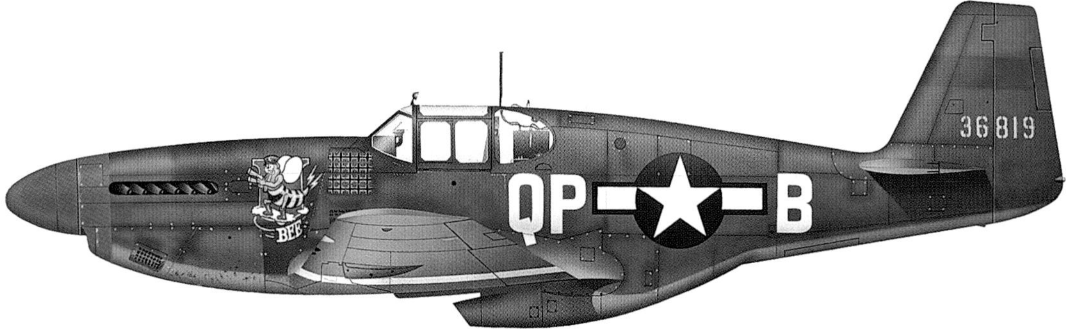

18
P-51B-5 43-6819 *BEE* of Capt Duane Beeson, 334th FS, Debden, April 1944

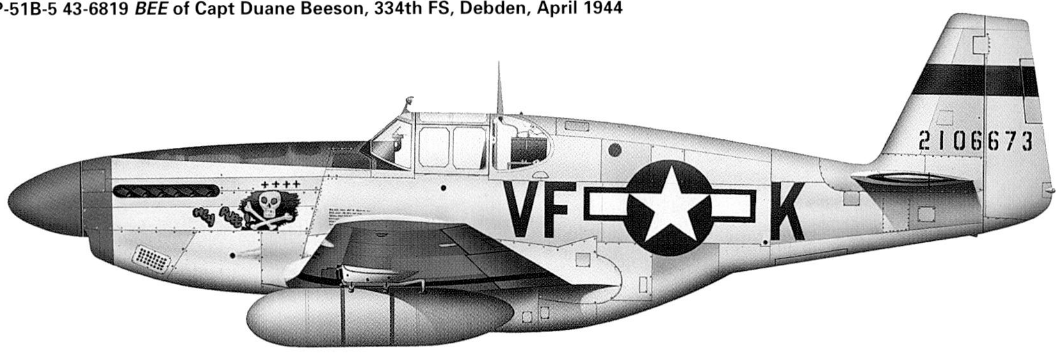

19
P-51B-10 42-106673 *Hey Rube!* of 1Lt Reuben Simon, 336th FS, Debden, April 1944

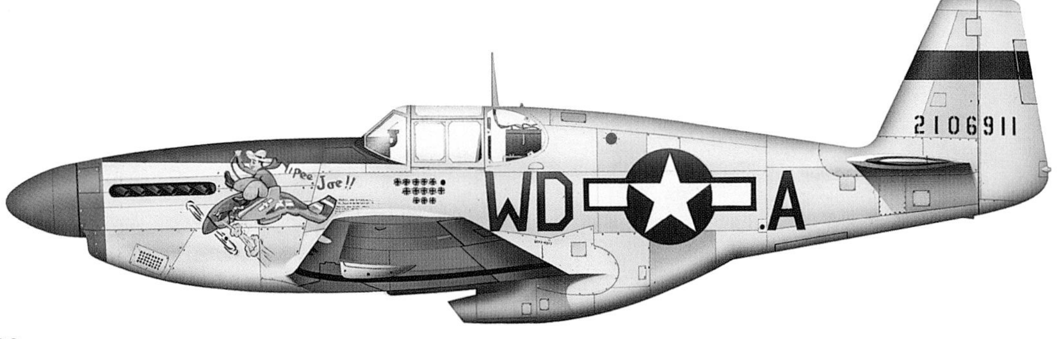

20
P-51B-15 42-106911 *Yipee Joe* of 1Lt Pierce McKennon, 335th FS, Debden, April 1944

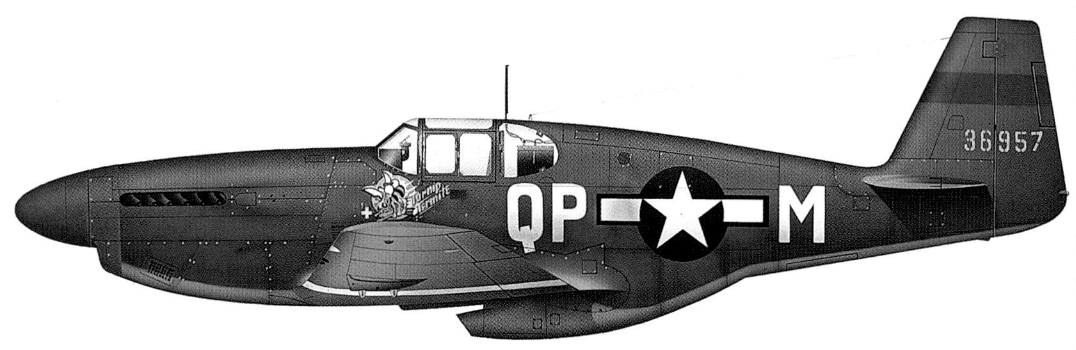

21
P-51B-5-NA 43-6957 *Turnip Termite* of 1Lt Frank Speer, 334th FS, Debden, May 1944

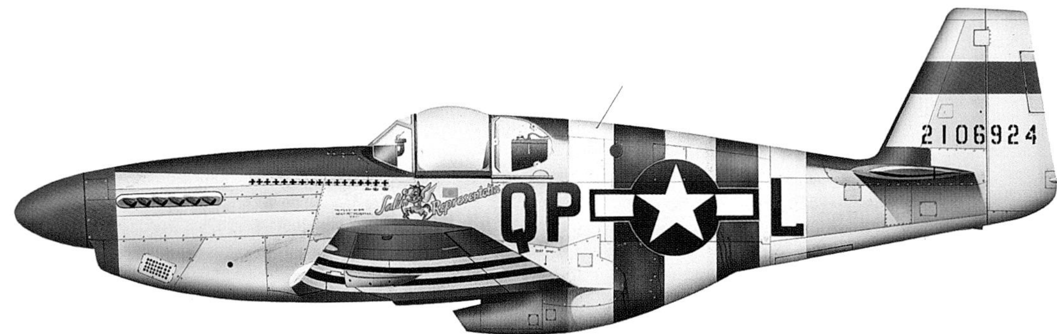

22
P-51B-15 42-106924 *Salem Representative* of 2Lt Ralph Hofer, 334th FS, Debden, June 1944

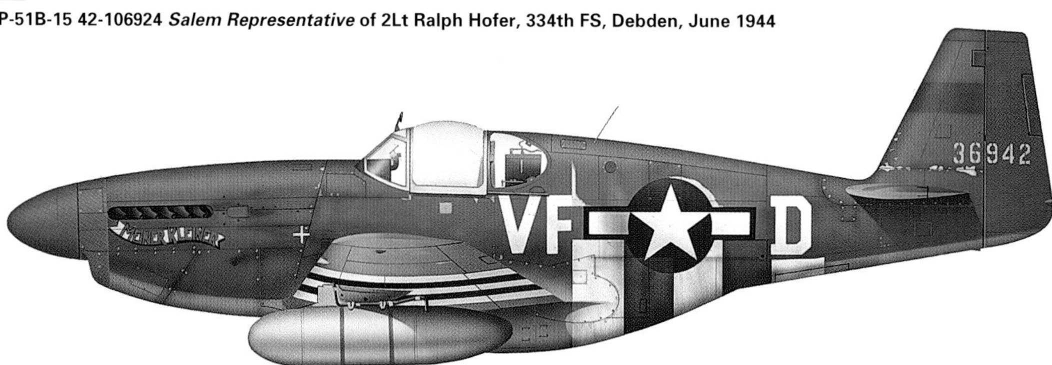

23
P-51B-5 43-6942 *MEINER KLEINER* of 1Lt Joseph Higgins, 336th FS, Debden, June 1944

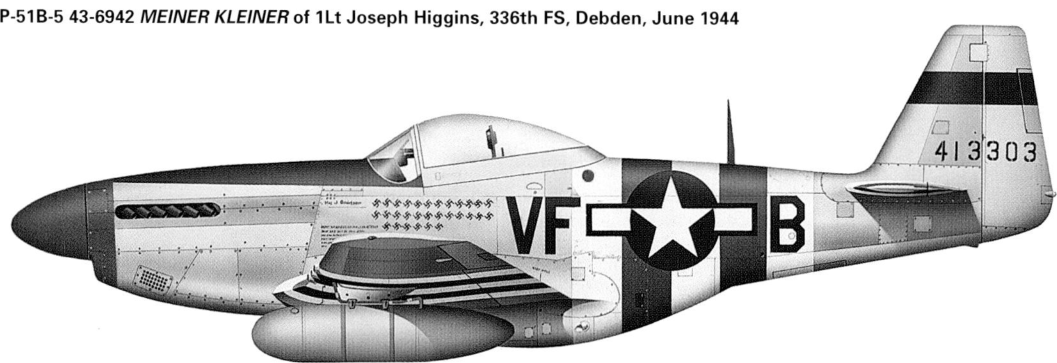

24
P-51D-5 44-13303 of Maj James Goodson, CO of the 336th Sqn, Debden, June 1944

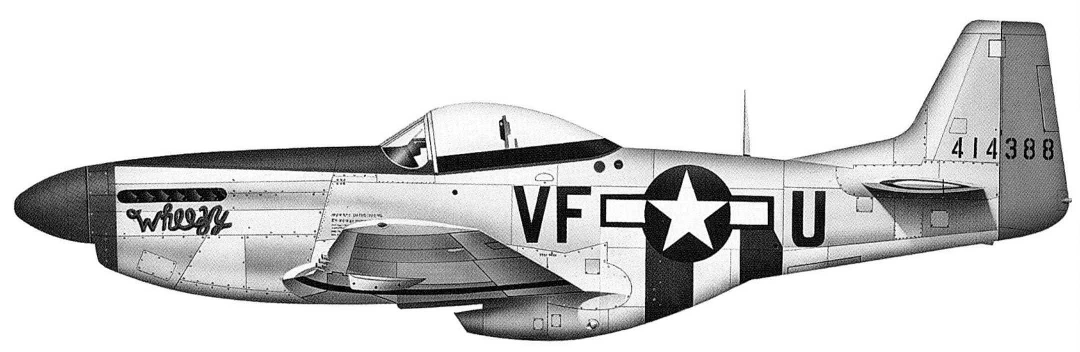

25

P-51D-10 44-14388 *Wheezy* of 1Lt Van Chandler, 336th FS, Debden, October 1944

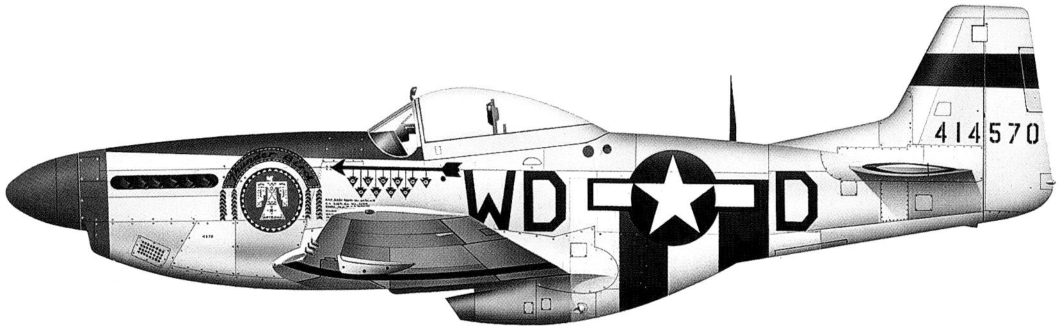

26

P-51D-10 44-14570 *THUNDERBIRD* of Capt Ted Lines, 335th FS, Debden, October 1944

27

P-51K-5 44-11661 *Iron Ass* of Lt Col Jack Oberhansly, Deputy CO of the 4th FG, Debden, December 1944

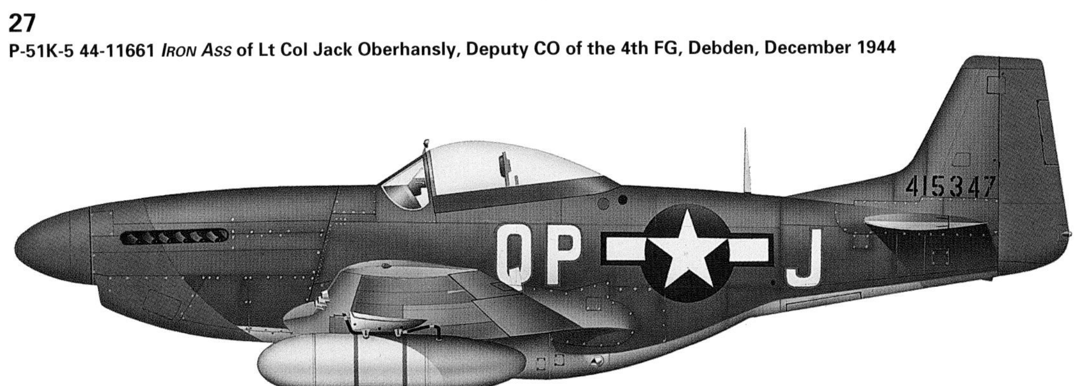

28

P-51D-15 44-15347 of Maj Howard Hively, CO of the 334th FS, Debden, January 1945

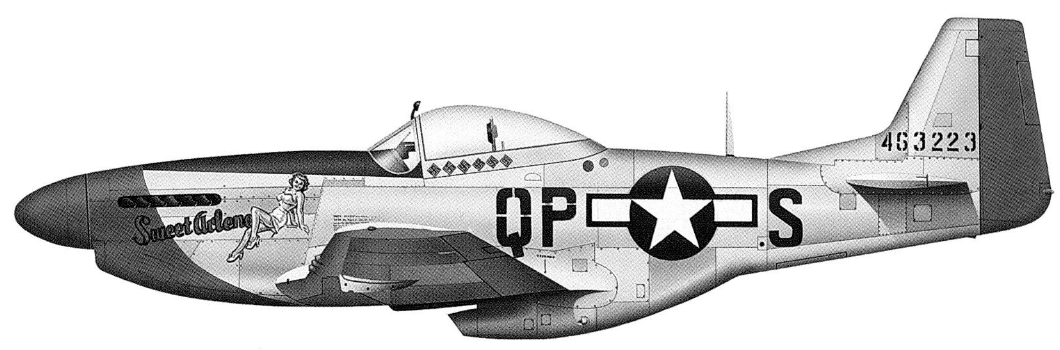

29

P-51D-20 44-63223 *Sweet Arlene* of 2Lt Arthur Bowers, 334th FS, Debden, February 1945

30

P-51D-10 44-14332 *Lazy Daisy/Dyer-Ria* of 1Lt Raymond Dyer, 334th FS, Debden, March 1945

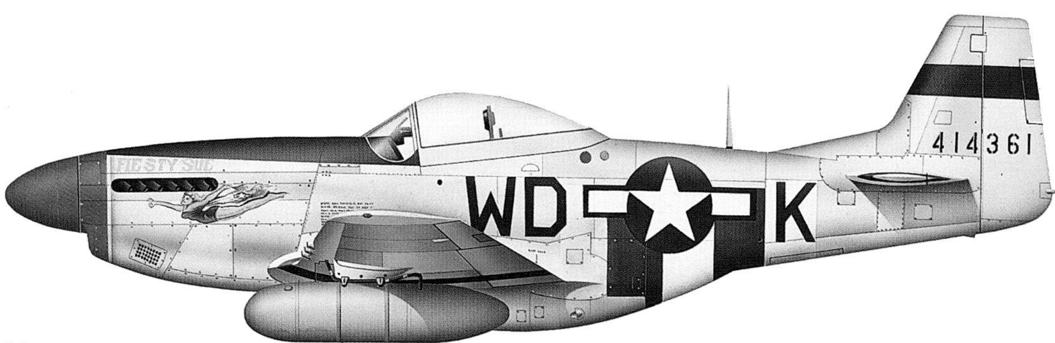

31

P-51D-10 44-14361 *Feisty Sue* of 1Lt Darwin Berry, 335th FS, Debden, March 1945

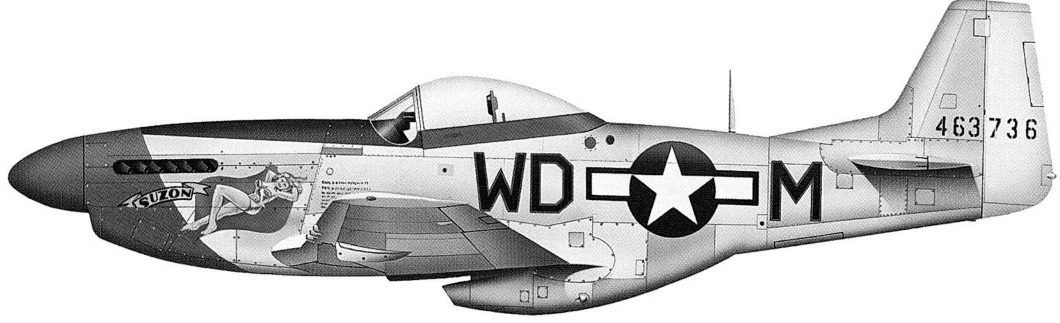

32

P-51D-20 44-63736 *Suzon* of 1Lt George Green, 335th FS, Debden, March 1945

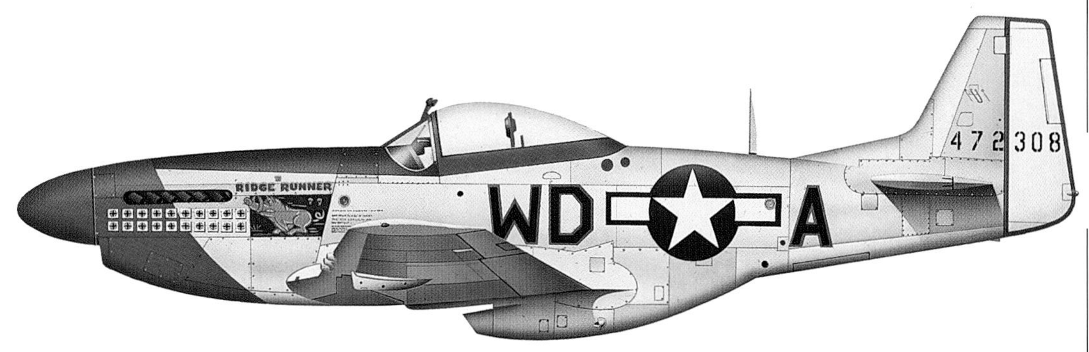

33

P-51D-20 44-72308 *RIDGE RUNNER IV* of Maj Pierce McKennon, CO of the 335th FS, Debden, April 1945

34

P-51D-10 44-14389 *Suzy* of 1Lt Robert Bucholz, 335th FS, Debden, April 1945

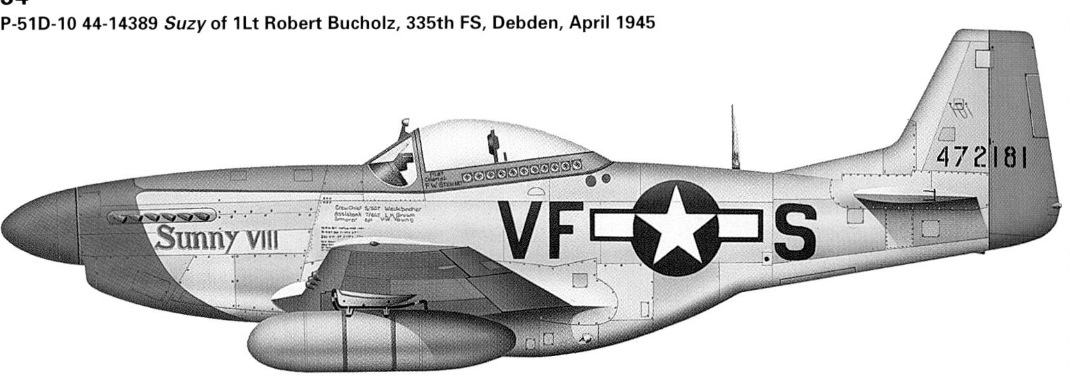

35

P-51D-20 44-72181 *Sunny VIII* of Col Everett Stewart, CO of the 4th FG, Debden, April 1945

36

P-51D-25 44-73305 *Blondie* of 2Lt Marvin Arthur, 334th FS, Debden, April 1945

The unofficial group badge of the 4th FG. The outfit officially had no group or squadron badges during World War 2

RUNNING UP THE SCORE

April Fool's Day 1944 was the first time that the 4th FG was able to conduct a full-strength mission with the Mustang, Col Blakeslee leading a Fighter Sweep/Withdrawal Support mission to the Ludwigshafen-Mannheim area. North of Lake Constance, two boxes of B-24s being protected by the group came under attack by fighters, and the 4th drove them off. Three Bf 109s were downed, with Capt Beeson scoring his 17th kill, Capt Gentile getting his theatre-leading 18th success and Flt Off Hofer taking his growing tally to seven victories. These successes pushed the 4th FG's overall score beyond the 300-mark.

Four days later, Col Blakeslee led a strafing attack on the airfields at Juterbog, Friedersdorf, Potsdam, Stendal, Plaue and Brandenburg-Briest. At Stendal, 'I covered a Ju 52/3m with strikes and then moved my sights onto an Fw 190', Maj Goodson reported. 'I would not have claimed the '190, but 1Lt Kendall Carlson says that I set it on fire. I pulled up and saw that about ten enemy aircraft were burning, and that there was no flak, so I ordered another pass and lined up on three Ju 88s parked wingtip-to-wingtip on the southwest corner. As I passed over, two were blazing, but at least one was shared with 1Lt Donald Emerson.

'I then attacked a Ju 88 in front of the north hangar, pulling up to see it burning. Capt Gentile and I then destroyed another Ju 88 on a hardstand

Fresh kill markings go on Don Gentile's P-51B 43-6913 *Shangri-La*, while the 4th FG's ranking ace attentively monitors the action. Gentile flew this machine for just 45 days, during which time he mowed down 15 German aircraft – half of them in this Mustang. The chequerboard below the exhaust was a device created by Gentile and his wingman Johnny Godfrey for quick identification in the air (*via Wade Meyers*)

on the northern extension – I was able to pull up and see that these two Ju 88s were burning nicely too. We left because we were out of ammunition, and the airfield was obscured by huge columns of smoke.'

Goodson claimed three and three shared aeroplanes destroyed on this mission. Although the group was credited with the destruction of 47 aircraft (only one of which was shot down), the attack had been costly. Both Capt Beeson and 1Lt Charles Carr were shot down by flak and taken prisoner, and squadronmate 1Lt Allen Bunte struck high-tension wires near Gardelegen and crashed into a lake. He too became a PoW. Finally, Capt Robert Hobert of the 336th FS baled out over the Channel when his fighter suffered mechanical failure. Although he was picked up alive by an ASR Walrus, Hobert died later in hospital from exposure.

The group's two highest-scoring aces pose for the camera in early April. Capt Don Gentile racked up 21.833 air-to-air and six strafing kills before being sent home on a war bond tour, and Capt Duane Beeson amassed 17.333 aerial and 4.75 ground victories prior to falling to flak and becoming a PoW on 5 April 1944 (*National Museum of the USAF*)

On 8 April, Maj Carpenter led a Freelance/General Support mission to Ulzen-Brunswick, and in a large-scale battle ranging over 30 miles from 23,000 ft down to deck level, the 4th destroyed 33 aircraft.

'Just about the time we reached the Celle area, 1Lt Clemens Fiedler reported many aircraft at "ten o'clock"', Carpenter recounted. 'These aircraft were flying close formation, and looked much like a box of bombers. We turned toward them and met them less head-on. There were 75–100 Fw 190s and Me 109s. We attacked at once, but were unable to

334th FS pilot 1Lt Allen Bunte, a native of Eustis, Florida, could not be brought down by German fighters, but a high-tension power line did the trick. On 5 April 1944 his P-51B (43-6837) hit wires near Gardelegen, causing the fighter to burst into flames. Bunte ditched in a nearby lake, knocking himself unconscious. The Mustang sank, but Bunte came to in time to release himself and bob to the surface. After paddling to the shore in his dinghy, Bunte was captured (*National Museum of the USAF*)

prevent some of the enemy aircraft from targeting the bombers and knocking four or five of them down.'

Carpenter picked out an Fw 190 and chased it down to 8000 ft before he could open fire. 'The aircraft then went into a spin, and I kept stalking him, thinking it was an evasive manoeuvre. However, the Fw 190 did not recover, and I saw it crash in a field with a great orange ball of flame.' Carpenter pulled up and got behind another Fw 190, sticking to him despite his evasive manoeuvres. 'I got a couple of good bursts into him, with several strikes in the cockpit area. He jettisoned his hood, but I did not see him bale out. I saw him crash three or four seconds later.'

1Lt Pierce McKennon, in RAF-style flying gear, climbs down from his assigned P-51B 42-6896. He downed five German fighters in this machine between 6 March and 18 April 1944, including his all-important fifth kill on 21 March (*via Wade Meyers*)

1Lt Pierce McKennon and his flight waded into what he estimated to be 85 enemy aircraft;

'I cannot give a very coherent description because it's the first fight like it I have ever been in. Fw 190s were all over the place, and every time I turned around I started shooting. Looking over at one side of the fight, there was a '190 and a P-51 going round and round, neither getting deflection on the other. I dived toward the '190 and clobbered him pretty good. He straightened out, and I got in some more strikes in the wing root and fuselage around the cockpit. He went into a sharp dive, and I saw him hit and litter a field with pieces of the aircraft.'

'We found two Mustangs from another group that were having some trouble with three or four Fw 190s', said McKennon's squadronmate, 1Lt Paul Riley. 'Having to use flap to turn inside these Fw 190s, I finally made a deflection shot as one of them tried to out-turn me. Greying out for a moment, I came to in time to pull a 30-degree deflection shot. I observed strikes on the engine and around the cockpit. The aircraft then dropped directly nose down straight under me and disappeared from my vision below 5000 ft. 1Lt Robert Church saw the aircraft, which was trailing white smoke, go down.' The Fw 190 hit the ground and burned.

1Lt Albert Schlegel also saw the white-nosed P-51s tangling with the Fw 190s. 'I got a few deflection shots on one, then he broke for the deck', he recalled. 'Before I could close on him, 1Lt Shelton Monroe got behind him, so I continued on down, covering him. After a long chase, Monroe got strikes all over the '190 and it crashed into trees, burning.'

Schlegel's flight soon came across an airfield, and he shot up a taxiing Fw 190. 'Just as I was about to make another attack on the airfield, 1Lt Monroe said that he was chasing an Fw 190, but as he was out of ammunition he'd keep him busy until I came up. After a short chase, I got quite a few strikes on the fuselage of the '190 and set its droppable belly tank on fire. Then large pieces started coming off, and he crashed into the deck and burst into flames.'

On 8 April 1944, 1Lt Shelton Monroe of the 334th FS destroyed an Fw 190, then, when out of ammunition, kept a second one busy until it could be destroyed by 1Lt Albert Schlegel of the 335th FS. Monroe would finish his year-long tour with the 4th FG in January 1945, having claimed 4.333 aerial and 4.5 strafing kills (*Julie Haynes via Peter Randall*)

This last-minute briefing of 336th FS pilots includes Capt Kenneth Peterson (top left), 1Lt Willard Millikan (left) and Capt 'Goody' Goodson (back to camera). Millikan downed three Bf 109s single-handedly during the 8 April mission to Tutow airfield. He went one better exactly two weeks later when he claimed four Bf 109s over Kassel (*National Museum of the USAF*)

The group's rising score attracted the 'big wigs'. An 11 April 1944 visit by the 'brass' to Debden was capped by this dinner, featuring a host of famous faces. On the far row in the centre is Supreme Allied Commander Gen Dwight Eisenhower, and to his left is Col Don Blakeslee, Lt Gen Carl Spaatz, commander of US Strategic Air Forces, and Capt Don Gentile. Second from left in the back row is Maj Gen William Kepner, head of VII FIghter Command. Sitting opposite Gen Eisenhower is Brig Gen Jesse Auton, 65th Fighter Wing CO, and to his left is Maj Jim Goodson and, turning, with his back to the camera, Maj Gen James Doolittle, commander of the Eighth Air Force (*National Museum of the USAF*)

By now Schlegel was ready to go home, but he spotted another Bf 109 and gave chase. 'After quite a long chase we were just getting into range of him when an Fw 190 came in from above.' Monroe and Schlegel turned into this new adversary, and the Bf 109 suddenly turned and crash-landed in a ploughed field. Schlegel stuck to the Fw 190's tail while Monroe made mock attacks, trying to straighten him out. Schlegel never hit the fighter, and 'after the fourth or fifth circuit, I was on the verge of flicking into the trees, so I broke off at this time', he said. Monroe saw the Fw 190 hit the trees and crash through them, leaving a path of small fires in its wake.

Also scoring big on the 8th were Gentile, 'Red Dog' Norley and Millikan, who each bagged three – the latter pilot also 'made ace'. 1Lt

Fiedler downed two, and no fewer than 13 pilots scored single kills. In exchange, however, Capt Howard Moulton of the 334th FS and 1Lt Robert Hughes of the 336th FS fell to enemy fighters near Celle and were made PoWs, and 1Lt Robert P Claus of the 334th FS and Capt Frank Boyles were killed in action by Fw 190s. For ex-No 121 'Eagle' Squadronn pilot Boyles, who was assigned to the 4th FG HQ and flying with the 335th FS, this was his first show since returning to operational status.

On 9 April, the group completed a bomber Withdrawal Support mission to Tutow airfield, then strafed two more aerodromes, but the Germans' use of dummy aircraft made confirming claims difficult. Capt David Van Epps of the 334th FS pulled up after the last pass at Tutrow and was not seen again. Hit by flak, he baled out and became a PoW.

The next day, Lt Col Clark led a mission targeting Romorantin airfield, in France, which was home to a large number of training aircraft that were dispersed in the woods that bordered the lightly defended base. The group destroyed 24 of them, with 'Goody' Goodson wrecking five himself and sharing in the destruction of a sixth.

These successes came at a price, however. The P-51B of 1Lt Clemens Fiedler (who had downed two Bf 109s 48 hours earlier) was hit by flak and he radioed that he was baling out. The pilot climbed and rolled the fighter onto its back, then went into a dive, before straightening out and going into a second dive, during which many objects flew out of the cockpit – but not Fiedler. To the horror of his fellow pilots, Fiedler was seen hanging halfway out of the aeroplane, and he perished seconds later when the Mustang hit the ground at high speed.

On 11 April, Maj Carpenter led a Withdrawal Support to Cottbus and Sagan. The bombers had been hit hard earlier in the mission, with no fewer

1Lt Robert Hills of the 334th FS, sat here in the cockpit of a P-47, destroyed a Ju 88 and an Fw 190 on 11 April 1944 during a strafing attack on an airfield southest of Stettin. Hills had flown with the RCAF prior to transferring to the 4th FG in September 1943. He would complete his tour in August of the following year with three strafing victories to his credit (*via Wade Meyers*)

Wear on the tail of 1Lt Bob Hills' P-51B 43-6717 is clearly evident. Assigned to the 4th FG in May 1944, this aircraft was eventually withdrawn from use three months later after suffering irreparable battle damage. The previous month, Hills had been named D Flight commander. Note the fighter's Spitfire-type rear view mirror (*via Wade Meyers*)

than 64 of them going down, but little enemy opposition was encountered on the way home. Just 4.5 aircraft were downed and four destroyed on the ground, all south of Stettin. 1Lt Biel got two Me 410s to 'make ace', with Flt Off 'Kidd' Hofer, 1Lt William Smith and Capt Raymond Care (who had achieved acedom three days earlier) sharing the remaining aerial successes.

Col Blakeslee led a Target Support escort mission to Oschersleben-Magdeburg the next morning. Northwest of Brunswick, four Bf 109s tried to get to the bombers. Maj Carpenter fired at one and overshot, but future five-kill ace 1Lt Frank Jones of the 335th FS was right there. He fired and 'saw strikes on the wings and cockpit. The aircraft headed for the clouds. I fell in behind him and gave him a long burst until he disappeared. I was about to fire when he blew up. All that was left was a cloud of black smoke above the ground and a trickle of blue smoke to the ground.'

1Lt Charles Anderson picked out the No 4 man in the formation and fired, 'seeing one strike right in the cockpit', he reported. 'He fell off on his left wing and did a spiral dive into the deck. The plane did not explode, but the aircraft broke up into small pieces. I then went after No 2.

'While firing at him, I saw No 1 coming at me from "nine o'clock". I could see he was not getting any deflection, so I kept after No 2. I believe No 1 was trying to ram me, but he passed about five feet behind my tail. I saw strikes on No 2, and he started streaming glycol from his starboard radiator. No 1 came in behind me and started firing, but as he began closing in, I tightened my turn for a few seconds until Maj Carpenter attacked him and made him break off. I then returned to my attack on No 2, and fired once more as he pulled up to about 5000 ft and baled out. His aircraft crashed and exploded.'

Carpenter 'hit the enemy aircraft in the left wing and cockpit. I watched him go down toward the ground, well under control but with no power. Then 1Lt McKennon came in and hit him a few times. The enemy aircraft had its wheels down and was trying to force-land on the airfield just beneath us. He went into a very small field, and his aeroplane broke up into many pieces. The fighter spread itself over a considerable area.'

On 13 April, Col Blakeslee led a Target Withdrawal Support mission to Schweinfurt that lasted five hours. The bombers were already coming under attack when the P-51s reached the rendezvous point south of Aschaffenburg, and the 4th was immediately engaged by a group of 20 Fw 190s.

Hailing from Dalton, Georgia, Capt Vasseure Wynn became commander of No 334 Sqn's B Flight in March 1944, only to be shot down by Fw 190s during a mission to Schweinfurt on 13 April. Wynn, who had seen action in the defence of Malta flying Spitfires with the RAF in 1942, became a PoW (*National Museum of the USAF*)

Capt Don Gentile's *Shangri-La* awaits its pilot at Debden on the day of its final mission – 13 April 1944. Boasting a red spinner, nose and wheel hubs, it also has all 30 of Gentile's claims (air and ground) on the victory scroll below the cockpit. By the end of the afternoon, this famous aircraft would be broken in two and Gentile would be on his way home for a war bond tour. The Airspeed Oxford parked behind the Mustang was the 4th FG's heavy communications and liaison aircraft. Coded AS 728, it was used to haul vital spares from VIII Air Service Command depots to Debden when parts were needed urgently (*Jack Raphael vis Wade Meyers*)

The P-51B of 334th FS pilot Capt Vasseure Wynn was quickly shot down, but his squadronmate 1Lt 'Cowboy' Megura settled the score when he promptly shot down the victorious Fw 190. Sobanski, Carpenter, McKennon and Norley also scored single kills. In addition to Wynn, who became a PoW, 1Lt Ralph Saunders of the 335th FS was killed when he was downed by a German fighter northwest of Schweinfurt.

The 13 April mission was Capt Don Gentile's last operation before rotating home, and to celebrate in front of the assembled media at Debden he beat up the field with a low pass. Buzzing the field or doing victory rolls was forbidden by Blakeslee because of the danger of battle damage. 'Gentile knew that, but did it anyway', his CO recalled in 1999.

Gentile failed to anticipate the gentle crown of the field, so halfway down its length his prop chewed a 50-yard furrow. The ace pulled the crippled aircraft up, then hit the ground directly in front of the photographers who were there to film the buzz, just missing them and the operations hut, and demolishing his P-51B *Shangri-La*. Blakeslee, who was still getting out of his aeroplane when Gentile crashed, spluttered, 'that pilot will never fly for me again!' Gentile walked away from this embarrassing end to his epic combat tour and promptly embarked on a war bond drive across the USA.

Two days later, Capt Care led a strafing mission intended to target Juterbog airfield, but weather broke the group up and three different bases were attacked by small sections of fighters. Care and 'Tom' Biel went after a yellow-nosed Ju 52/3m at one airfield, but in the process the former was hit by flak. He baled out near Celle and was picked up by German civilians immediately upon landing. He was interrogated for seven days before being sent to a prison camp near the Polish border.

1Lt Willard Millikan led nine 336th FS Mustangs against Hagenow airfield, where they destroyed two He 177s, an Fi 156 and a Bf 110. The unit had lost 1Lt Robert Siefert to mechanical failure as it flew across the Channel – the pilot baled out, but he was never seen again.

On 18 April, Col Blakeslee led the 4th to Berlin once again. Prior to reaching the German capital, 25+ Bf 109s and Fw 190s went after the bombers, and they were chased into the clouds by the escorts. 1Lt McKennon chased after one of the fighters, subsequently reporting that the Fw 190 'was different from any I had seen before. The fuselage seemed longer and smaller from the cockpit forward. After several bursts, I finally hit him, knocking off a few pieces. He flicked and went into a dive, with me following. He hit the deck at about a 45-degree angle and burned. Three Fw 190s then jumped me on the deck, but I outran them, climbed up and came home.'

Maj Carpenter's section jumped eight Fw 190s. 'I saw Maj Carpenter fire at one of them', reported one of the pilots in the flight. 'There was an explosion on it, and I saw it spin down. As the enemy aircraft was going down, the complete elevator and stabilizer on the port side fell away.' Carpenter then despatched a Bf 109, leaving it 'smoking and in a diving turn', recalled visiting pilot Maj Jenks, who 'fired at the rear Me 109, which half-rolled and split S'ed. I followed it down, thinking it was not damaged badly, but it never pulled out. It hit the ground and exploded a few miles northwest of Nauen.' Unfortunately, Maj Carpenter could not make these claims himself (which took his tally to 13.833 kills), as he had been shot down by a Bf 109 near Rathenow and captured.

After the group left the bombers, it strafed Juterbog airfield, where eight Ju 52/3ms were wrecked, before targeting Fassberg. Here, three He 177s and an He 111 were destroyed. North of Genthin, four Bf 109s were caught trying to land, and one was shot down. Chasing his fifth aerial success, Victor France, who had been promoted to captain the day before, was in hot pursuit of a Messerschmitt when his Mustang hit the ground near Stendal. He was killed instantly. 'Cowboy' Megura quickly jumped on the Bf 109 and shot it down. Also lost during the mission was 335th FS pilot 1Lt Lloyd Henry, who died when his fighter was downed by enemy aircraft. Seven other Mustangs returned to Debden with battle damage.

The following day, Capt Sobanski led an escort for 'heavies' returning from Eschwege. The rear boxes in the bomber formation came under attack from at least 60 enemy aeroplanes northwest of the target area, and as 1Lt McKennon's section came over the bombers, the ace spotted contrails above the B-17s and B-24s. McKennon recalled;

'We sighted 15+ enemy aircraft coming in from "ten o'clock" below us. We went after these, but then saw four Me 109s much closer and went after them instead. I looked back to clear my tail, and to see what the bunch back at contrail height were doing – I saw them dive toward the bombers. I got behind two silver-coloured Me 109s. At 75 yards I got strikes all around the cockpit and wing roots. Parts went flying in every direction, and at 4000 ft the enemy aircraft half-rolled and went into a cloud almost straight down. I didn't see him crash, but I'm quite sure he never pulled out. I started to climb after the No 1 who was ahead and to one side. I chased the son of a bitch all over the place, but I couldn't hit him. He finally shook me by going into a cloud.'

1Lt Bernard McGrattan spotted the same bandits, but they were broken up before he could reach them. Instead, he dove on three Bf 109s flying line abreast. 'Two of them broke right and one broke left', he said. 'I went after him. He tried to evade by a steep turn to the left, but after two complete turns I was able to draw deflection. I saw hits on his port wing and fired again. I saw many hits around the cockpit, and the aircraft fell earthward from the turn. He crashed almost straight down from where he was hit. I went down to the deck and was joined by 1Lt Megura.' The two spotted an Fw 190 and gave chase, only to see the panicky pilot bale out before either man could fire. McGrattan 'made ace' with these kills.

Sobanski, Millikan, Megura and 1Lt Robert Kenyon also downed a fighter apiece, but Capt Charles Anderson, a high scorer in the 335th FS with ten victories, suffered mechanical failure in his Mustang and was killed when the aircraft crashed near Brussels.

Col Blakeslee was again at the head of the group on 22 April when he led a Fighter Sweep between Kassel and Hamm. The 4th bounced 20 Bf 109s near Kassel, and the group was credited with the destruction of 18 fighters in the ensuing melee. 'I led the 335th and 336th FSs down to attack in a diving starboard turn, losing height and getting up-sun to the enemy aircraft', Blakeslee recounted. 'The 334th FS stayed up to provide cover. We attacked the aircraft, and as we approached they were flying in a Lufbery formation, making it difficult for any individual attacks until two of the Me 109s broke away, leaving a gap. Our P-51s attacked by sections, and the fight was on, with many enemy aircraft going to the deck.

'I saw one headed northeast up a shallow valley just skimming the trees. I gave a short burst at 300 yards, then closed to 200 and gave him a second burst. I was closing fast when I saw his tank strike the ground. I was not more than 15 ft above as I passed over him and saw his prop churn into the ground, throwing pieces, and the aircraft then crashed violently.

'I sighted another Me 109 3000 ft below me, being chased by other P-51s. I dumped flaps and dove – the enemy aircraft straightened out as I got to him, and I fired a two-second burst as he was pulling up over some trees. My fire hit the enemy aircraft on the wing roots and cockpit, and his prop and wing hit a tree top, cartwheeling him into the deck.'

The biggest victor for the day was 1Lt Willard Millikan, who destroyed four Bf 109s in quick succession with just 666 rounds. Godfrey downed three and 'Red Dog' Norley and Schlegel each claimed two apiece – the latter pilot 'made ace' with this haul. The group's only loss was 1Lt Robert Nelson of the 336th FS, who suffered mechanical failure in his P-51B in the middle of a fight and baled out near Kassel. He was taken prisoner.

Despite the group's recent successes, on 23 April Col Blakeslee expressed his concerns about his pilots' generally lax behaviour of late when out of the cockpit at Debden in a letter addressed to all personnel at the Essex base. In part it said;

'I want to say that we are just beginning to work – the busy season is at hand. We have been living under very easy conditions for a long time, and some of us still want to be "babied". Already I hear complaints of overwork, references to rotation, promotions and petty problems. For these I have no sympathy. The next few months will test the "guts" of a lot of people. I hope you stand the test. Let's go to work and keep the finger out – way out!'

As if to prove his point, on the 24th Col Blakeslee led his third mission in six days when the group flew a freelance escort to Munich that cost the Luftwaffe 12 aeroplanes. North of Worms, the colonel spotted 20 German fighters flying in a perfect V formation 15,000 ft below them,

Capt Charles Anderson had scored ten aerial victories and 5.5 strafing kills victories at the time of his death on 19 April 1944, when his Mustang suffered mechanical failure and he crashed near Brussels (*National Museum of the USAF*)

Capt Albert Schlegel 'made ace' on 22 April 1944 with two Fw 190s downed south of Kassel. He was killed on 28 August 1944 when his P-51D was struck by flak near Strasbourg (*via William Hess*)

closing in on the bombers from behind. Blakeslee damaged one Fw 190 and entered a turning fight with several more. Finally, one of his bursts hit a fighter. 'I was getting strikes on him when he jettisoned his hood and helmet. I overshot him, and as I did so I saw him unfastening his straps and watched him jump at 600 ft. His 'chute opened just above the ground.'

'I tacked onto a section of four Fw 190s', said Lt Schlegel, 'opening fire on the last one. I changed my deflection and got strikes in the area of the cockpit. The enemy aircraft fell into a dive and crashed in some woods.' After a head-on pass with another fighter, Schlegel latched onto an Fw 190. 'He rolled and pulled up into a turn. I hit him from about 200 yards and with about 20 degrees of deflection. The strikes were just behind and on the cockpit. It started burning in the cockpit and I watched it going almost straight down until it was below 1000 ft.'

'I climbed to rejoin the battle and, at 6000 ft, I saw an Fw 190 diving away to the south', recalled Col Blakeslee. 'I dove after him, and at 2000 ft he started a left turn. I opened fire and saw strikes along the cockpit. The enemy aircraft then straightened out and glided for an open field as if to crash-land.' Blakeslee overshot, but Schlegel was above the fight. 'I opened fire at about 300 yards and got some strikes. The enemy aircraft's right wing hit the deck and the rest of it broke up.'

1Lt George Stanford and his section leader dove on the formation at the same time. 'My leader picked out one and went after him', he said. 'Another enemy aircraft came up behind him, and I opened fire on it from dead astern, getting many hits. The Fw 190 exploded in front of me, throwing oil and debris all over my windscreen. What was left of it fell towards the ground in flames.'

1Lt Paul Riley had already shot down an Fw 190 when another Focke-Wulf got on his tail. 'I broke down hard left just as another one came directly into my flight path. I was boomeranged through the air by a collision with this aircraft. The stick was wrenched from my hand. I recovered control and found that one quarter of my left wing had been sheared off. Below me, I could see the pilot of the enemy aircraft with red parachute silk streaming after him, but the 'chute did not open. He went straight into the deck. I set course for home, and while climbing from 10,000 ft I had my left wing blown off by flak. I immediately baled out and landed about 60 yards from the AA battery.' Riley became a PoW.

In the same fight was 1Lt Milton Scarborough. When the Mustangs broke to attack, 'I blacked out temporarily', he said. 'Coming to, I discovered the only aeroplanes in sight were Fw 190s. One was climbing into my flight path, and I fired, observing strikes in the left wing root, cockpit and engine. It went into a lazy spin and crashed. Shortly thereafter, an enemy aircraft made a stern attack on my aeroplane, hitting the engine and setting it on fire.' Scarborough floated down into captivity.

Scarborough and Riley were not the only losses, as ace 1Lt Tom Biel was shot down and killed south of Darmstadt.

Uneventful escort missions followed on 25 and 26 April, and on the 27th the group took the 1st Air Task Force to Blainville/Toul airfield. A follow-up strafing attack on the base by the 335th FS saw 1Lt Leighton Read destroy a single-engined aeroplane, with four more damaged.

After an escort to Berlin on 29 April, single sections from the 334th and 336th FSs strafed Nordhausen airfield, west of Berlin. Flak was intense, and 1Lt John Barden was hit and forced to bale out to become a PoW. 'Cowboy' Megura was also wounded in the arm by a rifle bullet. The attack destroyed seven aeroplanes and damaged two more. On the way home, 1Lt Pete Kennedy suffered engine failure after he too had been hit by flak. Baling out near Flechtorf, he also became a PoW.

334th FS pilots 1Lt Hipolitus 'Tom' Biel and Capt Vasseure 'Georgia' Wynn strike a heroic pose in front of a Mustang in early April 1944. Biel scored 5.333 aerial and six strafing victories prior to losing his life in aerial combat near Darmstadt on 24 April. Wynn also fell victim to the Jagdwaffe, being shot down by an Fw 190 on 13 April and made a PoW (*National Museum of the USAF*)

Col Blakeslee led the final mission of a busy month on the 30th, when the group flew a Freelance General Support mission to Lyon. The only aerial victory was a Bf 110 spotted and despatched by Capt Sobanski, 1Lt Shelton Monroe and future 7.833-kill ace 2Lt Joseph Lang. A twin-engined aeroplane and four Do 24 flying boats were strafed and destroyed in Lyon harbour. Flt Off Fred Glover suffered a glycol leak in his P-51B after it was hit by flak, and he 'hit the silk' north of Lyon. Picked up by the French Resistance, he successfully evaded and made it back to England.

When the kills for April were tallied up, the 4th FG had indeed achieved Col Blakeslee's stated aim of passing the 500-mark by 1 May. Its pilots had destroyed 207 enemy aircraft in the air and on the ground, taking the group's total to 503.5. It was now the most successful fighter group in the ETO. The 4th would subsequently be awarded the first of its Distinguished Unit Citations for destroying 323 enemy aircraft between 5 March and 24 April 1944, for the loss of 44 pilots killed or captured.

Following a memorable party in the Debden mess on the evening of the 30th, some sore-headed pilots covered the 'heavies'' egress from Saarbrucken during a late afternoon mission on 1 May – as usual, Col Blakeslee was in the vanguard. A dozen Bf 109s were spotted east of Luxembourg, and Capt Godfrey went after one and chased it down to low altitude, where the German pilot baled out to give the 336th FS ace his 14th kill. Newly promoted 2Lt Ralph Hofer also downed a Bf 109, the pilot 'baling out in front of me so close that I could see his dress uniform and his black shiny boots glistening in the sun', the ace recalled. 'He waved as I flew by within 50 ft of him.' Hofer's tally now stood at ten kills.

Capt John Godfrey took his tally to 14 aerial victories when he downed a Bf 109 on 1 May 1944 (*via Sam Sox*)

335th FS pilot 1Lt Frank Jones chased a Bf 109 into a cloud, and when he pulled out he saw three enemy aircraft pursuing a Mustang. 'I turned into one and fired a good deflection shot as he turned into me. He rolled over on his back and went straight down. His canopy came off, but I did not see him bale out or a 'chute open. I followed him straight down and saw him hit and blow up in a great ball of flames. He crashed in a large town behind some houses.' A fourth Bf 109 was scored by 1Lt McGrattan, taking his tally to 7.5 kills.

The group failed to add to its tally for more than week, not claiming an enemy aircraft destroyed until 9 May. On this date, Capt Millikan led a bomber escort mission to the airfield at St Dizier. The group flew over the

Capt Herbert Blanchfield of the 334th FS claimed 4.333 strafing kills within days of receiving this P-51B in early April 1944. One of the first natural metal Mustangs issued to the 4th FG, its successful run came to an abrupt end on the morning of 9 May when it was shot down, with Blanchfield at the controls, during a strafing attack on a flak tower at Reims-Champagne airfield. Although initially evading capture, Blanchfield was eventually found by the Gestapo, and he spent the rest of the war as a PoW (*via Roger Freeman*)

base soon after the 72 B-17s had left, but no aircraft were sighted. It then checked out three more airfields in the area, and these too were devoid of German aeroplanes. Finally, a handful of Ju 88s were spotted at Reims-Champagne, and one was destroyed and two damaged. 'We came over the field in a dive from 200 ft down', said 1Lt Frank Speer. 'I believe Capt Herbert Blanchfield was shooting at a flak tower, as was his No 2. As we passed the field, I saw his P-51 streaming white smoke as he slowly pulled up to 3000 ft on a course of 240 degrees from the field. His jacket was covered in oil, which also covered the side of the aeroplane. He seemed to have lost both oil and glycol, and the engine was detonating violently.

'Blanchfield climbed out of the cockpit as the aeroplane half-rolled to the left. When he jumped it was doing about 150 mph, and his 'chute opened immediately. He landed in a small wood. His P-51 burst into flames and burned furiously about a half-a-mile from where he landed.'

Blanchfield ran from the wood and eventually encountered a farmer, who put him in contact with a man who hid downed Allied flyers. A few days later the Gestapo discovered his hiding spot. He spent five months in the hands of the Gestapo, and was then shipped off to *Stalag Luft I.*

Also shot down by flak on this mission were 1Lts Vernon Burroughs and Lloyd Waterman, whilst 1Lt Robert Sherman struck the ground with his propeller and ended up bellying in. All three became PoWs.

On 11 May, 1Lt Robert Tussey suffered mechanical difficulties and baled out into the Channel. He was picked up by a rescue boat, but he subsequently died from the head injuries he had sustained baling out.

The following day, 1st Air Task Force bombers received an escort to Brux, in Czechoslovakia – the furthest that the 4th FG had been to date. During the run in to the target, eight Bf 109s from JG 27 tried to attack the bombers, and three were destroyed by Capt Hively, 1Lts Pierce and Siems and 2Lt Hofer. In another attack, Maj Goodson and 1Lt McDill each bagged a Bf 109, and four pilots combined for five more kills. 1Lt George Stanford from the 335th FS was among the latter group of victors;

'At 10,000 ft, we spotted three Me 109s below us, and we went down to attack them from the rear. I picked the one in the middle, and he broke right and down onto the deck. I fired at him continually, starting at about 350 yards. I observed only one group of hits on his starboard wing. For some reason, however, he seemed to think his jig was up, for he pulled up in a steep climb, started to roll over, and jettisoned his canopy.'

Squadronmate 1Lt Elliot Shapleigh dove for the same three Bf 109s, his section weaving to lose speed so as not to overshoot. 'I opened fire, getting strikes on the wings and fuselage', he said. 'I pulled up as the aircraft went into the deck and exploded.' At that point Shapleigh made a starboard turn and found himself on the tail of Stanford's Bf 109. He opened fire, and the Bf 109 completed its roll and went into the ground on its back.

Future ten-kill ace 2Lt Ted Lines and his wingman spotted a pair of Bf 109s, and the two dropped their tanks to pursue. 'They split up and headed for the deck', recalled Lines. He saw his wingman destroy one Bf 109, 'and just then the other one cut right in front of me. I got on his tail and started firing. I followed the enemy aircraft for about 20 miles, and he led me into a flak area. By that time, I was out to get him. I cleared my tail, and just as I faced forward, I saw the Me 109 hit the ground and blow up.' Other fighters fell to Capt James Happel and 1Lt Robert Homuth.

The 4th FG ranged east once again on 13 May, when the group covered bombers returning from a strike on Poznán, in Poland. 1Lt Leonard Pierce's P-51B suffered a mechanical problem that forced him to bale out over the Channel soon after departing Debden. Once in the water, Pierce struggled to free himself from his parachute and drowned. When the ASR launch arrived, its crew found only his dinghy.

All 4th FG Mustangs were grounded between 14 and18 May so that groundcrews could install permanent fuel lines for the new 108-gallon paper drop tanks that would now replace the 75-gallon teardrop ones.

On the 19th, the group escorted bombers over the German capital and back to the Baltic. 'About four minutes after we had left the bombers, the leader of Red Section reported one aircraft circling above the cloud at "ten o'clock"', reported Capt Howard Hively. 'I told him to go down and I would follow. As he started down, I noticed there were three of them in a wide vic, with one way in front. The two wingmen half-rolled immediately, with Mustangs right behind them, but the leader continued in a straight line. I picked him, flew up almost beside him, identified him as a '109 with green markings on the side, let down my flaps, dropped to line astern and clobbered him from about 150 yards. He went down streaming black smoke. The pilot did not get out.'

Hively ordered his unit to form up. Soon, he saw six Bf 109s at 21,000 ft, 'a mile to our "ten o'clock", flying north. We swung onto their tails. I started to gain, but slowly. I saw 1Lt David Howe clobber the straggler in the starboard three, then the rest broke to the left and down. I was covered with so much oil from the first '109 that I could not see very well, and lost the port three for a time, but dove to where I thought they were going.

'At 9000 ft, I found what I thought were only two flying very good formation. I half-rolled, attacking the right one. I got hits on the tail and starboard wingtip of one, who evidently flicked to the left and smashed into another on the bottom of the turn whom I hadn't seen before. The one who was shot baled out immediately, and then his fuselage broke in half about three feet back of the cockpit. I followed the one who had hit him, still shooting deflection. He flicked again, and what appeared to be part of his starboard wing flew off, and he baled out.'

Both Hively and Howe had achieved acedom with their successes on this mission. Maj Michael McPharlin and 1Lts James Scott and Joseph Lang also claimed kills.

1Lt Donald Patchen of the 336th FS was hit by flak over Berlin, and he nursed his fighter as far as Hanover, where he baled out. His wingman saw him on the ground, where he had to make a choice between a field of wheat set afire by his P-51, a mob of farm-implement-wielding civilians or Wehrmacht troops. Opting for the latter, he was soon a PoW.

On 21 May, the 4th performed its first Chattanooga mission against rail targets, damaging ten locomotives and numerous trucks and warehouses. Five aircraft were also destroyed on Rathenow airfield, but 1Lt Bill Hunt of the 335th FS was hit by flak and killed attacking the rail yard at Zossen.

336th FS CO Maj James Goodson is seen here in the cockpit of his assigned P-51B 43-24848 in late May 1944. He claimed his 14th, and last, aerial victory in this fighter on 25 May. Goodson was officially credited with 14 aerial and 15 strafing kills, so the 30th swastika applied to this Mustang almost certainly signifies his solitary probable claim, which came at the controls of P-47D Thunderbolt 42-7959 on 3 September 1943 (*via Roger Freeman*)

An escort mission to Kiel the following day saw the 336th FS sweep ahead and engage ten Bf 109s. Capt Millikan and 2Lt Hofer each scored a kill, and Capt Megura shared a third with a P-38, but stray rounds from the latter fighter also holed Megura's glycol system. He was forced to head for Sweden, where he was interned for more than a month.

During the 24 May Penetration Target Withdrawal Support mission to Berlin, eight enemy fighters fell to the group's guns. The 4th was being led by 336th FS CO Maj Goodson, who was the first to spot 40 enemy aircraft near Hamburg. 'We got fairly close to them and started firing before they broke', reported 1Lt Frank Speer. 'Only the two we fired on broke. I got strikes on the first burst, and the enemy aircraft split-S'ed with me on his tail. He went straight down, skidding, rolling, and he took violent evasive action. I kept firing short bursts. Pieces were coming off him all the time, two of which damaged my P-51. I was directly above him, going straight down, when he seemed to hit compressability. His aeroplane was shuddering violently. I had to put down 20 degrees of flap to keep from overrunning him. I was indicating 500+ mph. The Me 109 started to pull out, and doing the same, I blacked out. When I came to, he was diving again, and I saw his canopy come off as he baled out.'

1Lt Joseph Lang saw the same gaggle of aeroplanes and ordered his squadron to drop tanks and give chase. 'The enemy aircraft circled port as we gained on them', he said. 'Some of them, seeing us, split S'ed away. I closed my section up astern of four Me 109s. I noticed another Mustang pull in front of one of the enemy aircraft. The P-51 was clobbered very badly and started losing altitude, smoking and burning.' This was probably the Mustang of 1Lt Harry Jennings from the 335th FS, who was last seen chasing enemy aircraft near Hamburg. He was killed.

Lang closed on a Bf 109. 'At 35,000 ft, he dived straight down. I fired and hit him in the starboard wing root and fuselage. I did this twice more. Most of the time he was rolling. At 18,000 ft, I noticed I had 675 mph "on the clock". He started burning, then the right wing broke off. He skidded and the fuselage broke in two. He then completely broke up.'

Lang pulled out of the dive and saw an Fw 190 on the deck. As he prepared to fire, he cleared his tail and saw six Fw 190s. 'I broke into them and was again bounced by a gaggle of 25 Fw 190s. As there were three gaggles of 20+ Fw 190s, I had a busy time with them. When I saw I couldn't keep turning, I pushed the throttle forward and started climbing. They queued up behind me and took turns shooting. Some of them kept climbing to the side and would make head-on passes at me. I finally hit some cloud at 18,000 ft and lost them.'

'We had climbed up to 30,000 ft when I sighted four Me 109s coming in below us', reported 2Lt Hofer. 'I attacked, but lost sight of them in the haze. I pulled up and sighted three Fw 190s attacking a B-17. We bounced them. We were trying to scare them off, but they didn't seem to see me. Finally I closed in on one, getting strikes. The aircraft started smoking, the hood was jettisoned and the pilot baled. The other two broke to the left.

'I then pulled up and saw 2Lt Thomas Fraser, my wingman, behind the other two Fw 190s. One of them made a split-S with 2Lt Fraser following. I then broke into the leader, preventing him from firing at 2Lt Fraser. He did a split-S, and I followed. I got a few scattered hits. Below the clouds, I got more strikes in a tight turn. He pulled sharply up into a cloud and jettisoned his hood. I did not see the pilot bale out, but the aircraft crashed in a field, burning, and its ammo exploded at intervals.'

Other victors during the mission were Capt Hively, 1Lts Russell and Gillette and 2Lt Fraser. In the afternoon, the group glide-bombed a railway bridge at Beaumont-sur-Oise with no visible results

Maj Goodson again led the 4th on its 25 May mission to Chaumont-Sarreguentines, in France, taking took two sections to protect the western flank of the bomber formation;

'We saw fighters and immediately went to investigate. These fighters turned out to be 20+ Fw 190s, with some 30+ Me 109s above as top cover. We split them up, but due to the fact that we were outnumbered 50-to-8, we were not able to destroy any. My wingman and myself ended up alone on the deck. As I started to climb up, I observed 24 Me 109s and Fw 190s in close formation in six vics of fours line astern. I told my wingman we would try to sneak up behind and knock off the last section and then run away in the haze. As we were closing on the last section, all the Huns broke, and a lengthy dogfight ensued, with the Fw 190s showing amazing fighting ability and aggressiveness. It was only after the most violent manoeuvring and excessive use of throttle and flaps that I was able to get good strikes on the most persistent '190. He pulled up and baled out.'

Capt Joseph Bennett of the 336th FS also enjoyed success, downing two Bf 109s, and squadronmate 1Lt Thomas McDill claimed a third. In the process, however, both pilots were shot down and became PoWs.

Two days later, an escort to Karlsruhe was unimpeded by German fighters, and pilots strafed targets on the way home. 1Lt Elliot Shapleigh developed engine trouble near Laon, in France, and he was forced to take to his parachute. He hid in some woods until darkness, and in the early evening stumbled across two farmers ploughing a field. When one of them left, Shapleigh approached the other and used his French-English phrase-book to ask for help. The farmer led him to a safe house, from which he was directed to a Resistance fighter, who hid him at his sister and brother-in-law's house. The pair built a false wall in their baby's room, behind which Shapleigh slept for four months. In September, US troops overran the area, and he was able to return to friendly forces.

Goodson was in command again on 28 May for an escort to Ruhland-Dessau. Some 20 German fighters attacked the bombers before the target, and in the ensuing fight, the 334th FS bounced the enemy aircraft and claimed 7.5 kills. 'Our squadron used its superior height and followed them in the turn in a shallow dive', said Capt Sobanski. 'We managed to split up the enemy formation, and I found a single bluish-gray '109 flying perfect line abreast formation with a P-51 at some 150 yards distance. They both didn't seem to realize their mistake, and only caught on when I attacked the '109. He dove straight down, and momentarily I lost him in the haze, finding him again when he started pulling back up. I fired a few short half-second bursts closing in, and was just going to position myself for a better shot at him, as I saw no strikes, when, much to my surprise, he jettisoned his canopy and baled out.'

2Lt Hofer scored his 15th, and last aerial kill, downing the Bf 109G-6 flown by Unteroffizier Heinz Kunz of 6./JG 11 near Magdeburg. The day's other victors were Maj McPharlin and 1Lts Siems, Kolter, Lang and Kenyon. In return, 1Lt Aubrey Hewatt was hit by a Bf 109 and baled out just before his P-51 exploded. 1Lt Richard Bopp became separated from the group and ran out of fuel. Like Hewatt, he ended up as a PoW.

On 29 May, Col Blakeslee led a Withdrawal Support mission to Poznán, which was vigorously opposed by the Luftwaffe. 'We dove on five Jerries attacking the lead box of the 2nd Combat Wing', reported 1Lt Robert Church. 'I saw an Me 109 open fire at the bombers and then climb up on the other side. I went after him. He saw me coming and started to wrack it in. Halfway through his turn, he suddenly reversed direction and dove straight down. I followed him, but did not fire. He jettisoned his canopy, but I did not see him bale out or spot a 'chute. At 4000 ft, we were both still going down at 450 mph, so I started to pull out. I saw his aircraft go straight into the sea about a half-mile southwest of Nysted.'

2Lt Ralph Hofer in his natural element (and his dog 'Duke', clearly not in his), in the cockpit of P-51B 42-106294 *Salem Representative*. Col Don Blakeslee's advocacy of the Malcolm hood resulted in most of the group's P-51B/Cs having the sliding canopy retrofitted. Note the single train and two sailing ship silhouettes applied beneath the more conventional German cross kill markings. Hofer was a keen strafer, and his addiction to attacking anything that moved on the ground would eventually cost him his life (*Bruce Zigler via Wade Meyers*)

Other fighters fell to Col Blakeslee, Capt Bernard McGrattan and 1Lts Conrad Netting and Don Emerson. 1Lt Orrin 'Ossie' Snell was chasing a Bf 109 at high speed when its tail section came off in flight. After leaving the target area, the 336th FS found a seaplane base on a lake and strafed it. In total, the squadron damaged 12 Do 18s and destroyed an Ar 196.

2Lt Hofer and 1Lt Frank Speer, meanwhile, attacked He 177s at Mackfitz airfield, in Pomerania. Having destroyed seven bombers between them, Speer's fighter was then hit by flak. Setting his P-51B down next to a village in Poland, he ran into the woods ahead of a mob of angry locals. After eluding them,

Speer hid in bushes and waited for nightfall, then used his knowledge of European geography to start an epic journey by foot. He travelled 400 miles, planning to walk to Denmark and stow away on a boat to Sweden. Having nearly made it, his plans were foiled when he was awakened from a nap by a German soldier. Speer ended up in *Stalag Luft III*, then survived the winter 'death march' to Nurnberg. When the PoWs were moved again, Speer and a fellow inmate escaped and were sheltered by French labourers. On VE Day, the pair took the surrender of 24 German soldiers.

Maj Goodson led a freelance sweep on 30 May that found a gaggle of 30–40 Bf 109s and Fw 190s near Genthin. When the 4th attacked, they discovered these aircraft were covered by 20–25 more fighters above them – these came down and bounced the Mustangs.

'We were at 34,000 ft where I saw two Me 109s in a circle', said 1Lt Oscar LaJeunesse. 'I made a pass at the second one, but a green-nosed P-51 came in from my left and almost hit me, and when I pulled up out of the way, I lost the Hun. I kept turning and got a little lead on the first one. I waited until I was 50 yards away so I wouldn't miss him. I hit him in the cockpit and on both wings. A big cloud of smoke came up and the '109 started down in a wide turn. I followed it, and when the pilot did not bale out I gave him another squirt. He let his canopy go then. Still he didn't bale out, so I urged him with another burst. That time he popped out and the aeroplane went straight down.'

1Lt Thomas Sharp dove to the deck and forced an Fw 190 to crash-land near Brandenburg. He was then joined by 1Lt Frank Jones, and they saw four aircraft landing in trail. 'There were 15+ Fw 190s on Oschersleben airfield as we attacked', said Sharp. 'We had made five passes when we were joined by 2Lt Hofer. On my first pass, one of the Fw 190s, located at the runway intersection, caught fire and burned. I then set another on fire on the south side of the field and damaged others that would not burn.'

1Lt Jones also made runs at the airfield. 'On my second pass, I hit one enemy aircraft that caught fire and burned, giving off a large column of smoke', he said. 'Several passes later, I hit another one that burst into flames. This one was later finished off by 2Lt Hofer, who left it burning fiercely.' Hofer destroyed an Fw 190 on his first pass. 'On my second pass, I set one of those at the runway intersection on fire', he reported.

In the fray, 8.5 fighters were destroyed, falling to 1Lt James Scott, Hofer, Jones, LaJeunesse and Sharp. Unfortunately, 1Lt Mark Kolter was killed in mysterious circumstances. He was heard calling for a homing, but he never responded. Kolter perished when his P-51B crashed. Also lost during the mission were Capt Willard Millikan and 1Lt Sam Young, who collided while dodging flak. Both men baled out and became PoWs.

Poor weather made the escort mission on 31 May a somewhat confused affair, so 2Lt Hofer broke off on his own and joined up with the 357th FG. He attacked Luxeuil airfield with the group, strafing 15 Bu 131 trainers and setting three of them on fire. Unfortunately, Capt Carroll McElroy and 1Lt Robert Homuth, both from the 335th FS, failed to return. Having aborted the mission because of the weather, they may have fallen victim to the guns of USAAF heavy bombers who mistook them for German fighters. McElroy became a PoW and Homuth was killed.

TOP COVER FOR D-DAY

Anticipation of the invasion of France heightened as missions became more tactical in nature. On 5 June, 4th FG operations officer Lt Col Jim Clark led a morning mission to the Lille area, where a large convoy of military vehicles was spotted. This information resulted in a hastily organized dive-bombing mission being flown that afternoon, led by Capt Hively. The 334th FS dropped 500-lb bombs and the 335th and 336th FSs provided top cover. Two trucks were destroyed.

As soon as the last planes landed at Debden, the group was grounded. At 1500 hrs, an order arrived that all aeroplanes would be painted with five alternating white and black bands on the wings and fuselage. Bombs were staged next to the fighters in advance of the next day's operations. At 2000 hrs, Col Blakeslee returned from a meeting and announced that the invasion would soon be underway. Three hours later, he briefed the group on the invasion plans.

On D-Day, all three squadrons operated individually, with Blakeslee leading the 334th and 335th FSs on a patrol east of Rouen between 0320 hrs and 0945 hrs to start the day. No enemy aircraft were seen, but 2Lt Ralph Hofer strafed two locomotives. The 334th lost 1Lt Thomas Fraser, who failed to respond to a vector at 0642 hrs. He had been bounced by German fighters near Rouen and shot down. Fraser became a PoW. The 336th FS was next off at 0635 hrs, led by Lt Col Clark, as it provided top cover for ships bombarding the landing beaches.

At 1120 hrs the 334th FS, led by Capt Hively, took off again, this time with two sections loaded with bombs while the other sections served as top cover. Heading for Rouen, a 15-carriage troop train was attacked, with

2Lt Ralph Hofer's *Salem Representative* at its most garish just after D-Day. The Mustang had olive drab paint on the wings and spine, which extended up the leading edge of the fin at this date, but which was later stripped back to the base of the tail. Also of note are Hofer's famous 'whitewall' tyres! He saw much combat in this machine during the D-Day period, strafing and bombing innumerable targets (*Keith Hoey via Wade Meyers*)

poor results, but things improved minutes later when ten Fw 190s were spotted preparing to land at Evreux. Four fighters were quickly downed, with 1Lts Shelton Monroe, James Scott and Siems claiming one apiece, and 1Lts Joseph Fernandez and Jack Simon sharing the fourth. Siems received a flak hit to the right side of his engine soon after downing his Fw 190, although he was able to nurse his crippled Mustang back to England. By then the 335th FS, led by CO Maj James Happel, had bombed the Fleury marshalling yards.

Maj Goodson took the 336th FS out on a fighter-bomber mission at 1335 hrs, and although no worthwhile targets were found, flak near Evreux downed 1Lts Harold Frederick and Oscar LaJeunesse. The former evaded and made it back, but the latter became a PoW.

The pilots returned to lunches and thermos bottles full of coffee, plus cots and blankets so that they could steal a few minutes of sleep before a third mission. Both the 334th and 335th FSs were led aloft by Col Blakeslee at 1820 hrs, and a radar station and road convoy were attacked near Rouen. A section from the 335th FS, led by 2Lt Ralph Hofer, raced to help in the attack, and they paid for it – 15 Fw 190s and Bf 109s from JG 2 and II./JG 26, led by Hauptmann Herbert Huppertz, bounced them. Only Hofer escaped with his life.

'As we approached Bernay, we spotted a formation of at least 12 Mustangs strafing German infantry near a bridge over the Risle', recalled Leutnant Wolfgang Fischer of 3./JG 2. 'Using the evening mist and setting sun for cover, we climbed to 1200 metres to take up a position for a classic bounce. The ensuing combat lasted just minutes, as we were each able to select a target before diving down on them.'

Capt Bernard McGrattan, Flt Off Walter Smith and 1Lts Harold Ross and Cecil Garbey were all killed in the one-sided action.

That same evening, Maj Michael McPharlin (formerly with the 334th, and temporarily on loan to the 4th FG from the 339th FG – he was flying a P-51B from this group) radioed that his left magneto was out and his engine was running rough as the 334th headed for France. He turned for home but was never seen again. 1Lt Edward Steppe took McPharlin's position in the flight. Later, while beating up a train, Capt 'Mike' Sobanski hit telegraph wires. Steppe reported that the damage was slight, and the pair continued to work over rail traffic. At 2035 hrs, about ten minutes before Hofer's section was bounced, Steppe was heard to radio, 'Watch those behind you, White Leader'. Nothing more was heard from either man – both were killed.

In all, the 4th had lost ten P-51s, and their pilots, on D-Day. No other group in VIII Fighter Command had lost more than three aircraft.

While serving as an infantryman in Poland in September 1939, Capt Winslow 'Mike' Sobanski was dive-bombed and injured aboard a train during the German invasion. He managed to escape to New York, and subsequently joined the RCAF before transferring to the 4th FG in May 1943. Sobanski and his wingman, 1Lt Edward Steppe, perished when they were bounced by German fighters during a disastrous evening patrol of Rouen-Dreux on 6 June 1944 (*National Museum of the USAF*)

Following its exertions of the previous day, the group rested until 1430 hrs on the 7th, when Col Blakeslee led a fighter-bomber mission to the Brest peninsula in search of targets of opportunity. Flt Off Donald Pierni and 2Lt Kenneth D Smith (both from the 336th FS) collided a mile south of Debden just after take-off, and although Pierini survived the mishap, Smith was killed.

The three squadrons split up to hit different areas. For the 335th FS, this comprised a marshalling yard at Quintine, a factory and a bridge, which were bombed with poor results. Lt Osce Jones was hit by flak over the marshalling yard, and although he tried to nurse the Mustang back home, ten miles south of St Malo the engine started to run rough and he crash-landed in a small field. He ran from his aeroplane to a treeline, and after discarding his parachute and dinghy he hid overnight in an orchard. Jones made contact with French civilians who took him in for a few days before betraying him to the Germans. He spent the rest of the war as a PoW.

The surviving pilots in the 336th FS undertook a bombing mission as well, getting better results, but Maj Goodson was hit by flak and crash-landed at Manston, destroying his P-51B.

On 8 June Blakeslee led a fighter-bomber mission to the area northeast of Le Mans, where six Mustangs attacked a marshalling yard with 500-lb bombs, cutting the tracks and damaging much of the rolling stock parked there. Six more bombed a pair of bridges, damaging both of them. In the process, as the 334th FS peeled off to attack the latter targets, 2Lt James Scott collided with the P-51B flown by 1Lt Eacott Allen and lost the tail off his P-51B at 2500 ft. Scott was killed, but Allen successfully evaded and eventually returned to England.

The interdiction missions in support of the invasion continued on 10 June. A Ramrod Area Support mission by the 334th FS (led by Lt Col Clark) to Morlaix airfield was followed by some train strafing. The 336th FS also attacked trains near Poix in a follow-up mission led by Col Blakeslee. 2Lt Conrad Netting of the 336th FS was hit by flak during his pass and crashed into trees and was killed. Squadronmate 1Lt Frank Caple force-landed at Le Touquet, on the French coast, a short while after his fighter was also struck by flak near Dieppe. He became a PoW. Maj Goodson led the final fighter-bomber mission of the day to the marshalling yards at Argentan, where 250-lb bombs damaged 40 rail trucks and several locomotives.

The following day, a nine-aeroplane fighter-bomber mission to the

1Lt Osce Jones (left) became a PoW on 7 June when his fighter was hit by flak. 2Lt Ted Lines (right), see here with his P-51B 43-7172 *Thunderbird*, survived a series of engine issues to become a ten-kill ace with the 335th FS (*National Museum of the USAF*)

Col Blakeslee pretends to brief the group in a scene staged for the benefit of *Illustrated* magazine's cameraman at Debden shortly after D-Day. Note Maj Goodson in the front row. A few days after this photograph was taken, Blakeslee navigated his group 1600 miles to Russia during the shuttle mission purely by dead-reckoning – the wartime feat of which he was most proud (*National Museum of the USAF*)

Bernay area saw the group unload 250-lb bombs on a 20-carriage train, six vehicles and a bridge. The day's second bombing mission, flown by the 334th FS, destroyed 37 trucks in a 70-vehicle convoy near Villedieu-les-Poels. Capt William Hedrick saw 2Lt Leon Cole's P-51C hit the ground while strafing, then the Mustang staggered back into the air, pouring black smoke. Hedrick circled, but he saw a flash behind him. In Hedrick's opinion, it was Cole's fighter exploding in mid-air, killing the pilot. Similarly, 1Lt Grover Siems saw 2Lt Harry Noon's P-51B strike trees while strafing, the fighter flicking over onto its back and exploding as it hit the ground – all while still carrying both its bombs. Finally, 2Lt Ralph Hofer's P-51B was hit in the oil system by flak, and the ace had to set it down on the beach. He returned to Debden the next morning after being given a tour of the frontlines.

After a day's break, Col Blakeslee commanded an Area Support mission for B-26s attacking a target near Dombrondt. Once the bombers had left, the group strafed road traffic near Pretteville, wrecking 14 trucks and damaging three more.

After an escort on 15 June, the group was briefed on plans for the first shuttle escort mission to Russia. Pilots were told that 16 aeroplanes from each squadron in the 4th FG, and 16 more from the 352nd FG, would fly from

1Lt Joe Higgins' P-51B 43-6942 *MEINER KLEINER* of the 336th FS displays just how much dirt and grime could accumulate on an aircraft's invasion stripes. Seen here taxiing out from Debden on a fighter-bomber mission, the aircraft carries a bomb marked with a tribute to 1Lt Harold Ross of the 335th FS, who who was among the seven 4th FG pilots killed on D-Day. This aircraft was lost to flak on 21 November 1944 (*National Museum of the USAF*)

Despite serving in a group known more for its air-to-air prowess, 1Lt Clarence Boretsky of the 334th FS was involved in several major air-to-ground missions in support of the D-Day landings, including a strike on bridges on 7 June and the destruction of half a 70-vehicle convoy four days later. Boretsky's crew chief was the seemingly ubiquitous Sgt Don Allen (*Danny Morris via Peter Randall*)

England to the USSR, then conduct missions in conjunction with the Russians, before returning home. A cadre of enlisted men would fly in B-17s to the Soviet Union, service the aircraft there, and come home during the bombers' return trip. The raid was to be held the next day, but on 16 June a postponement was announced due to poor weather.

A horse-drawn convoy became the target of an afternoon fighter sweep to the Combourg area on 18 June. 1Lts Robert Little and James Glynn of the 335th FS and 1Lt Harvie Arnold of the 336th FS all failed to return, with the latter being killed (his P-51D was the first of its type to be lost by the 4th in combat), Little becoming a PoW and Glynn eventually evading back to Allied lines. All had been hit by flak.

The next day's escort was recalled because of bad weather, but the group suffered a loss just the same. 2Lt Dean Hill of the 335th FS entered a cloud over the Channel and disappeared – apparently, he lost control, spun in and was killed.

Rushed orders for the 20 June Target Withdrawal Support mission to Politz meant that several of the group's aeroplanes were not serviced in time to catch up with the rest of the 4th FG. Form-up was confusing as a result, and there were numerous aborts. Those that did make the trip were rewarded by the sight of about 50 Me 410s below them near the target. As they dropped their tanks and dove on them, the dozen Bf 109s flying top cover for the *Zerstörers* tried to intercept.

'An Me 109 made a pass at me from overhead', reported 1Lt George Cooley of the 335th FS. 'As I turned into him, he made a 90-degree deflection shot and hit my starboard wing tank with a 20 mm shell. A P-51 crossed beneath me with an Me 109 on his tail. Catching the enemy aircraft in my sight, I gave him a short burst, observing strikes around the wing root and cockpit. I saw a fully-opened 'chute below me, but I did not actually see the Jerry pilot bale out.'

With racks devoid of ordnance, an unidentified P-51B/C in full invasion stripes returns to Debden following a mission just after the Normandy landings (*National Museum of the USAF*)

1Lt Robert Dickmeyer's 334th FS flight was above the German top cover. 'At 15,000 ft I saw an Me 109 coming from about "five o'clock" below us', he reported. As the Bf 109 passed through his section, he swung over his leader and started an overhead pass. 'I closed on him, firing all the time until I was directly astern of him. I observed a great many strikes and his canopy flew off, as did parts of his cowling. I passed him to the left and observed the pilot slumped over the side.'

Capt Frank Jones of the 335th FS came up behind four Bf 109s flying line abreast. 'They broke after I fired and went in four different directions. I picked one out that was making a climbing turn and fired. I hit him in the engine and around the wing root on the right side. A huge column of smoke came out. The pilot jettisoned the canopy, rolled the aeroplane over and baled out.'

As the Mustangs were fighting the Bf 109s, a lone Me 410 turned into them and continued on to make a firing pass on a bomber. 335th FS pilot Capt George Stanford and his wingman, Flt Off Lester Godwin, gave chase. Godwin hit the aircraft in the cockpit, wings and engine, as did Stanford. The Me 410 attempted to crash-land, but the pilot lost control and it flicked over at 100 ft and hit the ground inverted.

Lt Col Clark, Capt Thomas Joyce and 1Lts Otey Glass, Shelton Monroe, Donald Malmsten and Arthur Cwiklinski also claimed kills. 1Lt Don Emerson saw an Fw 190 pilot bale out before he had fired a shot at him. On the way home, the group strafed Neubrandenburg airfield, destroying four bombers. 1Lt Ferris Harris flamed a Do 217, but he was hit by flak and became a PoW.

Flak also struck Maj James Goodson's brand new P-51D, and the CO of the 336th FS force-landed. Still intact, the Mustang was strafed by his squadronmates until it caught fire. Goodson who had suffered a flesh wound when his fighter was hit, also became a PoW.

1Lt Joseph Lang's P-51D 44-13352 was one of the first 'bubbletop' Mustangs to reach the 4th FG. Claiming his fifth aerial kill on 21 June 1944 (flying his old 'QP-Z', P-51B 43-42841), Lang would increase his tally to 7.833 victories prior to losing his life on 14 October after aborting with engine trouble in P-51D 44-14123. Heading for home, he was set upon by Bf 109s, which eventually shot him down – but not before he had bagged two of them (*4th Fighter Group Association via Peter Randall*)

SHUTTLE MISSION

News that the Russian shuttle mission was back on reached Debden during the early evening of 20 June. The 4th FG would be heading east at 0755 hrs the following day! Groundcrews worked through the night to prepare three 16-aeroplane squadrons from the 4th, plus the 352nd FG's 486th FS, to escort more than 1000 bombers attacking Ruhland. The armada would then fly on to Piryatin, in the Ukraine, 580 miles from the take-off point.

Some 45 Mustangs from the 4th FG and all 16 machines from the 486th FS rendezvoused with the bombers over Leszno, in Poland, as briefed. Shortly thereafter, over Siedlice, 25 Bf 109s made a head-on attack on the B-17s and the group dropped tanks and gave chase, destroying two and damaging three – kills were credited to Capt Frank Jones and 1Lt Joseph Lang, who both 'made ace'. 1Lt Frank Sibbett of the 335th FS was killed when his P-51B was downed by enemy fighters, however.

The entire group, less Sibbett and 2Lt Ralph Hofer, made it to Piryatin on time. Disregarding orders, Hofer had chased after the fleeing Bf 109s until he ran low on fuel and was forced to land at an airfield in Kiev. He was the subject of much questioning before the Soviets accepted he was an American flyer. The mission ended at 1450 hrs. After almost seven hours in the air, many of the pilots had to be helped from their fighters as their legs refused to work after being sat for so long in their cockpits.

334th FS CO Capt Howard Hively gives a thumbs-up just before take-off on the first leg of the shuttle mission to Russia on 21 June 1944. Hively would be seriously wounded over Budapest on 2 July during a fight in which he claimed three Bf 109s destroyed, but he flew back to Debden with the rest of the group against doctor's orders (*National Museum of the USAF*)

The Russians put their guests up in tents, and though conditions were crude, the hosts were cordial. Just the same, the Germans crashed the party, bombing Piryatin that evening. A Ju 88 had trailed the American aircraft to the Russian fields, and at Poltova – one of the B-17 landing sites – half the bombers were destroyed, but the Mustangs were spared.

Following this attack, the P-51 units dispersed to Zaporozhe, Odessa and Chingueue, where they were met by more Soviet hospitality. Capt Howard Hively traded his western-style hand-tooled belt with its silver buckle to the general commanding the air army at Stalingrad, who gave him his belt with a buckle bearing a hammer and sickle.

The group returned to Piryatin on 24 June to have wing tanks fitted for the Mustangs' onward flight to Italy, then dispersed once again. The following day, groundcrews flown in from Debden aboard the B-17s escorted on 21 June inspected the P-51s to ensure their serviceability for the next leg of the mission. Finally, at 1405 hrs on the 26th, the 4th FG left Piryatin and headed for Brodye, in Poland, to escort bombers targeting the oil refinery at nearby Drohobycz. On the outbound leg of the mission, after breaking off from the B-17s over the coast of Yugoslavia and then crossing the Adriatic Sea, the group caught sight of Fifteenth Air Force Mustangs and duly landed at Lucera, in Italy, at 1935 hrs.

While the majority of the 4th FG was in Italy, Lt Col Clark led the 11 aircraft still in England on escort missions to Saarbrucken and Leipzig with the rest of the 352nd FG on 28 and 29 June. No kills were claimed.

Meanwhile, in Russia, 2Lt Hofer and 1Lts Gillette, Lang and James Callahan, who had stayed behind at Poltava with mechanical issues on the

26th, took off for Italy on 29 June in order to rejoin the group. Hofer took a different route than his three compatriots, and over the Mediterranean began to run low on fuel. Luckily, a flight of RAF Spitfires escorted him to Malta, where he refuelled and then left for Foggia the next day. Callahan also ran out of fuel and crash-landed in Sicily.

The 4th FG was 'volunteered' to fly a fighter sweep in advance of a Fifteenth Air Force strike on Budapest on 2 July. When the 45 Mustangs reached the target, a swarm of 80 German fighters and 18 Hungarian Bf 109Gs met the group, and a swirling dogfight erupted. Eight Axis fighters were destroyed, including three Bf 109s by Capt Hively.

After destroying his first victim, a 20 mm shell exploded adjacent to Hively's canopy, sending fragments of glass into the right side of his face and injuring his right eye. Despite these wounds, he pressed on with his attacks and destroyed two more, in part because Hively's squadronmate 1Lt Grover Siems spotted a Bf 109 on his tail and dove in to attack it, sending the fighter down in flames. Siems was then attacked himself, being so badly wounded in the shoulder, neck and chin that he was forced to return to Foggia. Upon landing, and unable to open his canopy due to blood loss, he was ignored by the airfield personnel until he fired his guns! Several mechanics removed Siems from his aeroplane, but he was so weak he could not move. The medics covered him with a sheet and sent him to the morgue, and only when Siems was able to wiggle a finger did an orderly notice him and give him a blood transfusion.

Aside from Hively, Capt William Hedrick destroyed a Bf 109 and damaged another, while Capt Frank Jones and Col Blakeslee achieved single kills (Jones' victory remained uncredited, however). Capt Joe Higgins of the 486th FS and 1Lt Don Emerson shared another Bf 109.

1Lt George Stanford's wing tanks refused to drop when the 98-aeroplane gaggle was spotted, but instead of aborting, he and wingman 2Lt Ralph Hofer pressed home their attacks. The extra throttle Stanford used to compensate for the drag of the tanks caused his engine to throw a rod. He radioed to Capt Frank Jones to take the lead, then bellied into a wheat field in Yugoslavia. Hofer buzzed him to make sure he was all right, but when Stanford looked up he saw a Bf 109 trailing his wingman. Hofer apparently shook his pursuer, but records unearthed in 2003 reveal that he then strafed Mostar-Sud airfield, where 4.Batterie/Flak Regiment 9 *'Legion Condor'* hit Hofer's P-51B and the ace crashed to his death. Stanford became a PoW, as did 1Lt J C Norris. Finally, 1Lt Thomas Sharp, who had also been unable to release his wing tanks, was killed when shot down by a Bf 109.

The 4th FG also provided Penetration Target Withdrawal Support

1Lt Grover Siems of the 334th FS relaxes on the wing of his P-51D 44-13322 *Gloria III*. Siems probably saved Capt Howard Hively's life during the 2 July mission to Budapest, but was badly injured himself in the process – so badly, in fact, he was put in the morgue after he landed at Foggia! An orderly spotted Siems wiggling his finger and medical personnel saved his life. He did not return to frontline flying with the 4th FG (*via Wade Meyers*)

2Lt 'Kidd' Hofer describes his latest escapades while clad in his trademark football jersey. He was initially forbidden from flying the shuttle mission by Col Don Blakeslee for refusing to take his shots, but he relented at the last minute. His CO, Capt Hively, was so fed up with him by then that he packed Hofer off to fly with another squadron and allocated his beloved *Salem Representative* to 1Lt Preston Hardy. Hofer was subsequently shot down over Mostar-Sud airfield in P-51B 43-6746 (*National Museum of the USAF*)

for heavy bombers hitting a marshalling yard at Arad, in Yugoslavia, on 3 July. Two days later, Col Blakeslee led the rest of the group back from Italy by way of an escort to the marshalling yard at Beziers, in France. All the P-51s that took off from the Italian base at Silinas made it to England safely following a gruelling seven-hour mission. Many were laden with souvenirs for the men who had remained at Debden during the group's foray abroad.

Nine late arrivals (five aborts from 5 July and four repaired late arrivals from Russia) made it back to Debden on the 6th. The entire tour had covered 6000 miles, ten countries and 29.24 hours of operational flying for ten enemy fighters destroyed. Of the 61 Mustangs that had started the trip, 52 made it back to Essex.

On 7 July, 1Lt Shelton Monroe led an escort to Aschersleben/Bernburg, and in the process the 334th FS engaged a mass of fighters preparing to attack the 'heavies' near Nordhausen. Charging into a gaggle of 70 Bf 109s and Fw 190s, Capt Thomas Joyce and 1Lt Willard Gillette got one apiece, while Lt Monroe damaged an Fw 190. A short while later, 75 single- and twin-engined fighters started lining up as if to attack the bombers, but for some reason they chose not engage the 'heavies'. Capt Joyce made a pass at them and felled his second Bf 109 of the day, with 1Lt Jack McFadden hitting the same fighter as its pilot baled out.

Meanwhile, 1Lt Charles Evans attacked an Me 410 from high and behind. 'Another P-51 (flown by 1Lt John Scally) came in behind the twin-engined aircraft as I was going down', said Evans. 'His port wing hit the starboard wing of the enemy aircraft. The P-51 immediately began spinning with one wing gone, and the enemy aircraft started a flat spin to starboard.' 1Lt Scally became a PoW. 1Lt Preston Hardy, climbing up from this engagement, bounced 14 Bf 109s and downed one, claiming a second as a probable. 1Lt Gillette also jumped Bf 109s near Blankenburg, probably destroying one of them. Finally 1Lt Gerald Chapman of the 336th FS got an Fw 190 and 1Lt John Goodwyn of the 335th FS jumped 30 Me 410s preparing to attack the B-24s and downed one of them.

On 11 July, 1Lt James Hanrahan of the 335th FS was lost during a mission to Munich. He was heard radioing for landing instructions, but suffered mechanical failure in his elderly P-51B and wound up being captured. Another escort to Munich two days later was notable for extremely heavy flak, which downed Maj Wilson Edwards from the 4th's HQ flight – he too became a PoW. These losses, and a recent lack of discipline in the air, rankled with Col Blakeslee. After this mission, he handed down a new set of rules 'intended to rebuild this group to its former status as the best outfit in the world', as he put it. Blakeslee also stated that any pilot viewed as undisciplined would be removed from operations and subjected to exhaustive training until he improved.

AIR, LAND AND SEA

Following three days of tedious Penetration Target Withdrawal missions, during which not a single Mustang from the 4th FG fired its guns, on 17 July the enemy was encountered once again. Group operations officer Lt Col Jim Clark was leading an Area Support mission to the Auxerre area when he spotted 20 railway wagons – his section dropped down and shot them up. Other sections strafed an ammunition train at St Pierre, with little flak to hamper them. This attack continued until one of the cars detonated in a massive explosion, which was felt by pilots several miles away. The 4th FG then worked over some armoured vehicles being transported by train south of Cosne.

No enemy aircraft were seen during the 18 July escort to Kiel, but the next day Bf 109s were up in large numbers over Munich. In the resulting fight, 336th FS pilots 1Lt Ira Grounds downed two and 1Lt Francis Grove got one. 2Lt Kermit Dahlen of the 335th FS was killed, however, his fighter being seen to explode after it was attacked by Bf 109s. Squadronmate 1Lt Curtis Simpson was more fortunate, finding himself over neutral Switzerland leaking glycol from his P-51B;

'This particular escort flight was the sixth straight flight that we had made to Munich in six days. We were jumped by a group of Me 109s and fought all the way into Austria. I had my P-51 on full throttle for far too long a time and my electrical system on the coolant shutters went out. They closed and the engine overheated. I lost all of my coolant, and if I had not been so close to Switzerland I would have ended up as a PoW or dead. I was looking for a place to land, since I did not want to jump.

'I found this very short meadow that had some white signs on it so I thought that I should try it. I had no other choice. I used full flaps with no power from the engine and I landed slightly on the tail wheel. There was no one there when I landed, but as soon as I stopped the aeroplane, here they came. The Swiss had helmets similar to the Germans, and I was not sure where I was. I stood up in the cockpit with my hands raised and asked if they were Swiss – luckily they said yes!'

1Lt Curtis Simpson of the 335th FS successfully put his ailing P-51B down on the short grass runway at Ems-Plarenga airfield, in Switzerland, on 19 July 1944. The fighter was subsequently dismantled by Swiss air force mechanics and transported to Dübendorf, where its engine maladies were repaired. Repainted in Swiss colours, the Mustang returned to the skies on 1 August (*Swiss air force*)

Simpson had landed at Ems-Plarenga airfield. His Mustang was subsequently dismantled and transported by truck and train to Dübendorf, where it flew again on 1 August 1944. Eventually escaping from internment in Switzerland, Simpson reached Debden on 15 October.

The 4th FG encountered intense flak over Dessau, Kothen and Leipzig on 20 July, and 1Lt Lester Godwin of the 335th FS was forced to bale out near Antwerp. Evading, he too returned to the group.

On the evening of 22 July, Col Blakeslee led a unique mission that saw 27 Mustangs escort four H2X radar-equipped B-17s from the 303rd BG to Bremen, Hamburg and Kiel to drop propaganda leaflets that provided details of the failed 20 July assassination attempt on the *Führer*. As a result of the darkness, 1Lts Carl Brown and Willard Gillette of the 334th FS collided just after take-off, but both managed to land their damaged fighters back at Debden. 1Lt Lloyd Kingham of the 335th FS was not so lucky, as his P-51D suffered engine failure on take-off and he perished when it spun in near Audley End. Two more P-51s were written off in crash-landings upon their return to Debden due to mechanical failures.

Col Blakeslee was aloft again two days later when he led a strafing mission to the Weingarten area of Germany. Lechfeld airfield was the assigned target, but poor weather over the base saw the 4th FG attack a power station at Weingarten instead. Several trains were also strafed along the north shore of Lake Constance, prior to the group heading home.

Capt Neil Van Wyck of the 335th FS took the lead for an escort mission to Merseburg on 28 July. Capt Hively had a wing tank fall off his P-51D on take-off, then returned, got a new tank and set out again. He could not catch up with the 4th, so instead joined up with the 355th FG. They encountered six fighters, and Hively claimed one of them as a probable.

July ended with an uneventful Penetration Target Withdrawal Support mission to Munich on the 31st. Although the group's kill tally now stood at 623, morale was low due to the lack of aerial activity that had characterized the air war in the ETO since D-Day. The Luftwaffe now seemed reluctant to oppose USAAF 'heavies' in significant numbers, and things were not expected to change in the near future. On a more positive note, the 336th FS had received the first K-14 computing gunsights to reach VIII Fighter Command.

The shattered remains of P-51D 44-13372 of the 334th FS after it suffered a structural failure in a dive during a test flight from Debden by 1Lt Willard Gillette on 10 August 1944. The aeroplane, formerly Lt Col Jim Clark's mount, lost its ammunition tray covers, then went out of control when its tail snapped off. Gillette baled out and landed on the cricket field in Haverhill Castle Camp (*National Museum of the USAF*)

Flying the P-51D nearest to the camera, Col Blakeslee leads 225th FS CO Capt Bob Church and Capt Bob Mabie in a tight formation for the benefit of the photographer. All three aircraft are still carrying their 108-gallon tanks (*via William Hess*)

The first action of the new month occurred on 2 August when several trains, and the airfield at Beauvais, were strafed, despite ground haze and some heavy flak. Capt Thomas Joyce's fighter was hit by rifle-calibre bullets in the tail and carburettor scoop, and 1Lt Gerald Chapman of the 336th FS failed to return. Last seen leaving the Beauvais, he was later classified as killed in action.

Capt John McFarlane of the 336th FS led a Penetration Withdrawal Support mission for four combat wings to Joigny, in France, the following day. Again, no enemy fighters were seen, but the 4th suffered yet another loss when Maj Fonzo Smith from the HQ flight suffered mechanical failure in his P-51D south of Caen. He ended up in *Stalag Luft II.*

Five combat wings of B-24s hit Brunswick on 5 August, and after the target Col Blakeslee left 334th FS pilots Capt Roy Henwick and 1Lt Jack McFadden to escort them home while he took the rest of the 4th FG down to strafe. Oil storage tanks were set ablaze, a locomotive and some oil wagons were peppered near Meppel and Capt Johnny Godfrey shot up three Ju 52/3ms on an airfield near Munden. He also claimed the 4th's first aerial kill for August when he downed a Bf 109 near Osnabruck, taking his tally to 15.333. More significantly, fellow 336th FS pilot 1Lt Fred Glover 'made ace' when he too got a Bf 109 near Gardelegen.

One of the 4th FG's most successful pilots, Capt Fred Glover 'made ace' when he downed a Bf 109 on 5 August 1944. Promoted to CO of the 336th FS shortly afterward, he led the unit through to VE-Day, by which time he had claimed 10.333 aerial and 12.5 strafing victories. Glover is seen here standing in front of his last assigned P-51D, 44-64153 (*via William Hess*)

The following day Maj Leon Blanding of the HQ flight led a Penetration Target Withdrawal Support mission to Berlin, and after the bombers had headed home, several sections dropped down and went looking for the enemy. Four aircraft were destroyed at an airfield south of the German capital, and Capt Godfrey also downed an Me 410. His P-51C was then hit by flak, which crippled its fuel system. The ace jettisoned his canopy and prepared to bale out, but 1Lt Fred Glover talked him into using his hand-pump primer so as to keep the engine supplied with fuel. Godfrey kept on pumping for 2.5 hours until he landed at Beeches, in Norfolk.

Col Blakeslee led a strafing mission to the Dijon, Chaumont and St Dizier area on the 8th, with the group splitting up into sections and attacking German road and rail targets. 334th FS pilots 1Lt Donald Malmsten (334th FS) and future six-kill ace 2Lt William Whalen were attacking a locomotive along the track from Chalon-sur-Saone when they crested a hill and found themselves over Dijon. Greeted by a blizzard of light and heavy flak, they split up. 2Lt Whalen returned to Debden, but Malmsten bellied in nearby. Despite being wounded, he successfully evaded capture and returned to base on 12 September.

A similar fate befell 1Lt Sidney Wadsworth of the 335th FS, whose P-51B was hit by flak near Pont de Pany. When it lost its coolant, he tried to make it to Switzerland, but was forced to crash-land in France. He was quickly taken prisoner.

Leon Blanding began flying as a sergeant pilot with No 121 'Eagle' Sqn, and he rose to the rank of major over the course of two tours with the 4th FG. His time in the frontline came to an abrupt end when he suffered a fractured skull after his Mustang was hit by flak during the 8 August 1944 mission to Norway. Blanding was by then assigned to the 4th HQ flight, having previously been CO of the 335th FS (*via Wade Meyers*)

The next day, Col Blakeslee led an escort for 30 RAF Beaufighters sent to attack a convoy of 14 ships near Varhaug, on the coast of Norway. When they had finished, four of the vessels were sinking and three others were afire. Just as the Beaufighters ended their attacks, 1Lt Thomas Underwood of the 334th FS was hit by flak and forced to bale out when the engine in his P-51B burst into flames. He too became a PoW.

One section remained with the Beaufighters as they headed back south, but the rest of the 4th FG went north to attack the airfields at Sola and Kristiansand. Finding these bases devoid of aircraft, the group turned for home. En route, Capt Frank Jones, who was flying his last mission before rotating home to get married, ditched his flak-damaged P-51D into the North Sea. The ace was unable to get out of the aeroplane before it sank.

A short while later, the 4th spotted a convoy of nine ships 15 miles off the coast. They dropped down to strafe, and were met by a curtain of flak. 1Lt Robert Fischer of the 335th FS was hit and radioed that he was heading for Sweden, but he never made it and was killed when his P-51B crashed into the sea. Maj Blanding was hit as well, with glass from his shattered canopy fracturing his skull and causing him to bleed profusely. 1Lts Darwin Berry and John Kolbe escorted Blanding back home, the pilot fading in and out of consciousness as they crossed the North Sea. He eventually landed his blood-streaked fighter at Acklington airfield.

On 9 August the group dive-bombed targets in Chalons-sur-Marne, claiming 35 goods wagons and several trucks destroyed, as well as attacking a railway tunnel, a marshalling yard, a road bridge and a factory at Vitry. 1Lt James Ayers was hit by flak and forced to land at Manston.

An escort mission to Sens and St Florentine on 10 August went unopposed, and a section dropped down to strafe trains. A dozen locomotives were damaged. The following day, more rail targets were attacked following an escort mission to Coulommiers airfield. 334th FS pilot 1Lt Willard Gillette suffered structural failure in his P-51D as he returned to base, forcing him to bale out south of Haverhill, in Suffolk.

On 12 August, after the Luftwaffe again failed to materialize, one section was detached to hunt for a train loaded with V1s in northern

France. The latter proved elusive, so 1Lts Lewis Wells and James Callahan of the 334th FS strafed a conventional freight train instead. The rest of the group also dropped down once released from its escort duties, with one section shooting up 15 locomotives in a marshalling yard.

Later that same day, the 4th FG sortied with its aircraft armed with two 500-lb bombs apiece. Although briefed to head for the Chalons-Troyes-St Dizier area, navigation errors took the group off course and its pilots dropped their bombs on targets of opportunity, with generally poor results. 1Lt Earl Walsh downed a road bridge, however, and 1Lts Clarence Boretsky, Norman 'Doc' Achen and C G Howard destroyed several staff cars and trucks. 1Lt Jerome Jahnke of the 334th FS was forced to bale out of his Mustang over Bradwell Bay, in Essex, when his engine caught fire.

The dive-bombing missions continued on 13 August, when targets in the Beauvais-Compiegne-Paris area were hit. The Mustangs claimed 17 locomotives, 74 rail trucks and several bridges destroyed. The group landed, re-armed and headed back to the Nantes-Gassicourt-Etampes-Chartres-Dreux area, where they added a further ten locomotives, 100 rail trucks, a bridge and two rail tunnels to the tally. Capt John Goodwyn flew so low while strafing that he returned with a tree branch embedded in his wing. A third mission was launched to disrupt road traffic west of Paris, and during this show 1Lt Stephen Boren of the 335th FS hit a tree in his P-51D while strafing near Troesnes and was killed.

Capt Don Emerson of the 336th FS commanded 15 August's escort mission to Bad Zwischenahn, and leaving elements of the 334th FS to take the bombers home, he took the rest of the group down to strafe ground targets. 1Lts 'Doc' Achen and Herbert VanderVate buzzed an airfield to see whether it was a decoy. 'I drew no flak on this pass', reported VanderVate. 'I looked around for 1Lt Achen, who had been slightly behind me on the pass, but could not locate him. I continued to climb west, and in about five minutes I heard 1Lt Achen call and say that he had made a crash-landing. He was on the ground at the time, and must have been safe. I wished him luck and signed off.' Achen became a PoW.

The next day, the group escorted 'heavies' to Dessau, where the 336th FS broke up a rare attack by 40 enemy aircraft. The only victor this day was 1Lt Ira Grounds of the 336th FS, who destroyed a Bf 109. Col Blakeslee had his P-51D badly shot up, but he made it home.

Capt Neil Van Wyck of the 336th FS led the escort on 17 August, when ten bombers targeted to Les Foulens, in France. The formation was greeted by a completely socked-in continent, and no action was seen.

Col Blakeslee was up again on the 18th, when he led an Area Support mission for fighter-bombers from the 56th and 356th FGs working in the Beauvais area, while Capt John McFarlane, CO of the 336th FS, commanded a strafing mission. When bombing a railway tunnel north of Meru, Capt Thomas Joyce was hit by flak. 'I could see that his starboard wing was in bad shape', said 1Lt Henry Clifton. 'About 18 inches or two feet of it was sticking up at a right angle to the rest of it. After flying for a while, Joyce's ship seemed to be in better shape than first thought.' He landed the Mustang safely.

Before others could bomb, the group was bounced by 50 Bf 109s near Beauvais, including eight machines from 10./JG 26. '1Lts Arthur Cwiklinski and C G Howard were my Nos 3 and 4', recalled 1Lt Preston

Capt Johnny Godfrey poses with the 336th FS scoreboard in the squadron's flightline HQ at Debden in August 1944 – 28.999 of the crosses in the destroyed column belonged to him. Although he returned to the US with Capt Don Gentile for a war bond tour between 30 April and 24 July 1944, Godfrey felt out of place, and requested an assignment back to combat. He duly returned to the 4th FG and claimed two more aerial victories prior to being shot down on 24 August (*National Museum of the USAF*)

Hardy. 'In the ensuing fight, I saw two 'chutes, which I think were both my pilots, although one could have been a Hun that was clobbered at the same time. I had shot an Me 109 off the tail of a P-51, and 1Lt Whalen shot one off my tail.'

In actuality, Cwiklinski had suffered an engine failure. After he landed, 'I left my 'chute and dinghy in the burning aeroplane and hid my helmet and "Mae West" in an oat stack', Cwiklinski later reported. 'Looking for a place to hide, I saw some farmers beckoning to me. I approached them, and they hid me in a wagon under some oats. They outfitted me with civilian clothes and moved me to a farm about five miles away. From there I rode a bike about five miles to Etrepagny, where I stayed in the mayor's home. On 29 August the town was liberated by the British.' Cwiklinski made it back to England on 5 September.

In all, the 334th and 336th FSs had destroyed seven Bf 109s, with two falling to 1Lt Cwiklinski and single kills for 1Lts Whalen, Hardy, Paul Iden, Donald Perkins and Brack Diamond. In return, the Bf 109s claimed nine victims – 1Lt Dean Lang (334th), who became a PoW, Capt Otey Glass (336th) and Cwiklinski (334th), who both evaded and returned to friendly lines, and 1Lts C G Howard (334th), Bernard Rosensen (335th), John Conley (335th), Robert Cooper (335th), Donald Smith (335th) and Leo Dailey (335th), all of whom were killed. These losses equalled the number of casualties suffered by the 4th FG on D-Day.

Fortunately for the group, VIII Fighter Command took a six-day break from operations, and this allowed the 4th to make good these losses before flying its next mission on 24 August, when Col Blakeslee led a Penetration escort mission for 96 B-24s to Misburg and a Withdrawal Support for six B-17s returning from Merseburg. While escorting some straggling B-24s, 1Lt Ted Lines' 335th FS section spotted two Bf 109s. 'I dropped my tanks and headed down', Lines reported. 'When I was at about 5000 ft, the '109s split up, so I took the nearest one, expecting my No 2 to take the other. I began firing out of range, and the '109 did a split-S and dove into the ground and exploded.

'I was getting intense light flak from the ground, so I started climbing in a port orbit. When I reached 12,000 ft, I spotted the second '109 and dove on him. I was closing fast, and again fired far out of range. The '109 started a slow port turn, and the pilot baled out, but we were right on the deck. When his 'chute opened, it caught on the tail and I saw the pilot and his aircraft hit the ground. It broke into a thousand pieces on impact, and the pilot was still hanging on to the tail when it crashed.'

The 336th FS attacked Nordhausen airfield, where 1Lt Melvin Dickey destroyed three Ju 52/3ms and Capt Pierce Wiggins flamed one as well. Capt John Godfrey destroyed no fewer than four Junkers transports, but he was hit by fire from his wingman, Dickey, and forced to make a crash-landing in his P-51D. After destroying 28.999 German aeroplanes, Godfrey found himself on hostile soil, suffering from cuts to his head and leg. He walked 13 miles and tried to catch a train, but was captured by railway guards. Godfrey wound up at *Stalag Luft III* at Sagan.

When the Germans began to move prisoners out of the camp in February 1945, Godfrey escaped in the confusion, but had to return to seek treatment for his frostbitten feet. He travelled with other PoWs to Nurnberg, but in early April he escaped again and traded clothes with a French slave labourer, then teamed up with two more escapees to venture to the frontlines. Unfortunately, they were re-captured and sent back to Nurnberg, where Godfrey escaped for a third time! Helped by a German farmer, he finally reached American lines.

1Lts George Logan and Harry Hagan from the 336th FS each destroyed a Bf 109 during an escort mission to Schwerin on 25 August. The group lost 1Lt Kenneth Rudkin of the 334th FS, however. According to his squadronmate 1Lt Leonard Werner, 'heavy flak started to come up. I broke up and to the right, and 1Lt Rudkin down to the left. After I was out of range of the flak, I called him, but received no reply.' Rudkin's P-51D had been hit by flak over Lübeck and he ended up as a PoW.

Following two uneventful escorts to Germany on 26 and 27 August, Col Blakeslee led a strafing operation to the Strasbourg area of France on the 28th. The group attacked rail and road targets as far east as Sarrebourg, with the count of damaged and destroyed including 56 goods wagons, 13 trucks, 22 locomotives, a factory and an oil storage tank.

This haul came at a cost, however. HQ flight pilot Maj Donald Carlson was flying with 1Lt Herbert VanderVate as his wingman, and he was directly behind him on the first pass made on the trucks strafed near Strasbourg, but he then lost contact with him. VanderVate was killed when his P-51D was downed by flak, as was 335th FS ace Capt Albert Schlegel. The third pilot to perish when hit by flak in this area was 1Lt Ferris Harris of the 336th FS. Capt Pierce McKennon's P-51D was also downed near Niederbronn, but he was spotted landing in his parachute. Maj Archibald Thompson of the 335th survived being hit by the deadly Strasbourg flak, and like squadronmate McKennon, he evaded.

After the devastation inflicted on the group on the 28th, the last three days of August proved uneventful. Strafing was proving to be the deadliest form of combat now undertaken by the 4th FG, and having seen the carnage inflicted on his outfit, Col Blakeslee wrote a briefing paper for VIII Fighter Command use. Released on 30 August, he offered the following advice to fighter pilots in the ETO;

'Once I hit the 'drome, I really get down on the deck. I don't mean five feet up – I mean so low the grass is brushing the bottom of the air scoop.'

Blakeslee knew that the lower you came in, the harder it was for the flak gunners to get a sound tracking solution. Therefore, skilled flying at zero feet gave you a far better chance of surviving than sitting up higher.

Capt Godfrey, seen here in the cockpit of his P-51B, was the consummate wingman, but seamlessly took on the roll of leading ace after Capt Don Gentile departed in April 1944. Indeed, he downed seven more enemy fighters before he was shot down by flak and made a PoW (*National Museum of the USAF*)

Having seen continuous combat since mid-1941, and with 1200+ combat hours in his log book, Blakeslee went on leave for a month on 1 September. Lt Col Jim Clark was made acting CO, and six-kill ace Lt Col Claiborne Kinnard came in from the 355th FG as deputy CO.

September started slowly with a series of routine escort missions producing little in the way of action. Indeed, the only real event of note in the first eight days of the month occurred on the 5th when Capt Jerry Brown, acting CO of the 334th FS, was forced to bale out of his ailing P-51D near Amiens. He returned to Debden the following day in a C-47.

Finally, on 9 September, the 4th FG engaged the enemy again when Lt Col Kinnard led 11 P-51s on a dive-bombing mission to Schouwen Island, off the coast of Holland. The bombs all missed, but strafing set three large boats alight off Walcheren. On the way home, however, the balky engine of 1Lt Earl Walsh's P-51D quit. 'I turned my ship up, got out on the wing and stepped off', Walsh, of the 334th FS, reported. 'I opened my 'chute at 4000 ft. I had no trouble getting in my dinghy. In 40 minutes, a Walrus arrived and tried several times to pick me up from the rough water. He ran me over twice, and I do not remember much after that until the Walrus started to sink. I remember nothing until I woke up on an ASR ship some time later. I returned to base the following day.'

Although best known for his service with the 355th FG, Lt Col Claiborne Kinnard successfully led the 4th FG during Col Blakeslee's extended leave in the US in the autumn of 1944. He ended the war with eight aerial and 17 ground victories to his name. All of Kinnard's kills with the 4th FG came on 11 (one aerial and one strafing) and 13 September 1944 (two strafing) (*via WIlliam Hess*)

On the 10th, 1Lt Ted Lines of the 335th FS became the first 4th FG pilot to 'make ace' in many weeks. The mission had not started well for him, as he had been forced to land his P-51D at an advanced base in order to rectify a minor mechanical fault. Hurrying to catch the group up as it headed for Ulm, in Germany, he spotted seven Bf 109s near Strasbourg. 'They were flying as a group of four, and a considerable distance behind them a group of three, one of which was smoking. I attacked the rear section, concentrating on the one that was smoking. I fired from 600 yards down to 100 yards, at which point he went into the deck and exploded.'

Lines picked out another Bf 109 and sent it crashing to earth, only to come under fire from two fighters that had worked onto his tail. He was also horrified to see six Fw 190s closing behind them. 'They turned out to be P-47s, and they got the Me 109s off my tail. I then went after the third Me 109, and followed him across an airfield, where they really threw flak at me. The Hun then made a very short port turn and tried to land, but he didn't quite make it – he crashed, with one of his wings flying off through the air.' On the way home, Lines also downed a Ju 88. The 336th FS lost 1Lt Robert White when he crashed at Boxted at the end of the mission.

The 11th saw the 4th FG enjoy its most successful day since May when the Jagdwaffe sortied 100+ fighters to stop the Eighth Air Force. The group claimed 11 aircraft shot down and ten destroyed on the ground during an escort mission to Halle. Capt Gerald Montgomery of the 334th FS got the day's first kill when he spotted a Bf 109 near Bad Frankenhausen and gave chase. During the pursuit, he spotted a further ten fighters getting ready to land at Plotzkau and called in the rest of the group. Montgomery destroyed the Bf 109, whose pilot baled out, and Lt Col Kinnard strafed and destroyed an Me 410. Then, as he prepared to come around for another pass, he caught a Bf 109 trying to land and shot it down too.

A short while later, 1Lt Richard Rinebolt spotted 50 enemy fighters below and to his right, and eight Bf 109s about 10,000 ft above him. 'I climbed and joined another Mustang as he clobbered a '109. Another one came in from my left, and I broke into him and dropped flaps to get behind him. He dove, and I began to fire, observing strikes on his right wing root. His canopy came off, and I saw a 'chute open.'

'I spotted an Fw 190 and went after him', reported 1Lt Leonard Werner. 'I fired and observed hits all over him. I pulled up to avoid colliding. Seeing another Fw 190, I positioned myself to attack. Noticing an Me 109 with a belly tank diving on my wingman, I turned sharply and made a turn-and-a-half with the enemy aircraft. He flicked and spun twice to the left, then once to the right, hit the ground and exploded.'

1Lt George Cooley was the high scorer on the 11th, claiming two Fw 190s downed, with other pilots claiming multiple strafing kills. These successes came at a price, however, with five Mustangs being lost, including that of 1Lt James Russell. After shooting down a Bf 109, 'I tried to turn into an Fw 190 that was firing at me from "ten o'clock", but a 20 mm shell exploded in my cockpit', he said. 'Blood got in my eyes, so I couldn't see. When I cleared them, I discovered that I had been hit in the coolant system and oil lines. I headed for home. I was afraid to bale out because one of my 'chute straps had been cut. Near Fulda, the engine froze and started to burn, so I crash-landed in a field. I got about 150 ft from my kite and passed out.'

Russell became a PoW, as did 1Lts Henry Ingalls and William Groseclose. Also lost were 1Lt Paul Iden, who died in his P-51B, and 1Lt Rufus Patterson, who baled out, but was too low. 1Lt George Cooley's fighter was also hit, but he nursed it to within 15 miles of Liège before baling out – he rejoined the group four days later.

On the 12th, the 4th FG bounced 14 fighters during an escort to Brux-Ruhland. 1Lt Robert Dickmeyer shot down an Fw 190, then finished off a second that had been damaged by 1Lt Earl Hustwit. Hustwit was one of five pilots who bagged single Fw 190s. Included in this number was 1Lt James Lane, who was in turn forced down by mechanical failure. He and Capt Thomas Joyce, who fell victim to flak, ended up as PoWs.

Lt Col Kinnard led the group to Ulm the following day, and seeing the bombers out of harm's way, the 4th dropped down and attacked Gelcheim airfield. 'On my first pass, I set an enemy aircraft ablaze. It exploded as I passed over it', said Flt Off Charles Poage. 'We made another

On 11 September 1944, 1Lt James Russell had just destroyed an Fw 190 when another fighter hit him in the cockpit with a 20 mm shell. Near Fulda, when his P-51D started to burn, 'I crash-landed in a field. I got about 150 ft from my kite and passed out', he said. 'I was picked up by a forest ranger ten minutes later' (*National Museum of the USAF*)

Capt Thomas Joyce of the 334th FS force-landed near Bernau after his fighter was hit by flak on 12 September. The Mustang was recovered by the Luftwaffe and sent to Göttingen to be rebuilt with parts salvaged from other wrecked P-51s (*via William Hess*)

336th FS Mustangs taxi out at Debden at the start of yet another escort mission in the autumn of 1944. These massed take-offs into the English overcast presented their own hazards for the unwary – several newly arrived pilots were involved in mid-air collisions on forming up (*Keith Hoey via Wade Meyers*)

pass from the same direction, and I observed strikes behind the engine of a second aeroplane. It blew up in front of me. On the third pass, I got strikes behind the engine of another aeroplane. After this last pass, we orbited the field and counted 11 aircraft burning, with possibly two left untouched.' Poage believed that he had destroyed Hs 123 biplanes.

In his first pass, Capt William Smith destroyed a twin-engined aircraft and damaged a second, but a flak battery hit him in the cockpit and engine. His P-51D pulled up to 400 ft, rolled over and crashed in flames on the airfield, killing him instantly. 1Lt Gillette damaged an Fw 200 during the attack and 1Lt Diamond destroyed three Hs 123s, Kinnard and 1Lt George Ceglarski two each and 1Lt Wilbur Eaton one.

Following three days of relative inactivity, on 17 September the 4th flew a fighter sweep in advance of the Operation *Market Garden* paratroop landings. It then escorted the vulnerable troop transports and glider tugs bound for Arnhem, after which individual sections provided a fighter screen east of the drop zone. Whilst performing the latter mission, the 335th FS was bounced by 15 Fw 190s near Bucholt, resulting in a furball in which 1Lt Ted Lines again scored multiple victories;

'My wingman hollered at me to break as I was trying to discard my right external wing tank. When I broke, I was head-on to five Fw 190s, so I immediately started firing, causing one Fw 190 to burst into flames. I turned to starboard, still trying to drop my tank, as two Fws came under me, heading in the same direction as I was. I got on the tail of the one nearest me and started firing, and the pilot baled out. At this point, a '190 closed on my tail and fired at me, hitting me in the tail and wing. My tank finally came off, and I was able to manoeuvre onto the tail of the '190 that had been firing at me. After three orbits, he broke for the deck, with me right on his tail. I fired and saw strikes on his engine, canopy, fuselage, wings and tail. He burst into flames, hit the ground and exploded.'

1Lt Nicholas Vozzy was not so lucky, as his P-51B was hit by fire from Oberleutnant Wilhelm Hofmann of 8./JG 26 and it burst into flames and crashed, killing him – Vozzy was Hofmann's 37th kill.

'The bandits had been flying at the base of a layer of haze, and with their light grey colour, they were very difficult to see', said 335th FS CO, Capt Louis Norley. Upon seeing Vozzy's fiery demise, he dropped his tanks and broke into the enemy fighters. Norley spotted an aircraft coming at him head-on, and he fired a short burst at long range;

'I then noticed two Fw 190s on his tail, the closest one firing. It became apparent that the aeroplane I had fired on was actually a P-51! I broke up, coming down on the tail of the lead Fw 190 as he broke off his attack and turned to port. I turned with him, the other '190 being attacked by my wingman, 1Lt Albert Davis. The '190 rolled and started to split-S, but levelled out and started to climb. I fired with no results. He levelled off and did some skidding evasion efforts as I closed, firing and skidding past him. He dove to port, allowing me to drop back on his tail. I fired, getting many strikes on his wings and fuselage. He flicked over on his back, went into a vertical dive and crased into a farm yard.'

1Lt Albert Davis also claimed two Fw 190s destroyed, but 1Lt Clifford Holske was shot down by German fighters and captured.

For the next seven days the only event of note occurred on 18 September when the 336th FS's 1Lt George Smith was bounced by an Me 262 during a bomber escort mission to Schwerin. Four of his squadronmates tried to engage the jet fighter, but without success.

Following a bomber escort to Koblenz on 25 September, two sections from the 335th FS dropped down to strafe a locomotive pulling six carriages. 1Lt Warren Williams of the 336th FS caught a lone Ju 88 on the ground at Lippsringe and destroyed it, but in exchange 334th FS pilot Capt Roy Henwick failed to return. His compass and radio failed, then he ran out of fuel near Castel Jaloux, where he crash-landed. The Maquis quickly picked him up – they were especially excited at the prospect of turning the Mustang's six 0.50-cals on the Germans! Henwick was taken to Bordeaux, then to Paris, and he returned to the group on 28 September.

Two days later, Maj Gerald Brown led an escort of B-24s to Kassel, and five enemy fighters were downed by 1Lts Arthur Senecal, Charles Dupree, John MacFarlane and George Smith. These victories pushed the 4th FG's overall tally past the 700-mark.

On the 28 September escort mission to Magdeburg, the group was confronted by 60+ Fw 190s taking aim on the bombers. 334th FS ace 1Lt David Howe passed them, and 'by the time I turned and got rid of my tanks, they were slightly higher than us, and climbing at "seven o'clock" to the bombers'. After a pass on the 'heavies', 'they all hit the deck, I picked out one and weaved down behind him. He flew over and through the tops of the clouds as I closed. Dropping a little flap to slow down, I opened fire at 450 yards, getting hits at once on the left wing. I corrected a little, and got hits on the motor, tail and wings. The enemy aircraft fell off on one wing, and I got in a good burst in by pulling negative Gs. I slid up in a turn to get ready for another pass when the pilot baled out.'

Maj Brown led an unopposed Target Support mission to Hamm on 2 October. Despite the Jagdwaffe staying on the ground, 1Lt George Logan of the 336th FS perished when his P-51D suffered mechanical failure over the Netherlands and suddenly spun in near Apeldoorn.

Four days later, following a Support mission to Berlin, 1Lt Donald Malmsten's 334th FS section bounced some Bf 109s trying to attack the last box of bombers. 1Lt Leonard Werner chased one, which went into a dive to escape. At 600 mph, the Bf 109 tried to turn left, at which point its wings ripped off and the fighter smashed into the ground. Werner then pulled up and spotted an Fw 190. He scored strikes on it as the two aeroplanes raced low over the western suburbs of Berlin. At one point, a rifle round burst through the floor of Werner's Mustang and ruptured his oxygen hose. He broke off the attack, and he was later credited with having damaged the Fw 190.

Elsewhere, 1Lts Elmer McCall and Ralph Lewis of the 335th FS spotted an Me 410 just prior to rendezvousing with B-17s north of Bremerhaven.

Capt Ted Lines of the 335th FS poses with his last P-51D (44-13555), named *Thunder Bird*, which wore this immense nose art made up of native American symbols. Lines had a knack for finding trouble on his own. On 9 October 1944 he turned back because of engine trouble and ended up downing two Bf 109s, and 15 days later he destroyed a pair of Fw 190s whilst trying to catch up with the rest of the 4th FG following engine problems with his Mustang. None of these victories was officially credited to Lines, however, and he finished the war with a score of ten aerial kills to his name (*4th Fighter Group Association via Peter Randall*)

'My section started to climb after the enemy aircraft', McCall reported. 'At 300 yards, I took a short burst and observed strikes. The right engine started to smoke, and he dropped his tanks as I fired again. He broke into 1Lt Lewis, who followed him through a diving turn, firing as he went. Two 'chutes opened and the aeroplane crashed into the sea.' 1Lt Joe Joiner of the 336th FS claimed the day's final kill when he downed a Bf 109.

Two days later, Flt Off Kenneth Foster of the 334th FS was forced to bale out of his elderly P-51B when its engine detonated over the Channel en route to Magdeburg. He was rescued within 30 minutes of landing in the water.

The escort to Giessen on 9 October was uneventful, but Capt Ted Lines still managed to scare up some action. 'Near Gedern, Germany, I developed engine trouble and started for home', he related. 'As I descended, my engine started running better. I came upon a fresh clearing with six Bf 109s sitting there with their engines running. One was just taking off, so I attacked him and hit him as he was just putting up his wheels. He started to turn, crashed and exploded. I turned and came back, attacking the one on the starboard side of the runway about to take off. I got strikes on the fuselage and engine area and he flamed and exploded. He was still burning as I left the area.' As Lines was flying alone, and there were no witnesses to these victories, they remained officially uncredited.

After an escort to Rheine-Salzbergen on 12 October, two sections of 334th FS fighters dropped down to strafe. They shot up trucks, boats and locomotives, and set two oil storage tanks afire. Ground fire hit 1Lt Raymond Dyer's Mustang, while 1Lt Edward Wozniak struck a tree, damaging both wings, but they were able to nurse their fighters home.

The group shepherded bombers to Kaiserslautern on 14 October. During the mission, seven-kill ace Capt Joseph Lang of the 334th FS peeled off and told 1Lt Lynd Cox to take over the section. 'Thinking he was aborting, we thought no more of it', said 1Lt Jerome Jahnke, Lang's wingman. 'At 1130 hrs, Capt Lang called, saying, "This is Lang, I am down below the clouds with 10 Me 109s. I got two. I don't know where I am, and I need help". We could not contact him thereafter'. Lang was shot down and killed.

On 20 October, Col Blakeslee returned from leave in the US, and he led the group on an escort to Minden six days later. No German fighters rose to attack the bombers, but Capt Ted Lines again found action. He was trying to catch up after suffering more engine problems in his assigned P-51D when he was attacked by six Fw 190s, one of which struck his right drop tank and set it on fire;

'I went into a spin at about 8000 ft. My wing tanks were now gone and my elevators were damaged, so I headed for the overcast, with the Fws still after me. I came out of the clouds. Three were still above me, and three were behind me. I began to manoeuvre onto the tail of one of the two still carrying drop tanks. When I started firing, I immediately saw strikes on his engine, fuselage and drop tank. He blew up right in front of me. I turned onto the other one with a drop tank and fired, hitting him hard. He started to burn furiously and went straight down. Since my engine was still acting up, I entered the clouds and steered for home.'

Once again Lines was flying alone, and with no witnesses present, these kills remained officially uncredited too.

BREAKING THE LUFTWAFFE'S BACK

Orders were received at Debden from VIII Fighter Command on 27 October to remove the black stripes from the Mustangs' vertical stabilizers and to paint the rudders red for the 334th FS, white for 335th FS and blue for 336th FS. Three days later, Col Blakeslee led an escort to Hamburg. Upon his return, he learned that Col 'Hub' Zemke, formerly CO of the 56th FG but now head of the 479th FG, had been taken prisoner after he had been forced to bale out of his Mustang in bad weather over Germany. Blakeslee was immediately grounded to prevent the other senior group commander in the theatre from suffering a similar fate. Lt Col Claiborne Kinnard assumed command once again.

During a sweep around Brunswick and Magdeburg on 2 November, 'We sighted jets going up through the haze to attack the bombers, and waited for them to come back down', reported Capt 'Red Dog' Norley of the 335th FS. When he spotted an Me 163, he followed it down. 'The jet started to level off and make a port turn, with his speed dropping considerably. I closed rapidly. Using the K-14 gunsight for the first time, I got a couple of strikes on his tail.' Norley overshot, pulled up, and got on the Me 163's tail again. 'At 400 yards I again got strikes on his tail. He rolled over and went straight down from 8000 ft, with fire coming from his port side and exhaust. He crashed in a small village and exploded.' 336th FS ace Capt Fred Glover also destroyed an Me 163, whilst 335th FS pair 1Lts John Kolbe and Charles Brock each destroyed Bf 109s.

After an escort mission to Karlsruhe on 5 November, the group shot up ground targets while the 336th FS provided top cover. Flak downed the P-51D of 335th FS pilot 1Lt Russell Anderson, who became a PoW.

Two unnamed pilots pose alongside the last Mustang (P-51D 44-13779) assigned to Col Don Blakeslee when CO of the 4th FG. After Col 'Hub' Zemke of the 479th FG was forced to bale out over Germany in bad weather on 30 October 1944, Blakeslee was immediately yanked from operational status. By then the veteran pilot had flown an estimated 1200+ combat hours and been credited with 14.5 aerial and 1.5 strafing kills (*Keith Hoey via Wade Meyers*)

Pre-mission apprehension shows on the face of 1Lt Louis 'Red Dog' Norley, seen here with crew chief TSgt Vincent Andra. Norley was one of only a handful of pilots to serve with all three squadrons within the 4th FG during World War 2. Joining the 336th FS in July 1943, he was made CO of the 335th FS in August 1944. Norley was subsequently given command of the 334th FS in January 1945. The 10.333-kill ace also claimed aerial victories with all three units as well (*via Wade Meyers*)

Lt Col Kinnard led 6 November's escort to Minden. Near Rheine, Capt Montgomery heard 1Lt John Childs of the 334th FS radio that he had a German fighter on his tail. 'Later, I spotted two Me 109s at about 7000 ft firing on a red-nosed Mustang', Montgomery said. 'I dove to assist, but the Mustang was taking no evasive action and was shot down before I could help him.' Childs was killed. His squadronmate 1Lt Earl Walsh was also shot down in the same action, although he became a PoW. The group evened up the score when 1Lts Jack McFadden and Van Chandler shot down a Bf 109 apiece, with the latter pilot's victim crashing into a revetment on Rheine/Salzbergen airfield.

On 8 November, with the bombers safely on their way home after targeting Merseberg, the 4th FG strafed rail targets near Vechta, in Germany. Seven locomotives were damaged, but the group lost 2Lt Earl Quist of the 336th FS in the process – he became a PoW.

Poor weather then severely hindered operations for the next ten days. Conditions improved sufficiently for the group to mount a strafing attack on Leipheim airfield on 18 November. Led by Lt Col Kinnard, the 335th and 336th FSs made two passes each to neutralize the flak, then the 334th FS made four passes on the enemy aircraft at the base.

1Lt Wilbur Eaton spotted three Me 262s and fired on one, which caught fire. 'I also got hits on the one next to it. As I crossed over the second jet, it exploded and I flew through the mud and debris of the explosion. My windscreen was covered with mud, so I couldn't make another pass.' 1Lt Carl Brown and Flt Off Charles Harre were credited with the destruction of two Me 262s apiece, and six other pilots each destroyed a jet. 2Lt Ralph Lewis of the 335th FS was the group's sole loss, the pilot being killed when his P-51D was hit by flak near Günzburg.

The escort mission to Koblenz on 20 November was fouled up by more bad weather. Worse, while climbing through clouds from 14,000 ft to

27,000 ft, 1Lts Leonard Werner and Donald Bennett of the 334th FS collided. Bennett became a PoW, but Werner was killed.

During the escort to Merseberg on 21 November, the 335th and 336th FSs ran into Bf 109s west of Merseburg. Capt Fred Glover downed three of them to take his score to 9.333 aerial kills, while 1Lt Douglas Groshong destroyed two and 1Lt John Kolbe claimed one. The latter pilot recalled;

'When I had identified him as an enemy aircraft, I slowed down and fired at him from behind. I immediately got strikes around the cockpit and wing roots. He pulled into a vertical climb and I lost him in the thick clouds. When I could no longer see him, I feared collision. I dropped below the overcast and made an orbit, at which time I saw a fire and wreckage of an aeroplane. I believe he spun out of the cloud and crashed.'

However, these victories, had came at a cost. During one tangle in poor weather, 334th FS pilot 1Lt Carmen Delnero was shot down, possibly by his own flight leader. He was killed when his plane exploded and crashed. Also lost was 2Lt George Klaus of the 336th FS, his P-51B being hit by flak when the group went hunting for ground targets. He became a PoW.

November ended with a series of uneventful Penetration Withdrawal Support missions. Finally, on 2 December, the 4th FG was vectored by fighter controllers to an area south of Kolbenz, where 30 Fw 190s were forming up for an attack on B-24s returning from a raid on Bingen. The bombers were vulnerable, with their formation strung out. The German fighters were arranged in three groups, and were ready to attack when the 4th and 361st FGs broke them up. Both kills that were claimed went to 334th FS pilots, namely 1Lts Jack McFadden and Carl Brown.

Three days later, 334th FS CO Maj Hively led the escort for two B-17 drone controllers and two Project *Aphrodite* robot Flying Fortresses. The latter were war-weary machines loaded with explosives and flown by pilots who would bale out over England shortly after taking off. The drone controllers would then fly the bombers and crash them into their targets. One of the robots spiralled to earth near Steinfeld, where it blew up with an enormous blast that was felt by the P-51 pilots at 14,000 ft. The second B-17 crashed into an open field south of Dummer Lake, sliding 150 yards across a field before halting without exploding. A request for the Mustang pilots to strafe the downed aircraft was loudly rejected.

When the bombers headed for home, the Mustangs strafed near the Hague. Hively also managed to find a lone Fw 190 and shoot it down.

On 7 December Lt Col Harry Dayhuff took over the 4th FG, this veteran pilot having previously served with the 78th FG. Four days later, he led his first mission with the group when it covered bombers targeting Hanau. Although no action was seen, 1Lt Paul Morgan of the 336th FS suffered engine problems and baled out over France. He made it back to Debden two weeks later.

The group returned to Hanau the next day when it undertook a two-part escort mission for bombers hitting targets in this area once again – 334th and 335th FS COs Majs Hively and McKennon were in

The only olive drab P-51D in the 4th FG was this one, 44-15347. Originally assigned to Maj 'Deacon' Hively, it was passed on to 'Red Dog' Norley when he became CO of the 334th FS on 25 January 1945. The aircraft had the distinction of being the last fighter in the group to claim a victory, and the last to be shot down. Both events occurred on 25 April 1945. This photograph was taken at Debden some four months earlier following heavy snowfall (*Danny Morris via Peter Randall*)

charge of the two forces. 336th FS CO Maj Freddie Glover led the 15 December escort to Kassel. No enemy aircraft were seen during any of these missions.

On 18 December, Lt Col Dayhuff led the group on a Freelance Fighter Patrol of the area between Kassel and Frankfurt, and the Mustangs became split up while descending through the undercast to hunt for targets. Two sections of Mustangs ran across seven Bf 109s, and 1Lt Henry Clifton of the 334th FS was able to down one of them.

A short while later, Capt William O'Donnell of the 335th FS spotted an Fw 190 trying to get on Capt John Fitch's tail, and he succeeded in damaging the fighter and forcing its pilot to break off his attack. O'Donnell followed, in a tight turn, getting strikes as he closed on the tail of the aircraft. Smoking badly, the Fw 190 executed a half-roll and dove for the ground. Fitch and 1Lt Robert Stallings gave pursuit, and Stallings hit the fighter again. It slammed into the ground and exploded. Climbing back to altitude, Fitch saw four Bf 109s. Three of them ducked into clouds, but a fourth tried to get onto Stallings' tail. O'Donnell opened fire and scored hits all over the fighter. It too dove into the ground.

Although the 335th had downed two fighters, it had lost Capt Charles Hewes, who was last seen making a strafing at 4000 ft near Giessen. It appears that his P-51D was hit by flak and he was killed.

On Christmas Eve, Lt Col Dayhuff led an escort to Giessen, and two Bf 109s made the mistake of challenging the 335th FS. Lt Calvin Willruth spotted the first one flying far below him. 'It was a dull grey Me 109 with crosses on either wing', he said. 'I fired a burst, getting strikes. I continued to fire, and I saw the Me 109 burst into flames. I saw the pilot bale out at 50 ft, just as we were receiving a heavy barrage of flak.' Squadronmate 1Lt George Green claimed a second Bf 109 probably destroyed.

Capt Don Emerson's face shows the strain of a mission flown in his Mustang. On Christmas Day 1944, he took on six German fighters single-handedly and destroyed two, only to be hit by British anti-aircraft fire whilst returning home. Investigators claimed that Emerson, who was the 336th FS's operations officer, was dead before his Mustang hit the ground in Belgium (*National Museum of the USAF*)

Most pilots from the 334th and 335th FSs – 42 fighters in all – landed at Raydon, Wattisham, Warmingford, Castle Camps and bases in Belgium upon returning from this flight because of heavy fog at Debden. The mess secretary sent turkeys, whiskey and cigarettes to the re-located pilots to provide some Christmas Eve cheer.

The next day, despite having fighters spread over several locations, the group managed to escort bombers to Kassel-Bonn-Trier, where the Germans had a Christmas gift waiting in the form of 30 Fw 190s and Bf 109s. 'Huns were reported at "12 o'clock" to the bombers', said Maj McKennon. 'We spotted three Fw 190s at "two o'clock", which we immediately engaged. All four of us ended up with '190s on our tails. I yelled at 1Lt Charles Poage to break, but it was too late as the Fw 190 had just finished him off. His aeroplane went down burning, but he succeeded in baling out.' Poage, who would be credited with two Fw 190s probably destroyed, was shot down near Bonn – he became a PoW.

'The Fw 190 on my tail finally broke and dived to the deck', McKennon continued. 'I followed, shooting bursts at him and getting occasional strikes. I pulled up to clear my tail, and 1Lt Tim Cronin closed in and fired, also getting strikes. The Jerry pulled up, rolled over and baled out.'

At the same time, Capt Donald Emerson went after six enemy fighters on his own, and he shot down two of them. 1Lts Victor Rentschler and William Hoelscher each destroyed a Bf 109, and teamed up to knock down an Fw 190. 1Lt Cronin downed an Fw 190 in addition to the one he shared with Maj McKennon, and Maj Glover destroyed an Fw 190D. Finally, 1Lt Van Chandler bagged a Bf 109 and an Fw 190. The day's total was ten kills. Sadly, Allied ground fire claimed Capt Emerson on his way home, the veteran pilot crashing to his death in Belgium.

This proved to be the last action seen by the 4th FG in 1944. The group celebrated the New Year by flying a two-part escort to Derben-Stendal, with Majs Glover and McKennon leading. Glover's group was vectored to Wittenburg, where 15 Bf 109s were spotted at low altitude. Four more were above them as top cover. 2Lt Ben Griffin of the 336th FS was on his first mission, and he followed his leader, 1Lt Pierini, down on the bounce, watching as two Bf 109s were sent crashing into fields below him by 1Lts Franklin Young, Gilbert Kesler and Alvin Wallace.

Meanwhile, the high cover remained above them, 'and finally one began to dive behind our section', said 1Lt Chandler, who was also on Pierini's wing. 'I called him into 1Lt Pierini, and he told me to go after him and he would cover me.' Chandler lost sight of the Bf 109, but minutes later spotted two more Bf 109s on the deck at about 50 ft. Chandler fired a short burst and got strikes, and his target rolled over and crashed to earth – he had just 'made ace'. The second Bf 109 led Pierini across a town before he began getting strikes. It suddenly 'pulled up sharply, did a wingover into the ground and exploded', confirmed 1Lt Young.

At that point, the section spotted three Me 262s from III./JG 7, which were charged with supporting the piston-engined fighters of JGs 300 and 301. The Americans dove on them, and Young scored hits on the aircraft of Leutnant Heinrich Lönnecker, whose jet crashed west of Fassberg.

The next day, Maj McKennon led the 334th FS on a Freelance escort to the Ruhr area. The unit received a vector to the Cologne area, where 1Lt Arthur Senecal saw two Bf 109s hugging the deck. He and 1Lt Carl Payne dove, followed by 1Lt Victor Rentschler. Both German fighters were sent crashing to the ground. Flak then hit Senecal's P-51B, and he tried to make it home. However, after just ten minutes its engine caught fire and he baled out, but his parachute did not open. Senecal was killed when he hit the ground ten yards from the wreckage of his aeroplane.

As the weather worsened, the only event of note for the next two weeks occurred at the start of the 6 January mission when 1Lt Jerome Jahnke of the 334th FS skidded on the icy runway and banged into squadronmate Capt Don Malmsten's Mustang, ending both their missions prematurely.

1Lt Van Chandler destroyed an Fw 190 and a Bf 109 during the Christmas Day mission, and he followed these kills up with another Bf 109 destroyed on New Year's Day to become an ace. Almost 60 years would pass before Chandler discovered that this feat had made him America's youngest fighter ace at just 19 years of age. He claimed three of his five kills in this aircraft, P-51D 44-14388. Chandler would score three MiG-15 victories whilst flying F-86Es with the 25th FIS/51st FW in Korea in early 1952. He also saw combat in Vietnam in 1969–70, flying F-100 Super Sabres with the 31st TFW (*Don Pierini via Peter Randall*)

A pair of P-51Ds seem to huddle for warmth in their revetments at Debden during the particularly bleak winter of 1944–45 (*via Wade Meyers*)

SLAUGHTER BY STRAFING

On 16 January, the 4th FG at last got to fire its guns in anger once again. Maj Fred Glover had led a support mission to Ruhland-Dresden, and once the bombers had left the target area, the 336th FS attacked an airfield south of Berlin. 'Green Section, led by 1Lt Chandler, saw a bogie on the deck', reported Glover. 'I sent them down to engage. They lost him, but in climbing back up they saw another aircraft landing at Neuhausen airfield. I told them to attack, and in two passes they received no flak and had five aircraft burning on the deck by the time I got the rest of the squadron down.

'I told the other two squadrons to stay with the "big friends". We made seven or eight passes apiece, with the exception of myself. After three strafing passes, I made four others to take photos. On the re-form, I counted at least 25 fires, but could not count further due to heavy smoke from the burning aeroplanes. Altogether, we were over the airfield for about 20 minutes, but had to leave due to shortage of gas and ammo.'

In all, the group destroyed 26 aeroplanes at Neuhausen, plus two more at Neuberg, where 1Lt Victor Rentschler of the 334th FS was hit by flak. 'I noticed his kite was streaming a little coolant, but when he opened his coolant scoop it seemed to stop', reported 1Lt Edward Wozniak. 'We flew on for about 15 minutes, and his coolant started streaming again. He motioned me to move away and he baled out, Jack-in-the-box style. His kite hit and blew up in a woods. He came down, gathered up his 'chute and started for the woods.' Even so, Rentschler became a PoW.

Upon returning to the UK, 1Lt Fred Hall's flak-riddled P-51D crashed while he was trying to land at the forward field at Hawkinge, on the Kent coast, killing the 336th FS pilot. The P-51D of squadronmate 1Lt Harry Hagan was also hit, and he baled out over Hawkinge and ended up landing in a tree near Folkestone.

The next day, a squadron-sized escort accompanied bombers to Hamburg. There was no aerial opposition, but 1Lt Robert Stallings of the 335th FS suffered engine trouble with his P-51K and baled out over the Channel near Lowestoft. Only his empty dinghy was subsequently found.

Maj McKennon led Group A and Capt Joseph Joiner Group B when the 4th FG undertook a sweep of Frankfurt and Wertheim on 21 January. Group A attacked a locomotive and its 20 coal trucks, a marshalling yard, four dummy He 111s on an airfield and the train station at Donausworth – the latter target was also strafed by Group B. Bad weather then grounded the group until the 29th, when it escorted bombers to Koblenz. 1Lt Morton Savage of the 334th FS did not return from this mission until 1 February. He and his section had dropped down to strafe a convoy of trucks, but Savage had struck a tree instead. The damage forced him to land at St Trond for a wing change.

Lt Col Jack Oberhansly came to the 4th FG already an ace, and the deputy group CO did not score during his brief time at Debden. Sgt Don Allen resisted painting Oberhansly's *Iron Ass* nose art at first, but it soon became a favourite within the group (*National Museum of the USAF*)

The 4th FG had at least three two-seat hack Mustangs converted by the groundcrews. This one was given a striking overall light blue paint job (the 336th FS's rudder colour), set off by the 4th's standard late-war swept-back red nose flash (*National Museum of the USAF*)

Weather again precluded combat operations until 6 February, when deputy group CO Lt Col Jack Oberhansly led an escort mission to Magdeburg. Once the bombers were safely on their way home, the 335th FS did some strafing in the neighbourhood of Torgau, shooting up 13 locomotives, 18 wagons, 11 rail trucks and two carriages. Former RAF pilot 1Lt Paul Santos was killed by flak, however, and squadronmate Flt Off William Bates had to abandon his P-51D off the coast of Southwold, in Suffolk, when it fell victim to engine trouble. Despite ASR P-47s being quickly on scene, Bates was too weak to climb into his dinghy and rough seas kept an RAF Walrus from landing to pick him up. When a rescue launch finally reached him two hours later, he was dead.

Another break in the weather on 11 February allowed the group to conduct a fighter sweep and strafing mission to Osnabruck-Hanover-Soest. The 4th claimed ten locomotives and several wagons destroyed, a tug and six barges damaged and three barracks buildings and a number of oil tanks shot up in the Kassel-Hanover area. However, while strafing near Lemgo, 1Lt Henry Kaul of the 336th FS hit a tree and was killed. Back in England, poor weather forced the group to land at other airfields, and when 1Lt Morton Savage tried to return to Debden from Wattisham, he struck a radio tower near Nuthampstead and was killed.

On Valentine's Day, an escort mission to Magdeburg was followed by more strafing. Four locomotives and three signals towers were damaged, and the group dropped its tanks on three barracks buildings, setting them ablaze with machine gun fire.

Six days later, the group launched an escort to Nurnberg. The bombers aborted, so the group went strafing in the Neumarkt-Regensburg area. Unfortunately, Capt John Fitch's P-51D was hit by flak after strafing, and the 335th FS pilot baled out southwest of Neumarkt. He was seen to be safe on the ground, and he became a PoW shortly thereafter.

Near Nurnberg, Capt Joe Joiner of the 336th FS was on his way to strafe when he spotted a pair of Fw 190s at about 500 ft. 'The '190s were flying line abreast formation, and I took the one on the left. I fired a short burst from about 250 yards and his belly tank exploded. After the smoke cleared

I fired another long burst from about 150 yards and the '190 exploded in a huge ball of flame and went into the deck.'

The other Fw 190 broke to the right and tried to escape at treetop level. 'I started firing from line astern and saw a few scattered strikes on the wings', said Joiner. 'I had to stop firing then because Capt Kendall Carlson was making a pass at the same target from a 45-degree angle. I started firing again and closed to about 100 yards. I was firing at him when he crash-landed in a field, and as he made a good crash landing I came back and strafed the aeroplane.'

On 21 February, the group again escorted bombers to Nurnberg, after which it strafed yet more rail targets. Five locomotives, 66 wagons and several vehicles were destroyed at Donauworth. As he was going after a train, 1Lt Andrew Lacy of the 334th FS felt his P-51K being struck by three 20 mm flak shells. 'He was streaming gas and had no oil pressure', reported 1Lt Kenneth Helfrecht. 'He headed towards base, but his engine stopped and he baled out. He waved as he was floating down. I lost him after he landed, so I believe he hid his 'chute and started to evade.' Lacy was quickly apprehended, as was 1Lt August Rabe of the 335th FS, who hit a tree while strafing and bellied in southwest of Coburg.

That same day, back at Debden, command of the group passed to Col Everett Stewart, who had initially seen combat in P-40s in the Pacific – indeed, he had flown a sortie over Hawaii on 7 December 1941. Following a spell as CO of the 328th FS/352nd FG in 1943, Stewart transferred to the 355th FG as its executive officer in late January 1944, and eventually took charge of the group in November of that year. The bulk of his 7.833 kills came during his time with the 355th FG.

The 4th FG escorted B-24s to Hildesheim-Piene-Stendal on the 22nd, after which the group menaced traffic on the autobahn between Brunswick and Hanover, destroying trucks, oil storage tanks and a locomotive. Pilots from the 336th FS then found a handful of uncovered fighters and bombers at Halberstadt airfield and destroyed eight of them.

An escort on 24 February to Herford was followed up by strafing in Holland near the Zuider Zee. This damaged six barges, three locomotives and several wagons, but at a cost. While attacking barges, 334th FS pilot

Col Everett Stewart was the final wartime commander of the 4th FG. His brightly coloured P-51D *Sunny VIII* was one of only two Mustangs in the group to boast a light blue anti-glare panel, the other being Maj Freddie Glover's P-51D (*National Museum of the USAF*)

2Lt Marvin Arthur saw squadronmate Flt Off Alvin Hand pull up after a pass. 'I saw Hand was in trouble', Arthur recalled. 'Before I could locate him again, someone spotted the wreckage where he had bellied in.' Hand became a PoW.

During a fighter sweep of the Dessau area on 25 February, a section from the 334th FS found an airfield near Rohrensee filled with 60 aeroplanes hidden under freshly cut tree branches. The four Mustangs made several passes, with 1Lt Carl Payne shooting down an Me 262 he spotted coming in to land, and also sharing in the destruction of an Me 410 with 1Lt Thomas Bell, who got an Fw 190 on his own and two more Me 410s shared with 1Lt Gordon Denson. 1Lts Donald Malmsten and William O'Bryan spotted a single Fw 190 and destroyed it too, while 1Lt Arthur Bowers was credited with the destruction of an Fw 190, a Bf 110 and an Me 410.

336th FS pilot Capt Kendall 'Swede' Carlson, who called Red Bluff, California, home, was a six-kill ace (with four more ground victories). He inadvertently flew his fighter into the ground while strafing aircraft at Kothen airfield on 25 February 1945, and emerging unscathed from the crash, he acted as a forward air controller, radioing targets to his fellow pilots overhead until captured by the Germans (*National Museum of the USAF*)

The 336th FS targeted Kothen airfield, where Capt Kendall 'Swede' Carlson destroyed an unidentified aircraft, as did 1Lt James Hileman, and 1Lt Richard Corbett flamed an He 111. As Carlson made a second run on the base, he mushed into the ground and skidded to a stop. From this unique vantage point, he called in targets over his radio to the rest of the group, before finally being captured – these included an Fw 190 downed by 1Lts Beacham Brooker and 1Lt Paul Morgan. As they were orienting themselves for another pass, seven German fighters turned up, and the Mustangs, low on fuel and ammunition, sped away.

These victories pushed the 4th FG's overall score past the 800–mark, which rivalled the tally of the 56th FG.

Maj Glover led Group A on a Freelance to Leipzig on the 27th, and Col Stewart flew with the 4th FG for the first time when his Group B escorted B-24s targeting Halle. The 335th FS remained with the bombers while the 334th and 336th FSs strafed Weimar airfield. The results were devastating, with 1Lt Malmsten destroying six aircraft on his own, Majs Montgomery and Glover, 1Lt Kesler and Capts Bell, Clifton and Ayers each bagging three, and the latter sharing a fourth with 1Lt Voyles. A further 18 aircraft were destroyed by 15 other pilots for a total score of 43. Unfortunately, during his third pass, 1Lt Robert Voyles of the 334th FS pulled up streaming coolant, and he had to break away sharply to avoid being hit by a 336th FS fighter firing in his direction. A few minutes later, Ayers heard Voyles radio that he was baling out – he became a PoW, as did 336th FS pilot 1Lt Harold Crawford, whose P-51K was also hit by flak.

No further action of note occurred until 3 March, when Col Stewart and deputy group CO Lt Col Sidney Woods led two groups on an escort mission to Magdeburg-Brandenburg. Some 15 Me 262s made runs on the 4th FG, and Col Stewart managed to damage one of them. Completing the escort, the 335th FS dropped down to strafe some trucks. Capt George

Maj Pierce McKennon was trained in the RCAF and joined the 335th FS in February 1943. He opened his aerial account by downing an Fw 190 on 30 July 1943 while flying a P-47. By the end of his first combat tour on 26 May 1944, he had claimed 10.5 aerial kills, and been made CO of the 335th FS. There was just one more shared aerial victory to come before the end of the war following his return to combat in August 1944. Again made CO of the 335th FS, McKennon led numerous bomber escorts in the final months of the conflict, and scored six strafing kills in April 1945. Having survived the war, he was killed in a flying accident involving an AT-6D near San Antonio, Texas, on 18 June 1947 (*via William Hess*)

The last in a series of *RIDGE RUNNERs*, P-51D 44-72308 is seen here at Debden near war's end. Outfitted with a pair of RAF-style rear-view mirrors – and marked with two small parachutes near the nose art, denoting McKennon's two bale-outs – this machine was damaged by flak during the legendary 16 April 1945 attack on Prague/Kbely airfield. McKennon was wounded in the eye, effectively ending his career with the 4th FG. By then he had flown 560 combat hours and used up two P-47s and six P-51s (*National Museum of the USAF*)

Davis subsequently fell victim to flak, the pilot suffering a fractured ankle when he landed on a stump after baling out. Ending up a PoW, he returned to the group on 2 April after his camp was liberated. Also lost to flak was squadronmate 1Lt Kenneth Green, who began flying erratically when the 335th broke off their attacks and headed for home. 1Lt John Creamer's efforts to get him to follow him home went to no avail, as Green had to bale out near Rotterdam. He too ended up as a PoW.

Enemy fighters were next seen on the two-part escort to Swinemünde on 12 March, when Maj John McFarlane's group saw three aircraft, but they were unable to catch them. His Mustang then developed a coolant leak and McFarlane was forced to bale out over Fehmarn Island, in Germany. He managed to evade capture and escape to Sweden.

An uneventful escort on the 17th was followed the next day by a two-part escort to Berlin. After reaching the target, 335th FS CO Maj Pierce McKennon took his half of the group to Neubrandenburg airfield, where he circled and then made a low pass, intending to use the information he gleaned as he raced over the base to set up the attack. Instead, McKennon took a well-aimed flak round through the oil lines of his P-51D *RIDGE RUNNER*, and he was forced to bale out three miles west of Penzlin – his Mustang crashed and exploded in the same field that the ace landed in.

Capt George Green was covering his leader, and he fired a few rounds at two men and their dog who were headed for McKennon, convincing them to approach with far less enthusiasm. Then, Green did the unexpected – he dropped his landing gear and landed in the field! Discarding his parachute, he motioned for McKennon to get in. The two men crammed into the single seat of the Mustang, and Green gunned the engine. The fighter bounced across the field, then heaved itself into the air and headed for Debden.

On 19 March, the group flew another two-part escort to Ingolstadt-Donauworth. Maj Norley observed a Bf 109 heading straight for his group as they passed Frankfurt, and he 'did a sharp 180 with my section', he said. 'The Me 109 turned north and started a shallow dive. I closed to about 2000 yards, but before I could fire a shot he jettisoned his canopy. Feeling slightly cheated, I fired a couple of short bursts. The pilot of the Me 109 baled out and the fighter crashed and burned.' Meanwhile, another section was bounced by two Me 262s, and although the Mustang pilots gave chase, they were left behind by the jets.

Capt George D Green was flying his assigned P-51D *Suzon* on 18 March 1945 when he saw his CO, Maj Pierce McKennon, bale out over Germany. Green made the bold decision to land and rescue the downed pilot, the two squeezing into the cockpit of Green's P-51D for the long ride home (*National Museum of the USAF*)

Maj Montgomery led 21 March's escort for B-24s targeting Hesepe abd Ahlhorn airfields. The group made just one pass on Hesepe due to intense flak, losing Capt Albert Davis of the 335th FS in the process. Baling out at a height of just 50 ft, his parachute had no time to deploy and he was killed when he hit the ground. The group turned its attention to Achmer airfield instead. Waiting for the 353rd FG to clear the target area after conducting its strafing passes, all three units made a series of runs. Capt Carl Alfred of the 336th FS claimed three of the seven aircraft destroyed, but 1Lt Robert Cammer of the 335th was shot down and captured.

The following day, Lt Col Woods led Group A on a bomber escort to Ruhland. Group B, led by Maj McKennon, was vectored away from the bombers near Brussels to look for bandits detected by radar near Frankfurt. As Group A rendezvoused with the Fifteenth Air Force B-24s that it had been charged with protecting, several Me 262s were spotted and duly chased away. A short while later Lt Col Woods saw a lone B-17;

'The bomber made a 180-degree turn to the right and headed back toward the Russian lines. I was following the "Fort" east of Berlin when I saw four aircraft making a circle over Furtsenwalde. I chased them across the town and identified them as Fw 190s. They were all carrying bombs, and appeared to be forming up for a sortie over Russian lines. They were camouflaged a mottled brown, and had small crosses on dirty white roundels.

'I closed behind the No 4 man in the flight and gave him a two-second burst from about 50 yards. I got strikes along the fuselage, in the cockpit and along the left wing. My flight observed the enemy pilot slumped over in the cockpit and saw him nose over and hit the deck. I pulled up to clear my tail and observed an enemy aircraft firing at me from above, 90 degrees to my left. I shoved the stick down and he missed and went over the top of me. I pulled straight up and rolled off the top and came down behind his tail. I followed him down in an aileron roll, hit him during the roll and observed him crash on Furstenwalde airfield.

'Then I saw a flight of four Fw 190s turning between Eggersdorf and Furstenwalde airfields. I closed on the No 4 man and gave him two two-second bursts. He jettisoned his bombs, then his canopy and started smoking. The pilot baled out. After destroying this aircraft, I pulled up and looked down my left wing to see some gunners in a pit below me shooting light flak that was just coming by my tail. I broke to the right and observed two Fw 190s on the tail of a P-51. I closed behind one right on the deck, gave him several short bursts and he crashed and burned.

'I climbed back to 3000 ft and saw another flight of four aircraft circling between Furstenwalde and Eggersdorf. I closed in behind the No 4 man, and all four broke violently to the left. He pulled up in a steep, climbing turn to the left, and as he did I saw my tracers going just into his tail. I pulled back slightly on the stick and the tracers went into his cockpit. The aircraft caught fire, crashed and burned.'

Lt Col Woods had taken just 20 minutes to become the only 4th FG pilot to achieve the rare distinction of 'making ace in a day'. 1Lt William Reidel claimed two Fw 190s destroyed, while single Focke-Wulfs fell to 1Lts Jahnke, Fred Farrington, Robert Davis and Capt Harry Hagan.

The 336th GS suffered two more fatalities on the 26 March fighter sweep of the Worms-Plauen-Weimar-Crailsheim area. The 4th FG's trio of units had been broken up by poor weather, forcing them to patrol separately. 2Lt Earl Hustwit was killed when his Mustang suffered mechanical failure over Holland, while 1Lt Larry Davis was seen coming out of low cloud near Woodbridge with his port wing on fire upon the

2Lt Arthur Bowers poses on the wing of his P-51D. Sgt Don Allen painted the nose art using a photograph of Bowers' wife as a guide. The 334th FS pilot was a late war strafing ace, with six kills to his credit during 30 missions – most of them flown in this aircraft (*Keith Hoey via Wade Meyers*)

Viewed from the cockpit of a 486th BG B-24J, 1Lt Raymond Dyer of the 334th FS provides close escort on the bomber's trip home. Dyer destroyed one of four Me 262s downed by the group on 4 April 1945. This was his sole aerial victory, although he claimed three strafing kills (*Robert Burman*)

group's return to Essex. He had possibly been the victim of a mid-air collision. Like Hustwit, Davis went in with his fighter.

Aside from these fatalities, 2Lt Arthur Bowers of the 334th FS returned to base with superficial wounds to the neck after his aircraft was hit northeast of Erlangen by both 20 mm and 40 mm cannon shells and small arms fire, blasting eight holes through the canopy.

On the 31 March escort to Hassel-Berlin, Maj Norley's Group B was bounced by three Soviet P-39s, one of which put a cannon round through the propeller of 1Lt Carl Payne's Mustang. A 336th FS pilot got hits on an Airacobra, but the two formations then broke apart without further damage being done. Flt Off Ken Foster of the 334th FS suffered an engine failure at 17,000 ft and began gliding toward friendly territory. He crash-landed near Ommen, in Holland. Foster was greeted by Dutch civilians, one of whom told him to hide in the woods. Later, this man and two boys returned and brought food and clothing for the downed aviator.

In the late afternoon, one of the boys returned with another man, who pointed a gun at Foster and turned him over to the Germans. They put him in the local jail. Through a cell window, a boy brought him a worn hacksaw blade, and Foster and two RAF personnel took turns sawing the bars in the window. After their evening meal, the trio escaped and found a friendly farmer, who hid them and managed to make contact with the local underground. They hid for a week while the Allies advanced toward them, then travelled to the recently liberated town of Meppel. Foster returned to the group on 21 April.

The 4th FG's next encounter with the now scarce Jagdwaffe came on 4 April, during an escort mission to Parchim airfield. As the B-24s ran in on the target, they were attacked by eight Me 262s. A dozen Mustangs gave chase, with 1Lt Raymond Dyer bagging one and 1Lts Kennedy, Ayers, Fredericks and Donald Baugh sharing in the destruction of a second jet. Three more Me 262s attempted to hit the B-24s later in the mission, but they were driven off.

Three days later Maj Glover led an escort mission for bombers striking ammunition dumps at Duneburg and Krummel. Near Steinhuder Lake, two Fw 190D-9s began to menace the formation. Maj Norley climbed to attack one, and it dove through the bomber formation, slicing off the tail of a B-24 in the process. Later, a gaggle of Bf 109s tried to get at the bombers, but they were driven off. 1Lts Ralph Buchanan, William Hoelscher, James Ayers and Marvin Davis were each credited with shooting a fighter apiece.

On 8 April, 2Lt Homer Smith was killed during a local training flight in one of the P-51Bs flown by the group's operational training unit. The young pilot, who had not yet been rated combat-qualified, crashed to his death north of Cambridge.

Maj Gerald Montgomery's P-51D *Sizzlin' Liz* rests in its revetment at Debden between missions in 1945. A long-time member of the 334th FS, Montgomery served with the 4th FG between May 1943 and war's end. He claimed three aerial and 14.5 ground kills, the latter tally ranking him second only to Maj Jim Goodson in the list of high-scoring 4th FG strafers (*via William Hess*)

The next day, Maj McKennon commanded an escort for B-17s targeting Munich-Brunnthal airfield. Afterwards, the Mustangs swept down to clean up what the bombers had left behind. McKennon destroyed three aeroplanes, 1Lts Thomas Elffner and Mack Heaton two each and four other pilots one apiece. 1Lt Robert Bucholz of the 335th FS also destroyed three enemy aircraft, but during his last pass his Mustang was hit by flak and he died when the fighter crashed into the ground. A similar fate befell his squadronmate, 2Lt Herman Rasmussen, who baled out too low south of Neubiberg.

On 10 April, 61 Mustangs launched on an escort mission to the Rechlin-Lars airfield. Afterwards, a section of 334th FS aircraft strafed Wittstock airfield, where Maj Montgomery set an Me 410 ablaze, 1Lt McFadden destroyed a Ju 88, 1Lt Donald Lowther claimed a Ju 52/3m and 1Lt Robert Miller destroyed an unidentified twin-engined aircraft. He was wounded by flak during his strafing run, and was heard radioing for medical attention. Miller duly landed at B-78/Eindhoven. Elsewhere during the mission, 1Lt Wilmer Collins of the 336th FS claimed the group's sole aerial victory of the day by downing an Me 262 over Lübeck.

Maj Louis 'Red Dog' Norley describes a recent aerial engagement to Capt Ben Ezell, who was visiting the 4th FG at the time this photograph was taken. Norley claimed kills with all three units in the group, and also led both the 334th and 335th FS at various times in 1944–45. He was officially credited with 10.333 aerial and five strafing victories between December 1943 and April 1945 (*via William Hess*)

Yet another Mustang was forced down by mechanical failure on 15 April, when 1Lt Edward Wozniak of the 334th FS force-landed near Wattau, in Belgium, after the engine in his fighter failed during an escort mission for A-26 Invaders targeting Ulm. Wozniak was injured during the incident, and he did not return to the group.

Maj Norley runs up the engine of his P-51D *Red Dog XII* at Debden soon after the 16 April 1945 strafing attack on Gablingen airfield, which saw him destroy four aircraft in this machine (*via William Hess*)

The following day, the 4th FG scored the biggest one-day bag in its history. Group A, commanded by Lt Col Woods, and Group B, under Maj Norley, flew an escort to Rosenheim and Prague, which was followed by a strafing mission around Karlsbad, Salzburg and Prague. The 334th FS attacked Gablingen airfield and devastated it. 'All sections pulled up in line abreast', said Norley. 'We made the first pass from southwest to northeast. Maj McKennon called and said that he could see no flak. We pulled up to starboard and came in for the second pass. On my third pass, I observed several columns of smoke and several more beginning to burn.'

The carnage was impressive, with 1Lts Kenneth Helfrecht and William Antonides each destroying five aeroplanes, Norley and 1Lt Gordon Denson getting four apiece, and 1Lts Dyer, William Spencer, Ayers, O'Bryan and Bowers each claiming three. Three more pilots bagged a pair, and four more pilots, including 1Lt Paul Burnett, one.

However, Burnett did not return from the mission. His target exploded violently, flipping Burnett onto his back. His Mustang was riddled with shrapnel, shredding the leading edge of one wing and bending the propeller out of position so it vibrated furiously. Burnett could see oil running out of the engine across the left wing root. He righted the P-51 and struggled for altitude, keeping the ailing fighter aloft for a further 30 minutes before the oil pressure reached zero and white smoke poured from the exhausts.

The five kills on 2Lt Arthur Bowers' *Sweet Arlene* represented his strafing victories in early 1945. Bowers destroyed three fighters at Rohrensee on 25 February and two fighters and a bomber at Gablingen on 16 April (*Keith Hoey via Wade Meyers*)

Burnett had been ready to bale out, so he rolled the aeroplane over and tried to drop out, but he was pinned half in and half out by the slipstream. He fought his way back in and righted the aeroplane. Burnett rolled the plane over again, and again was pinned against the headrest armour half-in and half-out. This time, he could not wiggle back in, but something jerked him out of the P-51 just as it hit the ground. Burnett came to six feet from his burning fighter, and crawled to a ditch, barely injured from this ordeal. He was soon surrounded by German civilians, but they were not hostile, and he was taken by Jeep to the US command post in Otterberg.

Meanwhile, at Prague/Kbely airfield, the 335th and 336th FSs were busy strafing lines of German aircraft. 'There were about 100 ships parked on the Prague/Kbely airfield', reported 1Lt Harold Fredericks. 'There were also 15 parked at adjacent fields. It seemed to be a receiving point for all types of aircraft.'

'I was flying No 3 to Lt Col Woods', said 1Lt Douglas Pederson. 'After the first pass, I never saw the men in my section again.' Woods was hit during his third pass across the field – he radioed that he was baling out, and became a PoW. The other two in the section, 2Lt Ben Griffin and 1Lt James Ayers, were also hit by 40 mm flak. 'I had been flying 1Lt Pierini's former plane, *Jersey Bounce II*, which I had renamed *Miss Marian*', said 2Lt Griffin. 'The third enemy aircraft I destroyed exploded violently as I flew over it. Flying debris cut the coolant line to the after cooler, which sprayed coolant over my face. In spite of this, I made one more pass and destroyed another aircraft. I then made a terrible error – I pulled up to 300 ft. This gave the flak gunners on the top of the buildings an opportunity to zero in on me.' Griffin became a PoW.

2Lt Ben Griffin's eventful few months with the 4th FG (he initially served with the 334th FS, before being posted to the 336th FS) came to an end when he was hit by flak strafing the airfield at Prague/Kbely on 16 April 1945. Despite having his coolant lines cut by flak, Griffin made one more pass before flak forced him down into captivity. He had claimed four German aircraft destroyed by the time he took to his parachute (*Nick King via Peter Randall*)

Fredericks also heard Capt Leroy Carpenter report he was baling out, but Carpenter was killed. 'I saw a ship going south of the airfield losing coolant', said Fredericks. 'I followed it and identified it as Capt Carl Alfred's ship. In a turn, I lost sight of him for a few seconds. I then saw his aeroplane in a shallow dive, streaming coolant, going into the deck and exploding on impact. Flying back to the aerodrome, I heard 1Lt Ayers say he was baling out too.' Alfred did not escape his from P-51D and was killed, but Ayers became a PoW.

1Lt Edward McLouchlin opened fire on a Ju 188 on his first pass and set it on fire. 'I found myself alone and made another pass. I got good strikes on another Ju 188 at the southeast corner of the field. I saw it burst into flame before I fired on the fourth Ju 188 in the middle of the field. I then fired into a hangar, with no apparent results. I pulled up to 5500 ft and was heading out when I got hit by flak and my P-51 began to burn. I baled out and saw my kite explode on impact with the ground.'

Also downed and captured were 1Lts Maurice Miller and Edward

This aerial view of Debden, taken near war's end, shows 336th FS Mustangs (and a war-weary P-47D) lining a taxiway, with a visiting 56th FG Thunderbolt on the far side of the tower (*National Museum of the USAF*)

Another view of Debden in 1945, showing more 336th FS Mustangs in their revetments. In the background is the runway, and beyond that more dispersed P-51s (*National Museum of the USAF*)

Gimbel, making a total of eight pilots lost during the mission. Maj McKennon's plane was hit by a 20 mm round that exploded in the cockpit and wounded him in the eye, but he nursed his Mustang home, as did eight other pilots whose fighters suffered flak damage. However, the cost to the Germans was staggering. 1Lt Douglas Pederson destroyed six Ju 52/3ms himself, Flt Off Donald Baugh wrecked five Ju 88s and 1Lts George Green, James Halligan and Loton Jennings were each credited with the destruction of four aeroplanes. The total was 51 at the Prague airfields and 110 for the entire day.

Despite the previous day's losses, the group flew an escort to the Karlsbad area on 17 April, and one squadron gave chase to an Me 262, which crash-landed on Ruzyne airfield. The 336th attacked Pilzen airfield, destroying four aircraft, but flak hit the Mustang of 1Lt Robert Davis, and he was killed when his fighter crashed.

1Lt Millard Jenks (centre), a member of the ground echelon, makes the first toast of VE Day. Jenks had been a teetotaller until 8 May 1945, finding the end of the war the ideal occasion to finally indulge at the officer's club (*National Museum of the USAF*)

On 25 April, Col Stewart led a fighter sweep to the Linz-Prague area, where 1Lt William Hoelscher of the 334th FS spotted an Me 262 and dove to attack. He scored strikes all over the jet, but while chasing it he too was hit by a 40 mm round over Prague/Ruzyne airfield that tore the left elevator off his P-51D and he had to bale out. Hoelscher landed amidst a group of Czech partisans, who hid him from the Germans. He hitched rides on motorcycles, Jeeps and aeroplanes and eventually made it back to Debden on 12 May. Although Hoelscher's Me 262 was officially credited him as a probable kill, the 4th FG recognized it as its last victory of World War II. He had certainly been the group's last loss of the war!

On 8 May, flights were suspended, the ammunition was removed from the Mustangs' wings and free beer started flowing at Debden at 1500 hrs. The war was over. Hoelscher's Me 262 brought the group's final score to 1011 aircraft destroyed in the air and on the ground – VIII Fighter Command subsequently reappraised all claims and credited the 4th FG with 1058.5 victories. A unit that had been formed from a motley group of USAAF washouts had amassed the greatest victory total of any American fighter group during World War II.

Five days after war's end, the 4th FG sortied a number of its P-51s as part of a group of 720 fighters from VIII Fighter Command in a victory review over southern England and London. The instincts of the pilots were not quick to adjust to peacetime life, for four days later, orders came to paint the squadron codes in very large letters under the port wing of the Mustangs so that pilots engaged in buzzing various parts of the countryside could be identified and punished.

In late May, the group began flying mock combat against No 453 Sqn of the RAF, with the Spitfires simulating Japanese Zeros. Soon, however, the Mustangs began to be ferried to Speke Air Depot for disposal. During one such flight, 1Lts Barnaby Wilhoit and Harold Fredericks of the 336th FS were killed when they hit the ground while trying to let down through heavy fog. Two weeks earlier, Capt Richard Tannehill of the 335th FS had perished when he spun into the ground near Llanbedr, in Wales.

In June, plans for the 4th FG to go to the Pacific were officially cancelled, and on 27 July the last personnel and equipment left Debden for a new station at Steeple Morden. This was to be a short stay, for by 12 September all Mustangs had been flown to depots, and pilots with fewer than 62 points were assigned to the Occupational Air Force to fly the UC-64 Norseman utility aircraft – a far cry from the P-51. The rest of the officers and men were loaded aboard RMS *Queen Mary* for the trip home. On 10 November 1945 – the day after the ship docked in New York – the 4th Fighter Group was officially inactivated at Camp Kilmer, New Jersey.

APPENDICES

APPENDIX 1

4th FG VICTORIES BY SQUADRON

Squadron	Air	Ground	Total
HQ flight	23.5	7.5	31
334th FS	201.17	178	379.17
335th FS	159.67	94.84	254.51
336th FS	165.67	180.92	346.59
Total:	**550.01**	**461.26**	**1011.27**

APPENDIX 2

4th FG WARTIME COMMANDING OFFICERS

Group Commander	(start date)
Col Edward W Anderson	27 September 1942
Wg Cdr Raymond Duke-Wooley (operational group CO)	27 September 1942
Lt Col Chesley G Peterson	20 August 1943
Lt Col Donald J M Blakeslee	1 January 1944
Lt Col James Clark (acting)	1 September 1944
Lt Col Claiborne Kinnard (acting)	15 September 1944
Lt Col Claiborne Kinnard	3 November 1944
Lt Col William A Trippett (acting)	29 November 1944
Lt Col Jack J Oberhansly (acting)	5 December 1944
Lt Col Harry J Dayhuff	7 December 1944
Col Everett W Stewart	21 February 1945

334th FS

Maj Gregory A Daymond	29 September 1942
Maj Oscar H Coen	3 March 1943
Maj Thomas J Andrews (acting)	13 April 1943
Lt Col John F Malone (acting)	19 May 1943
Lt Col Oscar H Coen	4 August 1943
Lt Col James A Clark	26 October 1943
Capt Duane W Beeson	15 March 1944
Capt Raymond C Care	5 April 1944
Maj Winslow M Sobanski	15 April 1945
Capt Howard D Hively	6 June 1944
Capt Gerald Brown (acting)	29 July 1944
Maj Howard D Hively	1 November 1944
Maj Louis H Norley	25 January 1945

335th FS

Maj William J Daley	29 September 1942
Lt Col Donald J M Blakeslee	22 November 1942
Maj Gilbert O Halsey	19 May 1943
Maj Roy W Evans	13 August 1943
Maj George Carpenter	5 February 1944
Maj James R Happel	18 April 1944
Maj Leon M Blanding	21 June 1944
Capt Robert C Church	29 July 1944
Maj Pierce W McKennon	18 August 1944
Maj Louis H Norley	28 August 1944
Maj Pierce W McKennon	22 September 1944

336th FS

Maj Carroll W McColpin	29 September 1942
Maj Oscar H Coen	28 November 1942
Maj John G DuFour	4 March 1943
Maj Carl H Miley	1 September 1942
Maj Leroy Gover	10 October 1942
Lt Col Seldon R Edner	29 November 1942
Maj Gilbert O Halsey	1 January 1944
Maj James A Goodson	8 March 1944
Capt Willard W Millikan (acting)	13 April 1944
Maj James A Goodson	10 May 1944
Maj Wilson V Edwards	21 June 1944
Maj John D McFarlane	5 July 1944
Maj Fred W Glover	24 August 1944

APPENDIX 3

4th FG AERIAL & STRAFING ACES

Name	Aerial Kills	Strafing Kills	Total	Notes
2Lt Ralph K Hofer	15	14	29	
Maj James A Goodson	14	15	29	(2 aerial 31st FG)
Capt John T Godfrey	16.333	12.666	28.999	
Capt Don S Gentile	21.833	6	27.833	
Lt Col Claiborne Kinnard	8	17	25	(7 aerial/22 strafing 355th FG)
Maj Frederick W Glover	10.333	12.5	22.833	
Maj Duane W Beeson	17.333	4.75	22.083	
Maj Pierce W McKennon	11	9.68	20.68	
Maj Gerald E Montgomery	3	14.5	17.5	
Maj George Carpenter	13.333	4	17.333	
Col Donald J M Blakeslee	14.5	1.5	16	(3 aerial RAF/1 aerial 354th FG)
Capt Nicholas Megura	11.833	3.75	15.583	
Capt Charles F Anderson	10	5.5	15.5	
Maj Louis H Norley	10.333	5	15.333	
Lt Col James A Clark	10.5	4.5	15	
Capt Willard W Millikan	13	2	15	
Capt Albert L Schlegel	10	5	15	
Maj Howard D Hively	12	2.5	14.5	
Capt Joseph L Lang	7.833	4	11.833	
1Lt Hipolitus T Biel	5.333	6	11.333	
Capt Frank C Jones	5	5.5	10.5	
Capt Donald M Malmsten	1.5	9	10.5	
Capt Ted E Lines	10	0	10	
1Lt Spiros N Pisanos	10	0	10	
Lt Col Sidney Woods	7	3	10	(1 strafing 479th FG/2 aerial 49th FG)
Capt Kendall E Carlson	6	4	10	
1Lt Paul S Riley	6.5	3	9.5	
Col Everett W Stewart	7.833	1.5	9.333	(all aerial kills with 352nd & 355th FGs)
Lt Van E Chandler	5	4	9	
Maj Shelton W Monroe	4.333	4.5	8.833	
Maj James R Happel	4	4.67	8.67	
Capt Victor J France	4.333	4.333	8.666	
Capt Joseph H Bennett	8.5	0	8.5	(5.5 with 56th FG)
Capt Bernard L McGrattan	8.5	0	8.5	
Capt David W Howe	6	2.5	8.5	
Maj William J Daley	8	0	8	(all with RAF)
Maj Carroll W McColpin	8	0	8	(all with RAF & Ninth Air Force)
1Lt William E Whalen	6	2	8	(5 aerial/2 strafing with 355th FG)
Capt Carl R Alfred	0	8	8	
1Lt James W Ayers	1	7	8	
1Lt Vermont Garrison	7.333	0.25	7.583	
1Lt Grover C Siems	4.333	3.5	7.833	
Lt Col Jack J Oberhansly	6	1.666	7.666	(all with 78th FG)
Capt Joseph H Joiner	3.5	4	7.5	
Capt William B Smith	3	4.5	7.5	

Name	Aerial Kills	Strafing Kills	Total	Notes
Maj Gregory A Daymond	7	0	7	(all with RAF)
Col Chesley G Peterson	7	0	7	(6 with RAF)
Capt Donald R Emerson	4.5	2.5	7	
1Lt William O Antonides	0	7	7	
Capt Raymond C Care	6	0.5	6.5	
Lt Col Roy W Evans	6	0	6	(1 with 359th FG)
Maj Michael G H McPharlin	5	1	6	(1.5 with RAF and rest with 339th FG)
Maj Henry L Mills	6	0	6	
1Lt Robert F Nelson	1	5	6	
1Lt Frank E Speer	1	5	6	
2Lt Arthur R Bowers	0	6	6	
1Lt Loton D Jennings	0	6	6	
1Lt Douglas P Pederson	0	6	6	
1Lt Archie Chatterley	4.5	1	5.5	
Capt Carl G Payne	2	3.5	5.5	
Capt Thomas R Bell	0	5.5	5.5	
1Lt Clemens Fiedler	4.333	1	5.333	
Maj Gerald C Brown	5	0	5	(all with 55th FG)
Lt Col Selden R Edner	5	0	5	(all with RAF)
Capt Kenneth G Smith	5	0	5	
Capt Vasseure H Wynn	3	2	5	(2.5 aerial victories with RAF)
Capt Harry N Hagan	2	3	5	
Capt Robert D Hobert	2	3	5	
Flt Off Donald P Baugh	0	5	5	
1Lt Gordon A Denson	0	5	5	
Capt Melvin N Dickey	0	5	5	
1Lt Kenneth G Helfrecht	0	5	5	
1Lt Gilbert L Kesler	0	5	5	
Capt Jack D McFadden	2	3	5	

COLOUR PLATES

1

Spitfire VB BL722 of 2Lt James Goodson, 336th FS, Debden, October 1942

2Lt 'Goody' Goodson and Capt 'Dixie' Alexander sought permission from squadron CO, Maj Don Blakeslee, to make the first flight of an American-marked fighter over the Continent, and he granted it with one proviso – they had to paint over the British roundels with white stars first. The only template handy was a crew chief's medallion, hence the somewhat-ironic use of the Star of David on these Spitfires. Goodson, who survived the torpedoing of the liner *Athenia* on the third day of the war, joined the RCAF in 1940 and began his combat career in 1942.

2

Spitfire VB BL255 *BUCKEYE-DON* of 1Lt Don Gentile, 336th FS, Debden, October 1942

1Lt Gentile's Spitfire wore two kill markings above the boxing eagle, denoting the Ju 88 and Fw 190 he claimed north of Dieppe during the ill-fated 19 August 1942 raid. BL255 served with Nos 133 and 611 Sqns prior to reaching No 121 'Eagle' Sqn. It went from there to No 610 Sqn in spring 1943, then on to No 118 Sqn and back to No 611 Sqn, before ending its service with No 61 OTU in May 1945.

3

P-47C-2 41-6204 of Capt Richard D McMinn, 334th FS, Debden, February 1943

Wearing the earliest version of the markings applied to 4th FG Thunderbolts, McMinn's P-47C carried the last two digits of its serial on the fuselage instead of the assigned codes. Subsequently marked as QP-M, this aircraft was shot down by an Fw 190 near Ostend on 15 April 1943. McMinn perished in the crash. He and squadronmate Capt Stanley Anderson, who was also killed by Fw 190s on this date, were the first combat fatalities suffered by the 4th FG in the Thunderbolt.

4

P-47C-5 41-6579 of Maj Carl 'Spike' Miley, CO of the 336th FS, Debden, March 1943

Miley, a former 'Eagle' Squadron pilot, joined the 336th FS in October 1942 and served as its commanding officer from 1 September until 10 October 1943, when he rotated home. Miley downed a Bf 109 east of Rotterdam on 28 July 1943 for his only victory. The Thunderbolt remained behind when Miley went back to the US, and was passed to 2Lt Conrad Ingold, who survived a crash on take-off in it on 22 September 1943.

5

P-47C-5 41-6538 *WELA KAHAO!* of Capts Walter Hollander and Stanley Anderson, 334th FS, Debden, April 1943

Hollander (also an 'Eagle' Squadron veteran) hailed from Honolulu, hence the nose art on this P-47, which means 'strike while the iron is hot' in Hawaiian. Anderson was flying 41-6538 on 15 April 1943 when it suffered an engine failure and was crash-landed at Langham. Later that same day, Anderson was shot down and killed by German fighters near Cassel. 41-6538 was repaired and transferred to the 495th FG, where it served until July 1944.

6

P-47C-5 41-6358 *CALIFORNIA OR BUST* of 1Lt Archie Chatterley, 334th FS, Debden, April 1943

Chatterley, who was raised in San Diego, California, joined the squadron in January 1943 and rose to become its assistant operations officer before being downed on 21 March 1944 and made a PoW. Chatterley collided with 1Lt James 'Wilkie' Wilkinson in this machine on 17 April 1943, but was able to dead-stick the Thunderbolt in. Wilkinson survived with back injuries, but returned to flying, only to be killed in combat with the 78th FG in June 1944. 41-6358 was repaired and transferred to the Ninth Air Force's 405th FG, and it flew with this group until it was shot down in the Channel near Jersey on 23 June 1944.

7

P-47C-2 41-6183 *Red Dog* of Capt Louis Norley, 336th FS, Debden, August 1943

Norley, who flew with all three squadrons in the group, amassed 554 combat hours over the course of three tours, most of them in aircraft named *Red Dog*. He received the nickname not for his red hair, but for his limitless ability to lose at 'red dog' poker! Norley claimed 2.333 of his 10.333 victories in P-47s, with one (a Bf 109) coming in this machine on 10 February 1944. This aircraft actually predated Norley's arrival at Debden, having been with the 4th FG since January 1943, and not transferring out until February of the following year. 41-6183 was lost on 15 July 1944 when it crashed in England while serving with the 2nd Air Depot Group.

8

P-47D-1 42-7945 *Miss Plainfield* of 2Lt Spiros 'Steve' Pisanos, 334th FS, Debden, May 1943

Pisanos' first Thunderbolt, named for a girl from the town in New Jersey in which he settled after emigrating from Greece in 1938, survived nine months of combat before being transferred out of the group on 28 February 1944. Pisanos transferred the cowling and nose art to this P-47D-1 in July or August. Having scraped together money to take flying lessons in the US, Pisanos was one of the first in the 4th FG with Mustang experience, having briefly flown Allison-engined examples with No 268 Sqn before being transferred to No 71 'Eagle' Sqn. In September 1942, Pisanos became the first person to be naturalized as an American citizen outside of the United States.

9

P-47C-5 41-6539 *Arizona Pete* of 2Lt Kenneth Peterson, 336th FS, Debden, June 1943

The art adorning Peterson's Thunderbolt referenced his hometown of Mesa, Arizona, as did his nickname 'Blacksnake'. He flew this aircraft until it was damaged in a crash on 28 June 1943. Peterson scored no victories in P-47s, but downed three in Mustangs, including two on 29 March 1944, when he tore into a formation of 12 Fw 190s single-handedly to rescue a crippled B-17. Peterson was shot down and taken prisoner during the fight, and was awarded the DSC for his actions. He remained in the USAF after the war, and was later killed in the crash of an F-80 Shooting Star at Nellis AFB.

10

P-47D-1 42-7876 *Miss DALLAS* of 1Lt Victor France, 334th FS, Debden, June 1943

After his original P-47C (41-6414) was lost when Lt Col Chesley Peterson baled out of it over the Channel on 15 April 1943, France received this machine, which was soon adorned with nose art saluting his Texas hometown. One of the earliest non-'Eagle' Squadron members of the 4th FG, France was killed in combat in a Mustang on 18 April 1944 when he hit the ground while pursuing a Bf 109.

11

P-47D-1 42-7890 *BOISE BEE* of 1Lt Duane Beeson, 334th FS, Debden, September 1943

Beeson's first victory came in a P-47C, but his second (a Bf 109) came in this machine on the very day he was assigned – 26 June 1943. He would score a further ten kills in this aircraft prior to it being replaced by P-51B 43-6819 in late February 1944. *BOISE BEE* was eventually transferred to the 495th FG, with whom it was written off in a forced landing on 16 June 1944.

12

P-47C-5 41-6529 *EAGER BEAVER/MISS BETH* of 1Lt Jack Raphael, 336th FS, Debden, October 1943

Hailing from Tacoma, Washington, Raphael flew with the RAF in Hurricanes, Spitfires and Typhoons before his transfer to the USAAF in March 1943. He was assigned this aircraft from August 1943 until February 1944, when the group re-equipped with Mustangs. After leaving the 4th FG in late June, 1944, Raphael was assigned to do liaison work with the French because of his fluency in that language. On 3 July 1945, while working with a team of lawyers investigating war crimes and damage caused by Allied forces, he was badly wounded by an anti-tank mine and was flown home to the US. Raphael lost his legs, but recovered and became a Fullbright scholar, eventually serving as a defence advisor for the Spanish air force. *EAGER BEAVER* started out as Ervin Miller's *Hi! R.P.M.*, and later transferred to the 404th FG, where it was involved in a fatal take-off accident on 13 April 1944.

13

P-51B-5 43-6636 *ILL WIND* of 1Lt Nicholas Megura, 334th FS, Debden, March 1944

Megura also flew a P-47C called *ILL WIND*, but he did not start amassing victories until this Mustang arrived. By May 1944 he had 11.833 kills, and would have likely scored more had his fighter not been mistakenly shot up by a P-38 on the 22nd of that month over Kiel, forcing him to crash-land in neutral Sweden. Political considerations meant this was the end of his combat career. 43-6636 did not last this long, for it fell to flak on 9 May while being flown by 1Lt Vernon Burroughs on a sweep of St Dizier airfield. Burroughs became a PoW.

14

P-51B-1 43-12214 *Rebel Queen* of Flt Off Fred Glover, 336th FS, Debden, March 1944

Glover joined the 4th FG as a flight officer in February 1944 and opened his scoring with two Bf 110s on 16 March in this aircraft. He claimed an Fw 190 and a one-third share in the destruction of an He 111 some 13 days later. Making ace on 5 August 1944, Glover had become the CO of the 336th FS by month-end. Having survived the war, he died in a crop dusting accident at Hazlehurst, in Georgia, on 7 July 1956. 43-12214 was passed on to the 555th FS/496th FTG in mid-1944, and its final fate remains unknown.

15

P-51B-5 43-6437 of Col Don Blakeslee, CO of the 4th FG, Debden, March 1944

Eschewing nose art on all his mounts, Blakeslee flew this aircraft during the first missions to Berlin. His enthusiasm for the Malcolm hood resulted in its installation on nearly all the group's P-51B/Cs. This machine, which was notoriously unreliable, was lost when it was hit by flak during a strafing mission near Dijon on 7 August 1944. The pilot at the time, 1Lt Sidney Wadsworth, became a PoW.

16

P-51B-7 43-6913 *Shangri-La* of Capt Don Gentile, 336th FS, Debden, April 1944

Shangri-La was Gentile's mount for just 45 days, from the start of March 1944 until it was 'pranged' on 13 April. During that period, Gentile destroyed 15 of his 21.833 victories. 43-6913 had started out as a P-51B-5, but was modified into a B-7 with the addition of an 85-gallon fuel tank in the US. The fighter went through an assortment of marking variations involving the nose and spinner – it also had red wheel hubs. Gentile claimed 7.5 of his 16.5 Mustang kills in this machine.

17

P-51B-10 42-106730 *REGGIE'S REPLY* of 1Lt John Godfrey, 336th FS, Debden, April 1944

Godfrey was assigned this aircraft after his return from leave on 21 April, and he gave it the same name that his earlier P-47 had worn, commemorating his brother who lost his life when his ship was sunk by a U-boat in the Atlantic. Despite only flying this aircraft on three missions in total, Godfrey used it to claim three Fw 190s on 22 April and a Bf 109 two days later. On 26 April it crashed at Martlesham when pilot 1Lt Robert Tussey's RAF-style flying boot caught on the landing gear lever and accidentally raised the undercarriage during a take-off run. This was one of three accidents Tussey was involved in over a three-week period, the first one of which damaged Godfrey's P-51B 43-6765 so extensively that it never saw combat again.

18

P-51B-5 43-6819 *BEE* of Capt Duane Beeson, 334th FS, Debden, April 1944

Beeson scored 5.333 kills in this P-51B between 5 March and 5 April 1944, taking his final tally to 17.333. Shortly after claiming a share in the downing of a Ju 88 over Plaue on 5 April, Beeson was shot down by flak while strafing bombers at Weissewarte airfield, near Brandenburg-Briest. He spent the rest of the war as a PoW. Remaining in the USAAF after the war, Beeson died of a brain tumour on 13 February 1947. His medals can be seen on display in the Duane W Beeson Air Terminal in Boise, Idaho.

19

P-51B-10 42-106673 *Hey Rube!* of 1Lt Reuben Simon, 336th FS, Debden, April 1944

Simon, a native of Los Angeles, California, used this

machine to stalk and destroy an Fw 190 on 8 April 1944. 42-106673 was lost on 7 June 1944 when its pilot, Flt Off Don Pierini, collided with 1Lt Kenneth Smith, who was killed in the crash.

20

P-51B-15 42-106911 *Yipee Joe* of 1Lt Pierce McKennon, 335th FS, Debden, April 1944

McKennon flunked out of USAAF flight training and joined the RCAF, transferring to the 4th FG as it was transitioning to P-47s, in which he scored 3.5 kills. McKennon's second P-51, *Yipee Joe*, survived for just 13 days after it was assigned to him. The fighter fell to flak on 9 May 1944 while being flown by 1Lt Lloyd Waterman, who become a PoW.

21

P-51B-5-NA 43-6957 *Turnip Termite* of 1Lt Frank Speer, 334th FS, Debden, May 1944

Speer was with the 4th FG for just over a month (17 April to 29 May 1944) before he was shot down and began an epic escape attempt that took him 700 miles on foot. He was captured, but then escaped again in 1945. *Turnip Termite* was named for a destructive pest in the *Lil' Abner* comic strip. 43-6957 met its end on D-Day when 1Lt Edward Steppe was shot down and killed while flying it.

22

P-51B-15 42-106924 *Salem Representative* of 2Lt Ralph Hofer, 334th FS, Debden, June 1944

The paint on 'Kidd' Hofer's Mustang, like the pilot, was rather non-standard, and included olive drab upper wings and rear fuselage. Hofer was assigned this aircraft in April 1944, named it after his hometown in Missouri and proceeded to go on a six-kill spree in May. Known for wearing a football jersey during missions, and for his go-it-alone approach, Hofer was the frequent target of Col Don Blakeslee's ire. The circumstances of his mysterious death – shot down by flak while strafing an airfield in Mostar, Yugoslavia – were only confirmed in 2003.

23

P-51B-5 43-6942 *MEINER KLEINER* of 1Lt Joseph Higgins, 336th FS, Debden, June 1944

Philadelphia native Higgins dubbed his aeroplane 'My Small One' in German, perhaps at the suggestion of crew chief SSgt Glessner Weckbacker. Higgins shared in the destruction of a Bf 109 with Donald Emerson near Budapest while the group was temporarily based at Foggia, in Italy. After Higgins had rotated home, 43-6942 was hit by flak near Merseburg on 21 November 1944 and pilot 1Lt George Klaus baled out and became a PoW.

24

P-51D-5 44-13303 of Maj James Goodson, CO of the 336th Sqn, Debden, June 1944

Goodson's 14 aerial kills were complemented by 15 strafing victories, earning him the unofficial moniker of 'King of the Strafers'. This aircraft wore all 30 kill markings (one of his strafing kills was also credited by mistake as an aerial success). On 20 June, Goodson was hit by flak while flying 44-13303 during a strafing run on Neubrandenburg airfield, and he was forced to crash-land. Once he was away from the fighter, his squadronmates strafed the Mustang until it was destroyed. Goodson became a PoW.

25

P-51D-10 44-14388 *Wheezy* of 1Lt Van Chandler, 336th FS, Debden, October 1944

Chandler claimed three of his five victories in this aircraft, prior to making ace in 44-15647 on 1 January 1945 when he shot down a Bf 109 near Ulzen. This earned him the distinction of being the youngest American ace of World War II. Chandler added four on the ground during an attack on the Neuberg airfield on 16 January. Chandler later destroyed three MiG-15s in Korea, and was deputy commander of the F-100-equipped 31st TFW in Vietnam.

26

P-51D-10 44-14570 *THUNDERBIRD* of Capt Ted Lines, 335th FS, Debden, October 1944

The third, and final, *THUNDERBIRD*, this was Lines' assigned fighter for his final three kills on 9 (a Bf 109) and 26 (two Fw 190s) October – none of these were officially credited to him. Born in Mesa, Arizona, Lines used native American imagery to reflect his origins. This aeroplane, the first of Pierce McKennon's *RIDGE RUNNERs*, was subsequently passed to 1Lt Chuck Konsler and survived the war, only to be scrapped in late 1945.

27

P-51K-5 44-11661 *IRON ASS* of Lt Col Jack Oberhansly, Deputy CO of the 4th FG, Debden, December 1944

Oberhansly transferred into the 4th FG already an ace in P-47s, having served as deputy group commander for the 78th FG. Sgt Don Allen painted the nose art onto this machine – it was Oberhansly's second aeroplane so named. Two days before he departed for the US, on 26 February 1945, Oberhansly's *IRON ASS*, with Flt Off Alvin Hand at the controls, was hit by flak while strafing barges. Hand baled out and became a PoW.

28

P-51D-15 44-15347 of Maj Howard Hively, CO of the 334th FS, Debden, January 1945

Hively's assigned aircraft following his late 1944 leave was this uniquely marked Mustang – the only olive drab P-51D in the group. The aeroplane passed to 'Red Dog' Norley sometime in February, and had the distinction of being the last aircraft lost in combat by the 4th FG in World War II when it was shot down by 40 mm flak over Prague/Ruzyne airfield with 1Lt William Hoelscher at the controls on 25 April 1945. The pilot successfully evaded.

29

P-51D-20 44-63223 *Sweet Arlene* of 2Lt Arthur Bowers, 334th FS, Debden, February 1945

Bowers scored no aerial kills, but he had a tendency for multiple strafing victories. On two separate occasions – 25 February and 16 April 1945 – he destroyed three aeroplanes while strafing German aerodromes. On 26 March, *Sweet Arlene* was hit by an assortment of German flak northeast of Erlangen, blasting a five-inch hole in one aileron, and leaving eight holes through the canopy. Bowers was wounded, but brought his P-51 home.

30

P-51D-10 44-14332 *Lazy Daisy/Dyer-Ria* of 1Lt Raymond Dyer, 334th FS, Debden, March 1945

Dyer, who hailed from Glassport, Pennsylvania, destroyed

an Me 262 in this machine on 4 April 1945. He later claimed three aircraft on the ground in the strafing mission to Prague on 16 April 1945. The rather unappealing play on Dyer's name appeared on the right side of the nose.

31

P-51D-10 44-14361 *Feisty Sue* of 1Lt Darwin Berry, 335th FS, Debden, March 1945

In exactly six months with the group, Berry amassed 270 hours of combat flying. On 8 August 1944 he was part of an escort for Beaufighters striking a convoy off Norway, and he and fellow 335th FS pilot 1Lt John Kolbe distinguished themselves by escorting Maj Leon Blanding, who was fading in and out of consciousness after suffering a fractured skull, to a safe landing at RAF Acklington. The career of *Feisty Sue* came to an end when she was hit by flak while strafing Achmer airfield on 21 March 1945. Pilot 1Lt Robert Cammer became a PoW.

32

P-51D-20 44-63736 *Suzon* of 1Lt George Green, 335th FS, Debden, March 1945

Green was flying this aeroplane when he rescued Maj Pierce McKennon. A little more than a month later, Green destroyed four aircraft on the ground during the 4th FG's anti-airfield campaign around Prague.

33

P-51D-20 44-72308 *RIDGE RUNNER IV* of Maj Pierce McKennon, CO of the 335th FS, Debden, April 1945

McKennon's fourth *RIDGE RUNNER* featured two parachutes in the upper right corner of the razorback hog logo, indicating his bale-outs. The previous *RIDGE RUNNER* was lost on 8 March 1945, and McKennon was rescued by 1Lt George Green, who landed and picked him up. The piano-playing major scored 11 aerial victories and 9.68 strafing kills – the full scoreboard was displayed on this aircraft. McKennon perished in a flying accident in July 1948.

34

P-51D-10 44-14389 *Suzy* of 1Lt Robert Bucholz, 335th FS, Debden, April 1945

Bucholz destroyed three aircraft during his final mission on 9 April 1945 – all ground victories at the Neuberg airfield. On his next pass across the base, his aircraft was hit by flak at low altitude and Bucholz was unable to escape. He was flying P-51D 44-13788 at the time.

35

P-51D-20 44-72181 *Sunny VIII* of Col Everett Stewart, CO of the 4th FG, Debden, April 1945

Stewart took command of the 4th FG on 21 February 1945 after serving as CO of the 355th FG, and remained in command through to war's end. He was able to get off the ground to fly against the Japanese at Pearl Harbor, and was a 7.833-kill ace when he arrived at Debden. A gifted pilot and organizer, Stewart may have been the best-liked commander of the group. *Sunny VIII* was the last of a sequence of *Sunnies* that included P-47Ds and a P-51B. This aircraft was lost on 29 May 1945 in a fatal accident as it was being ferried from Debden to the air depot at Speke.

36

P-51D-25 44-73305 *Blondie* of 2Lt Marvin Arthur, 334th FS, Debden, April 1945

One of Sgt Don Allen's most spectacular works of nose art, perhaps because he was the crew chief, *Blondie* was a latecomer to the group, arriving in April 1945. Arthur, a native of Indianapolis, Indiana, destroyed a Bf 109 on the ground and shared an Fw 190 with 2Lt Milton Spencer during the 16 April mission to Gablingen airfield.

BIBLIOGRAPHY

BISHOP, STAN D, AND HEY, JOHN A, *Losses of the US 8th and 9th Air Forces – ETO Area June 1942 – December 1943.* Bishop Book Productions, Cambridge, 2004

FRY, GARRY L, AND ETHELL, JEFFERY L, *Escort to Berlin: The Fourth Fighter Group in World War II.* Arco Publishing, New York, NY, 1980

GOODSON, JAMES, *Tumult in the Clouds.* St. Martin's Press, New York, NY, 1983

HALL, GROVER CLEVELAND, *1000 Destroyed: The Life and Times of the Fourth Fighter Group,* Morgan Aviation Books, Dallas, Texas, 1946

HAUGLAND, VERN, *Eagle Squadrons: Yanks in the RAF 1940–1942.* David & Charles, Newton Abbot, Devon, 1980

HESS, WILLIAM N, *Osprey Aircraft of the Aces 51 – 'Down to Earth' Strafing Aces of the Eighth Air Force.* Osprey Publishing, Oxford, 2003

MILLER, KENT D, *Fighter Units & Pilots of the 8th Air Force Pt 1.* Schiffer Military History, Atglen, Pennsylvania, 2001

MILLER, KENT D, *Fighter Units & Pilots of the 8th Air Force Pt 2.* Schiffer Military History, Atglen, Pennsylvania, 2001

OLYNK, FRANK, *Stars & Bars.* Grub Street, London, 1995

SPEER, FRANK, *One Down and One Dead: The Personal Adventures of Two 4th Fighter Group Pilots as They Face the Luftwaffe over Europe.* Xlibris Corp, Philadelphia, 2003

SPEER, FRANK, *Debden Warbirds: The Fourth Fighter Group in World War II.* Schiffer Military History, Atglen, Pennsylvania, 1999

WHITE, TROY, *Kidd Hofer – The Last of the Screwball Aces.* Stardust Studios, DeLand, Florida, 2003

INDEX